FAMILY FAVORITES COOKBOOK

THE ST@Y HOME CHEF

FAMILY FAVORITES COOKBOOK

RACHEL FARNSWORTH

Publisher Mike Sanders
Art & Design Director William Thomas
Senior Editor Brook Farling
Designer Lindsay Dobbs
Proofreader Monica Stone
Indexer Brad Herriman

First American Edition, 2022
Published in the United States by DK Publishing
6081 E. 82nd Street, Indianapolis, Indiana 46250
Copyright © 2022 Rachel Farnsworth
22 23 24 25   10 9 8 7 6 5 4 3 2 1
001-332664-SEP2022
All rights reserved.

Note: This publication contains the opinions and ideas of its author. It is intended to provide
helpful and informative material on the subject matter covered. It is sold with the understanding
that the author and publisher are not engaged in rendering professional services in the book. If
the reader requires personal assistance or advice, a competent professional should be
consulted. The author and publisher specifically disclaim any responsibility for any liability, loss,
or risk, personal or otherwise, which is incurred as a consequence, directly or indirectly, of the
use and application of any of the contents of this book.

Trademarks: All terms mentioned in this book that are known to be or are suspected of being
trademarks or service marks have been appropriately capitalized. Alpha Books, DK, and
Penguin Random House LLC cannot attest to the accuracy of this information. Use of a term in
this book should not be regarded as affecting the validity of any trademark or service mark.

Library of Congress Catalog Number: 2022934288
ISBN: 978-07440-6359-2

DK books are available at special discounts when purchased in bulk for sales promotions,
premiums, fund-raising, or educational use. For details, contact:
SpecialSales@dk.com

Author photo on page 9 © Ashton Kelley
Author photo on page 13 © Cali Stoddard

Printed in Canada

For the curious
www.dk.com

dedication

This book is dedicated to my family, my friends, and my fans.

acknowledgments

First and foremost, this book would not be possible without the support and help of my extremely patient and loving husband, Stephen. He has believed in me and my crazy ideas since day one. Without him, The Stay At Home Chef simply would not be possible. My children, Dexter and Adele, have been my taste testers their entire lives. When deciding whether or not to take on this project, it was them who provided the encouragement I needed to sign on. My siblings, Jennifer, Spencer, Cara, and Ammon all chimed in with their favorite recipes of mine and helped me decide which recipes absolutely needed to be included. Many of these recipes are specifically for them. My mom and dad have always been my biggest supporters, and I would not be who I am today without them. My entire family-in-law, grandparents, aunts, uncles, and cousins have cheered me on. I am so lucky to have such an amazing extended family.

Many people don't realize just how much work goes into running The Stay At Home Chef. I have an entire team helping me, and they've been with me every step of the way on this book: Dallan Anderson, Mike Downie, Stephanie Patterson, Caytlin McCleery, and Scott Warren. Thank you for everything you have made possible.

I would not be where I am today without my food blogger colleagues and dear friends: Alyssa Rivers, Amanda Rettke, Holly Nilsson, Trish Rosenquist, Aubrey Cota, Chelsea Lords, Jocelyn Adams, and Susie Bulloch. You have mentored me, taught me, inspired me, pushed me, and supported me in ways that cannot be repaid. Thank you.

Of course, this book would not exist without my publishing team at DK. Special thanks to Brook Farling who took a chance on me for my first cookbook many years ago. The talented William Thomas and Lindsay Dobbs are the ones who turned my crazy ideas into something so beautiful. And many thanks to Kelsey Curtis and the entire marketing team for helping this book see the light of day.

Finally, the most special of thanks to my fans. As much as this book is for my family, ultimately, it is for you and your families. May you treasure it for years to come.

contents

introduction

I'm Rachel, and I like food.

That's how I introduced myself to the world when I first started publishing recipes online in 2008. What started as an outlet to cope with postpartum depression by focusing on my passions has grown into a massive online food media publication where hundreds of millions of people from around the world have used my recipes and billions more have watched my video tutorials. The best way I could think of to honor my fans was to write the book that I want my children to have. This book is a compilation of not only my greatest hits with fans, but more importantly, the greatest hits with my family. I wanted to write a book that would not only provide readers with amazing recipes, but also one that would teach them to cook beyond the pages of this book and help them solve the constant question, "What should I make?"

And so I've written this cookbook. It is not your traditional cookbook that's a simple collection of recipes. It's an interactive guide to preparing food in your kitchen. It can operate completely as a standalone cookbook, but advances in technology have gifted us with the ability to connect this book to the virtual world where I can get in the kitchen and guide you through every step of the recipe. Yes, not only does this book have a photo for every recipe so you can see what the end result should look like, it also has a video demonstration for each and every recipe to guide you along the way. Gone are the days when you have a cookbook in hand but are otherwise on your own. Now I can be right there in the kitchen with you.

It is my hope that the recipes in this cookbook will continue to be made in the homes of millions of people across the globe. Over the years, you've allowed me into your homes. My recipes are part of your weekly routines, your special occasions, your holidays, your birthdays, and your most intimate events. With that comes great feelings of both appreciation and responsibility. I have thought of you and these moments as I've worked on this cookbook. These pages are filled with love.

I'm Rachel, and I like food. To be able to share that with each of you has been the honor and privilege of a lifetime.

1 getting started

about rachel

Rachel Farnsworth is a cookbook author and food blogger at the wildly popular website TheStayAtHomeChef.com, where she shares restaurant-quality recipes you can easily make at home.

Rachel started her first food blog in 2008 after the birth of her first child and when she became a stay-at-home mom. She wanted to use the culinary training she'd received in both high school and college, so she started cooking her way through culinary textbooks, which eventually led to her writing and developing her own recipes. Her friends and family started asking for the recipes, which at the time were just written in notebooks scattered throughout her kitchen, so she decided to find a simple way to share them. Back then, "mommy blogs" were all the rage, so she decided to use this same convenient format to share her recipes with anyone who asked for them.

In 2010, Rachel became pregnant with her second child. At first it seemed she was plagued with gravidarum hyperemesis, an uncommon condition in early pregnancy that is often described as "extreme morning sickness." Instead of improving, however, over time her symptoms worsened to the point that her organs were no longer functioning properly and she lost the ability to walk. Her doctors were baffled by this inexplicable illness that was unlike anything they had seen previously. After several hospitalizations, including a brief stay in intensive care, she was miraculously diagnosed with a rare chronic autoimmune condition commonly known as Addison's disease, and it happened just in time to save her life, but the condition also left her permanently disabled.

Struggling to find a new way forward in life, she took notice of the rise in popularity of food blogs as businesses and revenue-generating entities. Desperate to prove that she was still capable of contributing to her family and to society, she started a new blog in 2012 as a business venture to publish her recipes and unique spins on classic dishes. Rachel was living in the San Diego area at the time and had access to the amazing produce, fresh seafood, and local meats that are all so abundant in the region. What resulted was the same true farm-to-table, restaurant-quality cooking on a budget that she was doing as a stay-at-home mom, but this time it was for a much larger audience. Thus, The Stay At Home Chef website, where she would go on to share her restaurant-quality recipes, was born. The website slowly grew in popularity, and in October 2013, Brook Farling, an editor from Penguin Random House, contacted her about being the author for a slow cooker book for the Idiot's Guides series. She seized the opportunity and the project challenged her and pushed her recipe writing and photography skills to new levels.

Over the years, The Stay At Home Chef has grown into one of the largest food blogs in the world. Rachel has sought to include video demonstrations with each of her recipes, which early on was a unique feature that set her content apart from other websites. Since the start of The Stay At Home Chef website, hundreds of millions of people have used Rachel's videos and recipes, and she has gained a loyal following of over 10 million people across her social media channels. Beyond her cooking, she is also well known for her disability advocacy and for a viral inspirational video about her streaks of gray hair that has been viewed over 1 billion times. Rachel grew up in both California and Southern Nevada, including a brief stint in West Texas. She currently resides in the Salt Lake City area of Utah. Western United States and California cuisines are both huge influences in her cooking.

While being known around the world as a recipe publisher and disability advocate, Rachel is, first and foremost, a wife and mother. Her husband, Stephen, works with her behind the scenes on The Stay At Home Chef and is her biggest supporter. Her children, Dexter and Adele, have grown up right alongside The Stay At Home Chef, eating all of the dishes along the way and even appearing in some of the videos. Their personal family favorite recipes are central to theme of the recipes in this book—they're the same recipes Rachel feeds her family at home. Ultimately, this is a cookbook written with love and with the intention of passing these recipes down from a mother to her children.

how to use this book

Included with the recipes in this book are some additional features designed to make the book as user friendly as possible.

scannable qr codes

Each of the recipes in this book includes a scannable QR code on the same page as the recipe. By scanning the code with the camera app on your phone, you will be taken directly to the recipe on my website where you'll find a video demonstration that walks you through every step of the recipe. In addition to the video, you'll also find troubleshooting information, answers to frequently asked questions, reviews, nutrition information, and a built-in calculator where you can scale the recipe up or down based on your needs. You'll also find similar recipes and suggestions for what to serve with the recipe.

To use the QR code feature:

1. Open the camera application on your internet-connected Android or iOS smartphone or tablet. (An internet connection is required to use this feature.)

2. A notification will appear indicating your device is trying to open a link. Click the link or select "allow" to open the webpage in your preferred internet browser.

3. Once you're on my website, click the "jump to recipe" button to take you directly to the video demonstration and recipe. Or you can scroll through the additional information included with the recipe, like troubleshooting tips, answers to frequently asked questions, and recommendations for related recipes. That's it!

If you can't figure out how to get the QR codes to work on your device, visit my website (thestayathomechef.com/QRCodes) for both written and video tutorials that will teach you how to use the codes.

SCAN TO WATCH

related recipes on the website

Every recipe from this book is also featured on my website, and along with each recipe on my website is a related-recipes section. These related recipes may be variations of the same recipe, similar recipes that use the same main ingredient, or suggested side dishes to serve with the featured recipe. I want to give you an entire library of recipes that extends beyond the pages of this book, and the related-recipes section on my website will see to that!

recipe tags

Where applicable, the recipes in this book include visual tags that will help you easily find recipe ideas for your meal planning. These tags will help you quickly identify common dietary restrictions, preparation features, or alternative ways to prepare the recipes. The tags you'll find include:

GF **Gluten-free:** These recipes do not contain gluten. Gluten is a common allergen, and I always receive lots of requests for gluten-free recipes. Some recipes not tagged as gluten-free may be easily converted to gluten-free by using gluten-free replacement products.

VE **Vegan:** These recipes are naturally vegan and do not contain any animal products whatsoever.

VG **Vegetarian:** These recipes do not contain any meat but may contain eggs or dairy. Some vegetarians may not consume eggs or dairy, so please consult with any vegetarians you might be feeding.

FF **Freezer friendly:** These recipes can be frozen for later dinners. (If I couldn't fit freezer instructions in the book, you can find them on my website by scanning the QR code for the recipe.)

MA **Make ahead:** These recipes are great for making ahead of time. This feature can come in handy for parties, potlucks, and whenever you have guests over for a meal.

IG **Impress the guests:** These are special occasion recipes that will impress guests, while still being approachable enough to make. These recipes are great for holidays, anniversaries, birthdays, and special dinners where you want to really wow everyone at the table.

Q+E **Quick and easy:** These are go-to easy meals that require minimal effort and are on the table in 30 minutes or less. These are great for busy nights and last-minute meal planning.

SC **Slow cooker friendly:** These recipes can also be made in a slow cooker for your convenience.

PC **Pressure cooker friendly:** These recipes include alternative instructions for preparing the recipe using your electric pressure cooker.

PL **Potluck:** These recipes are ideal for large gatherings like picnics, holiday get-togethers, and other special occasions.

common substitutions

Most of the recipes in this book use basic ingredients that can be found in almost any kitchen. However, there may be instances where you don't have an ingredient and need to make a substitution or you need to make a substitution due to allergies or dietary preferences. Here are some simple substitutions that can be made in these instances.

flour

When flour is used as a thickening agent in a soup, gravy, or sauce, you can replace the flour with cornstarch or arrowroot powder for a gluten-free alternative.

- **For cornstarch,** simply use half of the amount of flour called for in the recipe.

- **For arrowroot powder,** use 1 teaspoon of arrowroot powder for every 1 tablespoon of flour called for in the recipe. (There are 4 tablespoons in ¼ cup.)

Note that the recipes in this book are not designed for the use of gluten-free flours and have not been tested using gluten-free flours or flour blends. If you are going to attempt to use a gluten-free flour replacement, use a gluten-free flour blend that is designed to be a 1:1 replacement for all-purpose flour

eggs

Whether you're baking for someone with an egg allergy or you are simply out of eggs, there are several egg substitute options to choose from. Which one you choose depends on a variety of factors, but it's mostly based on what purpose the egg serves in the recipe. Eggs are generally used in recipes in one of four ways: as a binder, a leavener, a glaze, or as a way to add more moisture to a recipe.

binder replacements for eggs

A binder holds ingredients together in recipes like meatloaf, meatballs, and breadings. Here are some common binder replacements for eggs. (Each replacement equals 1 large egg.)

- Combine 1 tablespoon ground flaxseed and 3 tablespoons water. Whisk together and let stand for 5 minutes before using in a recipe.

- Combine 1 tablespoon chia seeds and 3 tablespoons water. Whisk together before using in a recipe.

leavener replacements for eggs

A leavener helps things like cakes, muffins, or quick breads rise. Here are some common leavener replacements for eggs. (Each replacement equals 1 large egg.)

- Combine 1 tablespoon apple cider vinegar and 1 teaspoon baking soda.

- Combine 2 tablespoons water, 2 teaspoons baking powder, and 1 teaspoon vegetable oil.

- ¼ cup carbonated water

moisture replacements for eggs

The amount of moisture in a recipe is based on the ratio of liquid ingredients to dry ingredients. In some instances, recipes like cookies or brownies may use eggs for both moisture and emulsifying. Here are a few common egg substitutions you can use to add moisture to recipes that call for eggs. (Each replacement equals 1 large egg.)

- ¼ cup unsweetened applesauce

- ¼ cup mashed banana

glaze replacements for eggs

A glaze is brushed on top of breads to give them a shiny finish. Substitute 2 tablespoons of margarine or butter for 1 large egg. You can also purchase commercial egg replacers in both powdered and liquid forms. They will include specific instructions and recommendations for using them to replace eggs in a recipe.

wine

For white wine, you can substitute an equal amount of chicken broth or white grape juice.

For red wine, you can substitute an equal amount of beef broth or red grape juice.

garlic

For minced fresh garlic, you can substitute ¼ teaspoon granulated garlic or ⅛ teaspoon garlic powder for every 1 clove of fresh garlic called for in the recipe.

fresh herbs

For fresh herbs, you can substitute 1 teaspoon dried herbs for every 1 tablespoon of fresh herbs called for in the recipe.

cilantro

For those who don't like cilantro or have a genetic aversion to it, the most common substitute is parsley. You can also use other flavorful herbs like basil, dill, or tarragon.

sugar

There are a variety of reasons why you may want to include a substitute for sugar in a recipe, but here are some suitable alternatives.

- **Honey:** For every 1 cup of sugar in the recipe, use ⅔ cup honey and reduce another liquid ingredient in the recipe, preferably water or milk, if called for, by ¼ cup.

- **Stevia:** For every 1 cup of sugar in the recipe, use 18 to 24 stevia sweetener packets, ½ teaspoon of undiluted stevia powder, or 1 teaspoon of a liquid stevia extract.

- **Molasses:** For every 1 cup of sugar in the recipe, use 1⅓ cups molasses and reduce another liquid ingredient by ¼ cup, preferably water or milk, if called for.

- **Monk fruit:** For every 1 cup of sugar in the recipe, use ½ teaspoon monk fruit extract powder or 1½ tablespoons monk fruit extract. (Be sure to follow replacement instructions on the packaging.)

- **Maple syrup:** For every 1 cup of sugar in the recipe, use 1 cup of maple syrup and then reduce another liquid ingredient in the recipe, preferably water or milk, if called for, by ¼ cup.

2 breakfasts of champions

made-to-order baked frittata

BASIC CHEESE FRITTATA

6 large eggs
¼ cup heavy cream
½ tsp salt
¼ tsp black pepper
1 cup shredded cheese

POTATO FRITTATA

6 large eggs
¼ cup heavy cream
½ tsp salt
¼ tsp black pepper
2 medium Yukon Gold
   potatoes, finely diced
6 slices bacon, diced
3 garlic cloves, minced
½ tsp dried thyme
1 cup shredded Gruyère
   cheese

The frittata is a classic breakfast favorite that's perfect for everything from everyday breakfasts to holidays to special occasion breakfasts or brunches. This recipe features a basic cheese frittata along with three variations. You can customize any of the variations or mix and match your favorite add-ins to create your own custom versions.

Basic Cheese Frittata

1 Preheat the oven to 350°F (177°C).

2 In a large bowl, whisk together the eggs, heavy cream, salt, and black pepper. Add the shredded cheese and stir.

3 Pour the mixture into a 10-inch (25cm) nonstick oven-safe skillet or 10-inch (25cm) cast-iron pan.

4 Place the skillet in the preheated oven. Bake uncovered for 10 to 15 minutes or until the eggs are set and firm in the center.

Potato Frittata

1 Preheat the oven to 350°F (177°C). In a large bowl, whisk together the eggs, heavy cream, salt, and black pepper. Set aside.

2 Place a 10-inch (25cm) nonstick oven-safe skillet or 10-inch (25cm) cast-iron pan over medium-high heat. Add the potatoes and bacon. Sauté until the bacon is cooked through and crispy, about 7 to 10 minutes. Drain off any excess fat.

3 Add the garlic. Cook 1 to 2 minutes more or until the garlic is fragrant. Pour in the egg mixture and then stir in thyme and Gruyère.

4 Place the skillet in the preheated oven. Bake uncovered for 10 to 15 minutes or until the eggs are set and firm in the center.

·· NOTES ································

If you want to double the recipe, use a 12-inch (30.5cm) skillet and add 5 to 10 minutes to the baking time.

SCAN TO WATCH

BACON FRITTATA

6 large eggs

¼ cup heavy cream

½ tsp salt

¼ tsp black pepper

6 slices bacon, diced

½ cup cherry tomatoes, halved

1 cup baby spinach leaves

1 cup shredded cheese (cheddar, Monterey Jack, or mozzarella)

VEGGIE FRITTATA

6 large eggs

¼ cup heavy cream

½ tsp salt

¼ tsp black pepper

1 tbsp olive oil

½ cup frozen broccoli florets

½ cup sliced mushrooms

½ cup diced red bell pepper

¼ cup diced red onion

1 cup shredded cheese (pepper jack, mozzarella, or provolone)

Bacon Frittata

1 Preheat the oven to 350°F (177°C). In a large bowl, whisk together the eggs, heavy cream, salt, and black pepper. Set aside.

2 Place a 10-inch (25cm) nonstick oven-safe skillet or 10-inch (25cm) cast-iron pan over medium-high heat. Add the diced bacon and sauté until the bacon is cooked through and crispy, about 5 to 7 minutes. Drain off any excess fat. Add the tomatoes and spinach. Sauté just until the spinach begins to wilt, about 1 minute.

3 Pour in the egg mixture and then stir in the shredded cheese.

4 Place the skillet in the preheated oven. Bake uncovered for 10 to 15 minutes or until the eggs are set and firm in the center.

Veggie Frittata

1 Preheat the oven to 350°F (177°C). In a large bowl, whisk together the eggs, heavy cream, salt, and black pepper. Set aside.

2 Add the olive oil to a 10-inch (25cm) nonstick oven-safe skillet or 10-inch (25cm) cast-iron pan over medium-high heat.

3 When the oil is hot, add the broccoli, mushrooms, bell pepper, and onion. Sauté until the vegetables are tender crisp, about 5 to 7 minutes. Drain off any excess fat.

4 Pour in the egg mixture and then stir in the shredded cheese.

5 Place the skillet in the preheated oven. Bake uncovered for 10 to 15 minutes or until the eggs are set and firm in the center.

french toast

2 ½ cups milk
(whole, 2%, or 1%)

7 large eggs

¼ cup light brown sugar

½ cup all-purpose flour

3 tsp ground cinnamon

2 tsp vanilla extract

½ tsp salt

6 ½-inch to 1-inch thick
bread slices (challah,
brioche, or Texas toast)

FOR THE SYRUP

½ cup salted butter

1 cup granulated sugar

1 cup buttermilk

1 tbsp vanilla extract

½ tsp ground cinnamon

½ tsp baking soda

This French toast is easy to make and totally delicious, and it's freezable, so you can enjoy it even on the busiest of mornings. While you can omit the flour in the batter, it will give the crust more structure and texture. Use challah for the bread or try brioche or even Texas toast.

1 Whisk the milk and eggs together in a large bowl.

2 Add the brown sugar, flour, cinnamon, vanilla extract, and salt. Whisk until smooth.

3 Preheat a lightly oiled griddle or frying pan over medium-high heat.

4 Soak the bread slices in the mixture until saturated.

5 Cook the bread slices on each side until golden brown.

6 Serve warm and topped with berries and whipped cream, maple syrup, or my famous **Liquid Cinnamon Roll Syrup**.

Liquid Cinnamon Roll Syrup

1 Melt the butter in a large saucepan over medium-high heat. (You'll want to use a much larger saucepan than you think is necessary because the mixture will foam up when you add the baking soda.) Whisk in the sugar, buttermilk, vanilla extract, and cinnamon. Bring to a boil.

2 Once the mixture reaches a boil, reduce the heat to low and simmer for 2 minutes, whisking constantly.

3 Whisk in the baking soda and cook for an additional 30 seconds before removing from heat. (It will foam up like crazy, which is fun for kids to watch! The foam will dissipate after a few minutes.)

4 Serve warm drizzled over the French toast or allow to cool and transfer to an airtight container. Store in the fridge for up to 5 days. (The syrup will thicken as it cools.)

········· NOTES ·········

Freezing and reheating instructions: Cool the slices completely on a wire rack and then transfer to a parchment paper–lined baking sheet. Place a sheet of parchment paper between each layer and then transfer to the freezer. Freeze until solid and then transfer the frozen slices to a resealable plastic freezer bag for long-term freezer storage. To reheat the frozen slices, microwave on high for about 1 minute or until warmed through. (For a crispier texture, reheat the slices in a toaster until warmed through.)

SCAN TO WATCH

perfect pancakes

1½ cups all-purpose flour

2 tbsp granulated sugar

2 tsp baking powder

1 tsp baking soda

½ tsp salt

1 cup milk (whole, 2%, or 1%) or buttermilk

2 large eggs

¼ cup melted unsalted butter

1 In a large bowl, sift together the flour, sugar, baking powder, baking soda, and salt.

2 Whisk in the milk, eggs, and melted butter just until combined.

3 Preheat a flat griddle or large nonstick skillet over medium-high heat.

4 Scoop ¼ cup of the batter onto the hot griddle or skillet. Cook until the pancakes form bubbles on the surface and then flip. Cook until both sides are golden brown.

5 Serve hot with warm pancake syrup drizzled over the top.

······················· NOTES ·······················

To make dry pancake mix, sift together the flour, sugar, baking powder, baking soda, and salt in a bowl. Transfer to a resealable plastic bag or sealable storage container. When ready to use, combine 1¾ cup of the mix with 1 cup milk (whole, 2%, 1%) or buttermilk, 2 eggs, and ¼ cup melted butter. (You can double, triple, or even quadruple this dry mix.)

For a healthier version, replace the all-purpose flour with whole wheat flour, replace the sugar with an equal amount of honey, and replace the butter with an equal amount of unsweetened applesauce.

······················· VARIATIONS ·······················

Fold ½ cup blueberries or semisweet chocolate chips into the pancake batter or add them after you scoop the batter onto a griddle to form fun designs in the pancakes.

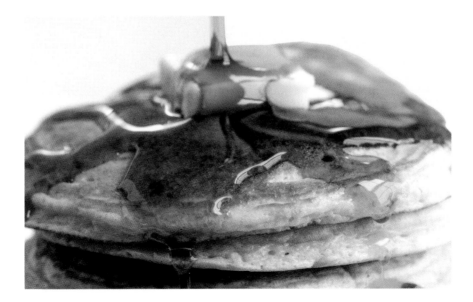

SCAN TO WATCH

simple quiche

This basic quiche recipe is filled with fluffy eggs and melty cheese and can be used as the base for any of your favorite quiche flavors. Make this simple version or try your hand at a classic quiche Lorraine by adding shallots, bacon, and Gruyère cheese. Or make a crowd-favorite broccoli quiche with ham, frozen broccoli, and shredded cheddar cheese. The possibilities are endless!

1 Preheat the oven to 400°F (204°C).

2 Gently transfer the crust to an ungreased pie plate, allowing the crust to hang over the edges of the plate. Roll and pinch or crimp the edges and then use a fork to prick holes in the bottom of the crust.

3 Place parchment paper on top of the pie crust to create a bowl. Add pie weights or dried, uncooked beans to the bowl. (This will prevent the pie crust from sliding or bubbling.) Placed the crust in the preheated oven and parbake for 10 minutes and then remove from the oven and set aside. Reduce the oven temperature to 350°F (177°C).

4 In a medium bowl, whisk the eggs, milk, heavy cream, salt, and black pepper until well combined. Stir in the cheese.

5 Remove the parchment paper and pie weights or beans. (If you're using any additional add-ins like meat or vegetables, add them in the bottom of the parbaked pie crust at this point). Pour the egg mixture over the top of the add-ins.

6 Bake for 40 to 45 minutes or until the center is set.

1 unbaked Foolproof Pie Crust (p. 342)

4 large eggs

1 cup milk

1 cup heavy cream

¼ tsp salt

¼ tsp black pepper

1 cup shredded or crumbled cheese (Gruyère, mozzarella, cheddar, provolone, or feta)

1½ cups add-ins

······················· **NOTES** ·······················

You can mix and match the following add-ins for this incredibly flexible recipe: ½ cup cooked, crumbled bacon; ¾ cup diced ham; ¾ cup cooked ground sausage; 1 cup chopped frozen spinach, thawed and drained; 1 cup frozen broccoli, thawed and drained; 1 cup steamed asparagus, cut into 1-inch pieces; 1 cup sautéed sliced mushrooms; ½ cup sautéed diced shallot or diced onion.

SCAN TO WATCH

simple sausage gravy

1 lb (454g) ground pork
sausage

¼ cup all-purpose flour

3 cups milk
(whole, 2%, or 1%)

Salt and black pepper
to taste

This simple sausage gravy is perfect served over toast, biscuits, potatoes, and even French fries! This dish originated in the Appalachian region of the U.S. in the 1800s and has become a quintessential American breakfast and brunch favorite. It's evolved over the decades into a wide variety of preparations, but you really can't go wrong however you choose to serve it. You'll love how versatile this gravy is and how easy it is to make.

1 Preheat a large skillet over medium-high heat. Add the ground sausage, and use a spatula to break the sausage into small pieces. Cook until the sausage is browned and cooked through, about 8 minutes.

2 Stir in the flour. Continue stirring until no flour specks are visible.

3 Slowly add the milk, stirring constantly. Bring to a boil and then reduce the heat to low. Simmer until the gravy is thickened, about 2 to 3 minutes.

4 Season with salt and black pepper to taste. Serve hot over toast or biscuits.

······· **NOTES** ·······

You can switch things up by using different flavors of ground sausage or sliced breakfast sausage links. If you're using sausage links, you may need to add some additional fat like butter or olive oil to replace the fat that otherwise would be rendered from the ground sausage. This added fat will combine with the flour to create a roux, which will thicken your gravy.

SCAN TO WATCH

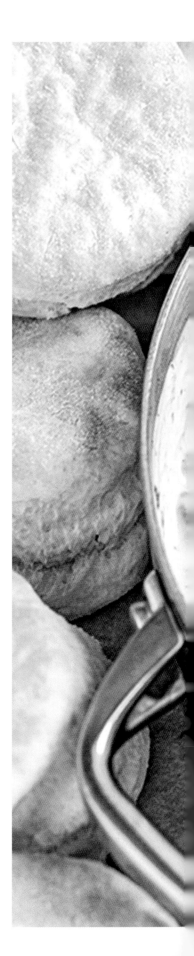

FF · VG

READY IN 30 MINUTES • MAKES 12 MUFFINS

best bran muffins ever

1½ cups 100% whole-
  wheat bran cereal*
1 cup buttermilk
⅓ cup coconut oil, melted
1 large egg
⅔ cup light brown sugar
½ tsp vanilla extract
1 cup all-purpose flour
1 tsp baking soda
1 tsp baking powder
½ tsp salt

Just because bran muffins are functional doesn't mean they can't also be delicious! This is a bran muffin recipe that actually tastes good. The secret is the coconut oil. Not only does it make the muffins healthier, it also adds delicious flavor.

1 Preheat the oven to 450°F (232°C). Lightly spray a muffin pan with nonstick cooking spray or line it with paper muffin cups.

2 In a medium bowl, combine the bran cereal and buttermilk. Soak for about 10 minutes or until the cereal is saturated and soggy.

3 Add the melted coconut oil, egg, brown sugar, vanilla extract, flour, baking soda, baking powder, and salt. Stir thoroughly to combine. (The mixture will be very thick.)

4 Divide the batter equally among the 12 muffin cups, filling them almost completely full.

5 Bake for 5 minutes then, without opening the oven door, reduce the heat to 350°F (177°C) and let the muffins continue baking another 8 to 10 minutes or until a toothpick inserted in the middle comes out clean. Remove the muffins from the pan and cool on a wire rack. Store for up to 5 days at room temperature.

SCAN TO WATCH

·· NOTES ··

* You can find 100% whole-wheat bran cereal in the breakfast cereal aisle at the grocery store. You can use flake-style or the cylindrical stick-like variety. (I like to use All-Bran cereal.) While the cereal may appear unappealing, I promise you'll be turning it into something delicious!

GF · MA

READY IN 1 HOUR 10 MINUTES · MAKES 12 SERVINGS

loaded hash brown breakfast casserole

1lb (454g) ground sausage or 8oz (227g) diced cooked ham

20oz (567g) package frozen diced or shredded hash brown potatoes

1 medium white or yellow onion, diced

1 medium red bell pepper, diced

4oz (113g) can diced green chiles, drained (optional)

10 large eggs

2 cups half-and-half

½ tsp salt

½ tsp black pepper

2 cups shredded cheddar cheese

A breakfast casserole is always a great option for feeding a crowd. You can easily customize this recipe based on what you have on hand. And the best part is that it can be put together the night before so all that's left to do is pop it in the oven in the morning.

1 Preheat the oven to 350°F (177°C) and lightly grease a 9 x 13-inch (23 x 33cm) baking pan.

2 If using ground sausage, preheat a skillet over medium-high heat. Add the sausage and cook 7 to 10 minutes until cooked through. Drain.

3 Add the frozen hash brown potatoes, onion, bell pepper, cooked sausage or ham, and green chiles (if using) to the prepared baking pan. Toss to combine.

4 In a large bowl, whisk the eggs and then pour in the half-and-half. Season with salt and black pepper and then whisk to combine. Stir in the shredded cheese.

5 Pour the egg mixture on top of hash brown mixture in the prepared pan.

6 Cover the pan with aluminum foil and bake for 45 to 60 minutes or until the eggs are set.

SCAN TO WATCH

································· NOTES ··································

To make ahead, prepare the recipe as instructed but do not bake it. Instead, simply cover and refrigerate until ready to bake.

FF

homemade breakfast muffins

½ cup salted butter, softened

1 cup granulated sugar

2 large eggs

½ tsp salt

1 tsp vanilla extract

2 tsp baking powder

2 cups all-purpose flour, divided

½ cup milk (whole, 2%, or 1%) or buttermilk

These simple but delicious homemade muffins can be eaten as a sweet breakfast treat or as an afternoon snack. They're amazing served warm and topped simply with a pat of butter. You can also use this recipe as a base to create a variety of other muffin flavors.

1 Line a muffin tin with paper liners. Lightly spray the liners with nonstick cooking spray.

2 In a large bowl, use a hand mixer to cream together the butter and sugar until smooth and creamy, about 2 minutes.

3 Beat in the eggs until combined, about 20 to 30 seconds. Add the salt, vanilla extract, baking powder, and any optional spices you might be using. Mix briefly.

4 Add 1 cup of flour and mix with the hand mixer until just combined. Add the milk and stir to combine. Use a rubber spatula to scrape the bottom and sides of the bowl and then add the remaining 1 cup of flour. Stir until just combined.

5 If desired, use a rubber spatula to gently fold in any desired add-ins. (Chocolate chips, berries, chopped dried fruit, or chopped nuts will all work.)

6 Preheat the oven to 425°F (218°C). Divide the batter among the 12 muffins cups and set aside to rest while the oven preheats.

7 Bake for 7 minutes. After 7 minutes, reduce the heat 350°F (177°C). (Do not open the oven door.) Bake for an additional 13 to 15 minutes or until the tops are golden. (Watch the muffins closely. The cooking time may vary depending on your oven.)

8 Remove the muffins from the oven and set aside to cool in the pan for 5 minutes before transferring them to a wire cooling rack to cool completely.

SCAN TO WATCH

······················· **NOTES** ·······················

Optional add-ins: Add 1 cup of any of the following to the batter: mini chocolate chips, white chocolate chips, cinnamon chips, fresh blueberries, dried cranberries, raisins, chopped walnuts, or chopped pecans.

For a streusel topping: Stir together ½ cup brown sugar, ½ cup all-purpose flour, ¼ teaspoon salt, and ¼ teaspoon ground cinnamon (optional) in a medium bowl. Use a pastry blender or two knives to cut 4 tablespoons cold butter into the flour mixture until it resembles small pebbles or sand. Spoon the topping on top of batter just before baking.

For spiced muffins: Depending on how prominent you want the flavor to be, add ½ to 1 teaspoon ground cinnamon or pumpkin pie spice to the batter.

For citrus-flavored muffins: Replace the vanilla extract with an equal amount of lemon or orange extract and add up to 2 tablespoons of orange or lemon zest.

Other flavor options: For poppy seed muffins, add 3 tablespoons poppy seeds to the batter; for almond muffins, replace the vanilla extract with an equal amount of almond extract; for chocolate muffins, add ½ cup cocoa powder with the sugar; for pistachio muffins, replace ¼ cup of the sugar with a 3.4 ounce (96g) package of instant pistachio pudding.

perfectly easy homemade waffles

2 cups all-purpose flour
1 tbsp granulated sugar
1 tbsp baking powder
¼ tsp salt
1¾ cups buttermilk
2 large eggs
½ tsp vanilla extract
½ cup salted butter, melted

These foolproof waffles are fluffy on the inside and crispy on the outside. There are many styles and shapes of waffle makers on the market. Belgian-style waffle makers create thicker waffles with deeper pockets that can either be circular or rectangular, while American-style waffle makers make waffles that are thinner with smaller gridlike indentations.

1 Preheat the waffle iron.

2 In a large bowl, combine the flour, sugar, baking powder, and salt. Stir.

3 Add the buttermilk, eggs, vanilla extract, and melted butter. Stir until well combined.

4 Add ½ cup of the batter to the preheated waffle maker for a Belgian-style waffle or add ⅓ cup of the batter to the waffle maker for an American-style waffle. (The amount of batter you use will vary based on the size and style of the waffle iron.)

5 Serve the waffles hot topped with warm syrup or fresh berries and whipped cream.

.... NOTES ....

The batter can be made ahead of time and stored in an airtight container in the fridge for up to 5 days, making it super easy for kids and adults alike to quickly make their own waffles in the morning. If you make the batter ahead of time, be sure to stir it well before using. Some discoloration may occur as the batter sits in the fridge, but stirring will make the discoloration disappear.

SCAN TO WATCH

cooked bacon
(two ways)

1lb (454g) bacon

My two preferred methods for cooking bacon are in the skillet and in the oven. Baking is a superconvenient way to cook a large amount of bacon for a large group without the need for any extra attention. The skillet option is preferred when making smaller amounts for crumbling or for smaller groups for breakfast.

FRYING

1 Place the bacon slices in a cold large skillet in an even layer and without overlapping.

2 Place the cold skillet over medium heat. Cook for 8 to 12 minutes or until the bacon is as crisp as you'd prefer, flipping the slices halfway through the cooking.

3 Transfer the slices to a paper towel–lined plate to drain.

BAKING

1 Preheat the oven to 400°F (204°C).

2 Place the bacon slices in a single layer on a parchment paper–lined baking sheet.

3 Bake for 15 to 20 minutes for chewy bacon or 25 to 30 minutes for crispy bacon. Remove the baking sheet from oven and transfer the slices to a paper towel–lined plate to drain.

SCAN TO WATCH

best homemade cinnamon rolls ever

1 cup warm milk
(whole, 2%, or 1%)

1 tbsp instant dry yeast

2 tbsp granulated sugar

1 tsp salt

3 tbsp plus ½ cup salted
butter, softened and
divided

1 large egg

3 cups all-purpose flour,
divided

FOR THE FILLING

1 cup light brown sugar

2 tbsp ground cinnamon

FOR THE GLAZE

4oz (113g) cream cheese,
softened

¼ cup salted butter,
softened

1 to 1½ cups powdered
sugar

½ tsp vanilla extract

1 to 2 tbsp milk
(whole, 2%, or 1%)

There's nothing quite like the smell of warm cinnamon rolls filling your house. To me, the perfect cinnamon roll is soft, fluffy, and gooey, and this recipe delivers on all three! You can alter this recipe to create other flavors. I've given you three variations to get your creative juices flowing.

1 Begin making the dough by combining the warm milk, yeast, sugar, salt, 3 tablespoons of the softened butter, and egg in the bowl of a stand mixer fitted with a dough hook. Add 1 cup of flour and begin turning the dough on low speed.

2 Once the flour begins to incorporate into the dough, increase the speed to medium. Continue adding flour in small amounts until the dough pulls away from the sides of the bowl. (The dough mixture should be soft and tacky but should not stick to your hands.)

3 Transfer the dough to a lightly greased mixing bowl. Cover the bowl with a towel and let the dough rise at room temperature until it has doubled in size, about 1 hour. Lightly grease a baking sheet or 9 x 13-inch (22 x 33cm) baking pan. Place the remaining ½ cup of butter in a microwave-safe bowl. Microwave until melted.

4 Transfer the dough to a lightly floured pastry board or wood cutting board. Punch down the dough and then roll it into a 12 x 18-inch (30 x 46cm) rectangle. Use a pastry brush to brush the dough with the melted butter.

5 In a small bowl, make the filling by combining the brown sugar and cinnamon. Sprinkle the topping over the dough. Roll the dough up tightly lengthwise until you have one long roll. Using plain dental floss or a sharp knife, cut the dough into 12 equal 1-inch (2.5cm) slices. (Start by cutting the roll in the center and then cutting it into smaller pieces.)

6 Place the slices flat side down on the prepared baking pan. Cover with a towel and set aside to rise for 30 to 45 minutes.

7 Preheat the oven to 325°F (163°C) degrees. Bake the rolls for 18 to 20 minutes or until they're just kissed with brown on top.

8 While the cinnamon rolls are baking, make the cream cheese glaze by using a hand mixer to whip the cream cheese and butter in a medium bowl until light and fluffy. Whip in the powdered sugar and vanilla extract. Add just enough milk to achieve a drizzlelike consistency.

9 Drizzle the glaze over the rolls while they're still warm. Serve immediately or allow to cool before storing. Store in the fridge for up to 5 days.

SCAN TO WATCH

Overnight instructions: After you've rolled and cut your cinnamon rolls, place them in the prepared baking pan, cover with plastic wrap, and place them in the refrigerator. The next day, remove from the fridge and allow to come to room temperature (about 45 minutes to an hour, depending on the temperature of your house) before baking.

Freezing instructions: Roll and cut the cinnamon rolls. Place them several inches apart on a baking sheet and transfer to the freezer. Once frozen, transfer the rolls to a resealable plastic freezer bag. When ready to bake, place the frozen rolls in a lightly greased baking dish and allow to come to room temperature before baking.

Caramel–Apple Cinnamon Rolls: Make the dough as instructed. Reduce the brown sugar for the filling to ½ cup. Once the cinnamon-sugar mixture is sprinkled on top of the dough, sprinkle two cored and finely chopped medium Granny Smith apples over the top. Replace the cream cheese glaze with ½ cup caramel sauce drizzled over the top of the baked rolls. If desired, sprinkle ½ cup chopped pecans over the glazed rolls.

Pumpkin–Cinnamon Rolls: Reduce the milk in the dough to ½ cup. Add 1 cup pumpkin purée with the milk. Use 2 tablespoons of brown sugar instead of white sugar in the dough. For the filling, whip together ½ cup softened butter with ⅓ cup pumpkin purée, ¾ cup brown sugar, 1½ teaspoons ground cinnamon, ½ teaspoon ground ginger, and ½ teaspoon ground nutmeg. Spread the mixture in an even layer over the rolled-out dough.

Orange Rolls: Replace ½ cup of the milk for the dough with ½ cup orange juice. For the filling, instead of the cinnamon-sugar mixture, mix 1 cup granulated sugar with 2 tablespoons orange zest. For the glaze, replace the vanilla extract with orange extract and substitute 1 to 2 tablespoons of orange juice for the milk.

3 tasty little things

authentic italian bruschetta

2 vine-ripe tomatoes, diced

5 fresh basil leaves, chiffonade

½ tsp dried oregano

3 tbsp extra virgin olive oil, divided

1 tsp balsamic vinegar

Pinch of salt

1 Italian-style baguette, sliced

1 garlic clove

This recipe was sent to me from my dear friend Becky, who was living in the Naples region of Italy at the time. She had told her Italian home cook friends what I did for a living and they insisted she send me the instructions for making authentic Naples-style bruschetta. The recipe was absolute perfection when I made it, and I didn't change a thing!

1 Combine the tomatoes, basil, oregano, 1 tablespoon of the olive oil, balsamic vinegar, and salt in a medium bowl. Stir and then transfer to the fridge to chill for 30 minutes.

2 Slice the baguette into ¼- to ½-inch slices. Cut off one end of the garlic clove and rub the garlic over both sides of the bread slices. Brush both sides of the bread slices with the remaining olive oil.

3 Toast the bread slices on a grill or in a hot skillet until they're browned on both sides. Place the toasted slices on a serving platter.

4 Top the toasted bread slices with the cold tomato bruschetta. Serve immediately.

SCAN TO WATCH

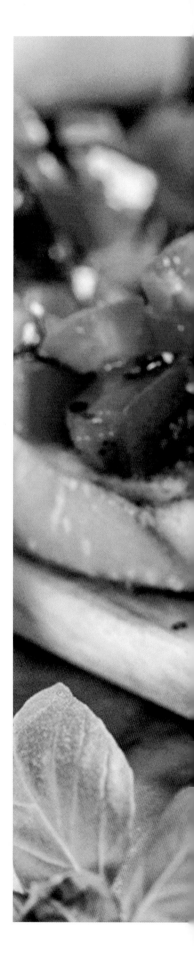

deviled eggs
(two ways)

DEVILED EGGS

12 large eggs

¼ cup mayonnaise

1 tbsp Dijon mustard

1 tbsp sweet pickle relish

1 tsp prepared horseradish

¼ tsp black pepper

Salt, to taste (optional)

½ tsp paprika

BLT DEVILED EGGS

12 large eggs

¼ cup mayonnaise

1 tbsp honey mustard

4 strips candied bacon, finely diced

2 handfuls small cherry tomatoes, quartered

1 handful fresh basil leaves, chopped

½ tsp chili powder, to garnish

·········· NOTES ··········

Because some mustards and relishes are saltier than others, your eggs may or may not need salt depending on your preferences. Taste the filling before filling the egg whites and add salt to taste.

SCAN TO WATCH

Deviled Eggs

The best deviled eggs use all of the classic ingredients but with one secret weapon: horseradish! It's an old chef's secret, and while it doesn't bring much heat, it does enhance the overall flavor. Most people will never realize horseradish is even in the eggs, but it will take your deviled eggs to the next level.

1 Hard-boil the eggs. Once cooled, peel the eggs and slice each in half lengthwise.

2 Gently remove the yolks and place them in a medium bowl. Transfer the whites to a serving platter.

3 Using a fork, mash the yolks and then stir in the mayonnaise, Dijon mustard, sweet pickle relish, horseradish, and black pepper. Mash until the ingredients are well combined. Taste and add salt, if desired.

4 Spoon the filling into the centers of the whites and dust with the paprika. Serve cold.

BLT Deviled Eggs

1 Hard-boil the eggs. Once cooled, peel the eggs and slice each in half lengthwise.

2 Gently remove the yolks and place them in a mixing bowl. Transfer the whites to a serving platter.

3 Add the mayonnaise and honey mustard to the yolks and mash with a fork until well combined and somewhat fluffy.

4 Fold in the diced bacon, tomatoes, and basil. (Reserve a small amount of the basil for garnishing.)

5 Spoon the filling into the centers of the egg whites and dust with the chili powder. Garnish with the reserved basil. Serve cold.

cheesy spinach–artichoke dip

8oz (227g) cream cheese, softened

¼ cup mayonnaise

½ cup grated Parmesan cheese

1 garlic clove, peeled and minced

½ tsp dried basil

¼ tsp salt

¼ tsp black pepper

14oz (397g) canned artichoke hearts, drained and chopped

10oz (283g) frozen chopped spinach, thawed and thoroughly drained

¾ cup shredded mozzarella cheese

Everyone loves spinach–artichoke dip! It's full of flavor and golden brown, ooey-gooey goodness. I love to serve it with a sliced baguette, but pita wedges, crackers, vegetables, or chips are also great for scooping.

1 Preheat the oven to 350°F (177°C). Lightly grease a small baking dish.

2 In a medium bowl, mix together the cream cheese, mayonnaise, Parmesan, garlic, basil, salt, and black pepper. Gently stir in the artichoke hearts and spinach.

3 Transfer the mixture to the prepared baking dish and top with the mozzarella. Bake for 25 minutes or until the cheese is bubbly and lightly browned.

NOTES

If desired, you can use fresh spinach. First remove any woody stems. In a skillet, add a couple teaspoons of olive oil and cook the spinach until wilted. Chop the spinach and then squeeze out any remaining moisture. For this recipe, 10 ounces (283g) of fresh spinach should cook down to about ¾ cup drained and is equal to about 5 ounces (142g) of frozen spinach. (For best results, use baby spinach.)

If you're throwing a party, you can make this recipe in a slow cooker. Combine all ingredients in a small slow cooker and cook on high for 2 hours or on low for 3 to 4 hours. Keep the slow cooker on the "warm" setting during the party.

SCAN TO WATCH

homemade salsa

½ small red onion, minced

2 tbsp lime juice

5 medium Roma tomatoes, diced

½ cup minced fresh cilantro

1 medium jalapeño, stem removed and finely minced

1 garlic clove, minced

¼ tsp salt, plus more to taste

This homemade salsa is so delightfully bright and flavorful; once you've mastered the raw, pico de gallo–style of salsa, it's easy to make slight adjustments to create other varieties. You can increase or decrease the heat level by using different varieties of peppers: a poblano will create a milder salsa, a serrano will make it more spicy, and a habanero will make it extra hot.

1 Place the minced onion in a large bowl. Drizzle with the lime juice and let it sit for 5 minutes.

2 Add the diced Roma tomatoes, cilantro, jalapeño, garlic, and salt.

3 Stir until well combined. Season with more salt to taste, if desired.

························· VARIATIONS ·························

Tomatillo Salsa (Green Salsa or Salsa Verde): Replace the Roma tomatoes with husked and diced tomatillos.

Roasted Tomato Salsa: Place whole Roma tomatoes on a baking sheet and place them 6 inches (15cm) beneath the broiler in your oven. Broil until the skins are blackened, rotating them every few minutes. Once the skins are blackened, let the tomatoes cool and then remove the skins. Dice the tomatoes and then proceed with the recipe as instructed.

SCAN TO WATCH

best buffalo chicken dip

16oz (454g) cream cheese, softened

1 cup blue cheese dressing

1 cup buffalo wing hot sauce (I like Frank's RedHot sauce, but any buffalo-style sauce will work)

2 cups shredded sharp cheddar cheese

2 cups shredded cooked chicken

6oz (170g) crumbled blue cheese (optional)

FOR SERVING

4 celery ribs, cut into sticks

4 carrots, peeled and cut into sticks

1 baguette, sliced into ¼-inch (.60cm) slices

Plain tortilla chips

This spicy party appetizer is full of classic buffalo wing flavors, but in dip form! The combination of three cheeses leads to the ultimate creamy dip with a blast of heat from cayenne-based hot sauce.

1 Preheat the oven to 400°F (204°C). Lightly grease an 8 x 8-inch (20 x 20cm) baking pan.

2 Using a hand mixer, beat the cream cheese until fluffy. Stir in the blue cheese dressing, hot sauce, cheddar cheese, and cooked chicken. Continue stirring until thoroughly combined.

3 Spread the cheese mixture out into the prepared pan and top with the crumbled blue cheese (if using). Bake for 20 to 25 minutes or until the cheese is melted and bubbly.

4 Serve hot with the celery sticks, carrot sticks, baguette slices, and tortilla chips on the side for dipping.

.... NOTES ....

Don't like blue cheese? You can swap out the blue cheese dressing for ranch dressing and skip adding the crumbled blue cheese on top. Or you can swap the blue cheese for an equal amount of additional shredded cheddar cheese or even shredded mozzarella.

SCAN TO WATCH

roasted guacamole

1 medium Roma tomato

1 garlic clove (unpeeled)

1 small serrano pepper

2 medium avocados

¼ cup chopped fresh cilantro

2 tbsp lime juice

¼ tsp salt, plus more to taste

This guacamole recipe is so simple to make and is so incredibly delicious. It has that buttery avocado flavor and goes with everything! The tomatoes, garlic, and serrano pepper are all roasted to add a layer of flavor that takes this guacamole to the next level.

1 Preheat a heavy skillet or griddle over high heat. Place the tomato, garlic clove, and serrano pepper in the skillet, turning each every few minutes until the skins are blackened. (The garlic will roast more quickly, so you'll want to remove it from the skillet first.)

2 Remove the skins from the tomato, garlic clove, and pepper.

3 Using a food processor (or a molcajete for a more authentic preparation), purée the tomato, garlic, and pepper.

4 Add the avocados, cilantro, lime juice, and salt. Pulse until well combined but still chunky. Season with more salt to taste, if desired.

.... **NOTES** ....

If you don't have a food processor, you can use a garlic press for the garlic clove, a knife to chop the cilantro, and a fork to smash the pepper and tomato. Mash the avocado with a fork until it's combined with the other ingredients but still a little chunky.

SCAN TO WATCH

cream cheese wontons
with quick sweet and sour sauce

2 cups vegetable oil
  (for frying)

8oz (227g) cream cheese,
  softened

1 large egg

1 tbsp water

24 wonton wrappers

FOR THE SAUCE

¾ cup light or dark
  brown sugar

2 tbsp ketchup

¼ cup rice vinegar

2 tbsp soy sauce

2 tbsp cornstarch

1 cup pineapple juice

These delicious wontons are paired with a flavorful sweet and sour sauce and make a great appetizer or finger food for a party. If you want to make them ahead of time, simply prepare them all the way up until the point of frying and then refrigerate or freeze them until you're ready to fry.

1 Make the sweet and sour sauce by whisking together the brown sugar, ketchup, rice vinegar, soy sauce, cornstarch, and pineapple juice in a small saucepan.

2 Bring the ingredients to a simmer over medium-high heat. Once the sauce begins to thicken, remove the pan from the heat and set aside.

3 Heat the vegetable oil to 350°F (177°C) in a medium saucepan over medium heat. (Monitor the temperature closely and adjust the heat as needed to ensure it stays 350°F [177°C]).

4 While the oil heats up, whip the cream cheese with a hand mixer until fluffy and smooth. In a small bowl, whisk together the egg and water to make an egg wash.

5 Lightly brush both sides of a wonton wrapper with the egg wash. Put about 1 teaspoon of the cream cheese in the center of each wonton wrapper, fold the wontons by bringing opposite corners together into the center, and then repeat with the remaining corners. Pinch the wrapper shut, making sure to remove any air pockets. Repeat with the remaining ingredients.

6 Fry the wontons, four at a time, in the hot oil until golden brown, about 1 minute per batch. Use a slotted spoon to remove the wontons from the oil and transfer to a paper towel–lined plate to drain.

7 Serve hot with the warm sweet and sour sauce for dipping.

SCAN TO WATCH

one-skillet queso fundido with chorizo

8oz (227g) Mexican chorizo, casings removed

1 small white onion, minced

1 large poblano pepper, seeded and diced

8oz (227g) shredded Monterey Jack cheese

8oz (227g) shredded Oaxaca cheese

2 medium Roma tomatoes, diced

¼ cup chopped fresh cilantro

Plain tortilla chips (for serving)

This ooey-gooey queso fundido is made in just one skillet and features chorizo, poblano peppers, and the perfect blend of melted cheeses. It's easy to make and worthy of serving in any restaurant! Grab some chips and enjoy this amazing dip.

1 Preheat a 10-inch (25cm) cast-iron skillet over medium-high heat. Add the chorizo and cook, stirring occasionally, until the chorizo is browned, about 5 minutes.

2 Add the onion and poblano pepper. Sauté until soft and the chorizo is completely cooked through, about 7 to 10 minutes. Drain any excess fat from the skillet.

3 Stir in both cheeses and then transfer the skillet to the oven, placing it about 8 inches (20cm) from the broiler flame. Broil on high 3 to 5 minutes or until the cheese is melted, bubbling, and starting to brown.

4 Garnish with the tomatoes and cilantro. Serve hot with tortilla chips.

NOTES

If you don't have a cast-iron skillet, you can make this dish in a regular baking dish. (A 7 x 11-inch [18 x 28cm] baking pan, 2-quart [1.89L] casserole dish, or even a pie plate will work.) Cook the chorizo, onion, and poblano peppers as directed in a regular skillet. Stir in the cheeses and transfer all of the ingredients to the baking dish. Broil as instructed.

SCAN TO WATCH

quick-and-easy hummus

¼ cup tahini paste

¼ cup lemon juice (about 1 lemon)

3 tbsp extra virgin olive oil, divided

2 garlic cloves

¼ tsp ground cumin (optional)

¼ tsp salt, plus more to taste

3 cups chickpeas (garbanzo beans), cooked or canned

2–3 tbsp water

This simple and delicious hummus is so easy to make at home. I've also included three popular flavor options: garlic hummus, roasted garlic hummus, and roasted red bell pepper hummus. You can easily alter the flavors to create your own versions. This freshly made hummus beats a store-bought version any day!

1 Add the tahini paste, lemon juice, 2 tablespoons of the olive oil, garlic cloves, cumin (if using), and salt to a food processor or blender. Purée until smooth, about 30 to 60 seconds.

2 Rinse and drain the chickpeas and remove any shells. Add the chickpeas to the food processor and blend for 3 minutes. (If the mixture is too thick, add 2 to 3 tablespoons cold water to thin the mixture to the desired consistency.) Add more salt to taste, if desired.

3 Transfer the hummus to a serving bowl and drizzle with the remaining olive oil. Optional garnishes include chopped parsley, paprika, pine nuts, chopped olives, or chopped roasted red bell pepper. Store in fridge for up to 5 days.

VARIATIONS

Garlic Hummus: Blend in 4 to 6 additional garlic cloves with the rest of the ingredients.

Roasted Garlic Hummus: Cut the top off the narrow end of a garlic bulb and then drizzle it with olive oil. Wrap the bulb in aluminum foil and roast in a 400°F (204°C) oven for 30 to 40 minutes. (Roasting tones down the strength and enhances the flavor.) Squeeze the cloves from the bulb. (This replaces the two cloves called for in the original recipe.) It is delicious!

Roasted Red Bell Pepper Hummus: You can make this either by roasting a fresh red bell pepper or using a 12-ounce (340g) jar of roasted red bell peppers that has been drained. (One 12-ounce jar contains about one whole red bell pepper.) Combine the roasted peppers with the chickpeas in the original recipe and blend thoroughly.

SCAN TO WATCH

cranberry salsa

¼ cup sliced green onion

2 jalapeños, minced

¼ cup minced fresh cilantro

2 tbsp finely grated fresh ginger

2 tbsp lemon juice

½ cup granulated sugar

12oz (340g) fresh cranberries

Cranberry salsa is a uniquely American appetizer that is made with fresh cranberries. Not only is it delicious, but the festive red and green colors play nicely with the holiday seasons that occur in parallel with the availability of fresh cranberries in the fall. It's great for snacking at home or taking to a holiday party. It's a staple in our home that we look forward to all year!

1 Rinse, drain, and sort the cranberries, discarding any that are soft or bruised. Place the cranberries in a food processor or blender and pulse until finely chopped but not mushy.

2 Transfer the chopped cranberries to a bowl and then mix in the green onion, jalapeños, cilantro, and ginger. Pour the lemon juice and sugar over the top and stir to combine.

3 Cover with plastic wrap and refrigerate for at least 1 hour to allow the flavors to develop. (It will be a bit tart to begin with but will develop even more flavor as it rests in the fridge.)

4 Serve with crackers or spread over cream cheese.

·············· **NOTES** ··················

A common and popular way to serve cranberry salsa is over an 8-ounce (225g) brick of softened cream cheese. You can also serve it plain, as you would any salsa. It pairs well with Wheat Thins, Ritz crackers, and plain tortilla chips.

SCAN TO WATCH

4 pork, the other red meat

bone-in marinated pork chops

4 bone-in thick-cut
  pork chops
¼ cup extra virgin olive oil
2 tbsp light brown sugar
5 garlic cloves, crushed
1 tbsp lemon juice
1 tbsp Worcestershire
  sauce
1 tbsp white wine vinegar
1 tsp ground mustard
1 tsp salt
½ tsp black pepper

Bone-in pork chops are easy to make and can rival any beef steak for flavor. For best results, I recommend purchasing chops that are sliced a minimum of 1-inch thick and preferably 1½ to 2 inches. A thicker cut is less likely to dry out, giving you a juicier chop. Use the marinade in this recipe or simply season with salt, black pepper, and paprika.

1 Place the pork chops in a resealable plastic bag. Preheat the oven to 400°F (204°C).

2 In a small bowl, make the marinade by whisking together the olive oil, brown sugar, garlic, lemon juice, Worcestershire sauce, white wine vinegar, ground mustard, salt, and black pepper.

3 Pour the marinade into the bag and over the pork chops. Seal and turn the bag gently to coat the chops in the marinade. Transfer to the fridge to marinate for 2 to 8 hours.

4 To cook, preheat an oven-safe heavy skillet over high heat. Remove the chops from the bag and discard the marinade.

5 Sear the chops for 2 minutes on each side and then immediately transfer the skillet with the chops to the oven. (Alternatively, transfer the chops to a baking dish.) Bake until the internal temperature of the chops reaches 145°F (63°C), about 15 minutes.

6 Remove the chops from the oven and set aside to rest for 5 to 10 minutes before serving. Season with additional salt and black pepper to taste.

··· NOTES ···

You have some options when it comes to choosing which type of pork chop you'll use:

Rib chop: This is the most desirable cut of pork chop. It comes from the rib section (hence its name) and has a large bone running along one side. This cut is very tender with a nice pork flavor.

Loin chop: This cut has a T-bone in the middle. It has two different kinds of meat: loin meat on one side and tenderloin meat on the other. These two meats cook at different rates, so this cut can be a bit more difficult to work with.

Shoulder chop: This is the least desirable cut of pork chop and is not commonly found in American grocery stores. It has lots of flavor, but also a lot of gristle and bones. This cut is best prepared braised.

SCAN TO WATCH

GF · **Q+E**

READY IN 25 MINUTES · MAKES 4 SERVINGS

baked boneless pork chops

4 boneless pork chops
  (¾ to 1-inch thick)

4 tbsp extra virgin olive oil

2 tsp salt

1 tsp black pepper

1 tsp smoked paprika

1 tsp onion powder

These juicy baked pork chops require only a few spices and just 20 minutes to make. For best results, use boneless pork chops that are at least ¾ to 1-inch thick so they can retain moisture and avoid drying out.

1 Preheat the oven to 400°F (204°C). Lightly grease a baking sheet.

2 Rub each pork chop with olive oil.

3 In a small bowl, stir together the salt, black pepper, smoked paprika, and onion powder. Rub all sides of the pork chops with the seasoning mix. Place the seasoned pork chops on the prepared baking sheet.

4 Bake for 15 to 20 minutes or until the pork chops reach an internal temperature of 145°F (63°C). (Actual baking time will depend on the thickness of the chops). Serve hot.

SCAN TO WATCH

sunday pork roast

This pork roast is an easy-to-make comfort food that is hearty, filling, and can easily feed the entire family for Sunday dinner. Pork roast tends to be a less expensive than beef roast. This recipe includes instructions for a classic oven-braise preparation as well as slow cooker and electric pressure cooker preparations.

1 In a small bowl, combine the salt, black pepper, garlic powder, onion powder, and paprika.

2 Rub the vegetable oil onto the pork roast and then sprinkle the seasoning mixture onto the roast. Place the roast fatty side up in a large roasting pan or cast-iron Dutch oven.

3 Roast, uncovered, for 30 to 45 minutes and then reduce the oven temperature to 350°F (177°C). Continue cooking for 1 hour more.

4 Remove the roast from the oven and place the onions, carrots, and potatoes around the roast. Pour the apple juice over the vegetables Place the rosemary sprig on top of the roast.

5 Roast an additional 1 to 1 ½ hours or until the vegetables are tender and the meat shreds easily with a fork. Season the vegetables with additional salt and black pepper to taste. Serve hot.

2 tsp salt, plus more to taste

2 tsp black pepper, plus more to taste

1 tsp garlic powder

1 tsp onion powder

1 tsp paprika

2 tbsp vegetable oil

3–5lb (1.35–2.25kg) pork shoulder or pork butt roast

2 large white onions, cut into 2-inch (5cm) chunks

1lb (454g) baby carrots

1½lb (680g) baby red potatoes

2 cups apple juice

1 sprig fresh rosemary

························· **NOTES** ·················

Slow cooker instructions: Season the roast as directed in step 2. Place the meat directly into a slow cooker, add all remaining ingredients, and cook on low for 8 hours.

Electric pressure cooker instructions: Season the roast as directed. Sear the roast using the "sear" setting on your electric pressure cooker. Deglaze the pot with the apple juice and then add the vegetables. Cook on high pressure for 60 minutes, followed by a 15-minute natural release. After 15 minutes, flip the steam release valve to the venting position. Remove the lid once steam has stopped coming out of the valve.

SCAN TO WATCH

crispy fried pork chops

2 cups vegetable oil
(for frying)

4 boneless pork loin chops
(¼- to ½-inch thick)

3 tsp salt, divided

2 tsp black pepper, divided

2 cups buttermilk

¼ cup buffalo hot sauce
(optional)

1½ cups all-purpose flour

½ cup cornstarch

2 tsp paprika

1 tsp onion powder

1 tsp garlic powder

These thinly sliced pork chops are covered with a flavorful buttermilk coating, dredged in seasonings, and then fried in oil. While thin pork chops can easily end up dry from other cooking methods, frying them in oil results in this inexpensive cut coming out tender and juicy.

1 Pour the vegetable oil into a large skillet. Heat to 350°F (177°C). (Monitor the temperature of the oil closely, and adjust the heat as needed to ensure the temperature stays consistent.)

2 While the oil is heating, season the pork chops with 1 teaspoon salt and 1 teaspoon black pepper.

3 Pour the buttermilk and hot sauce (if using) into a 9 x 13-inch (23 x 33cm) pan and then stir to combine. Submerge the seasoned pork chops in the buttermilk mixture and set aside. (You can refrigerate the seasoned chops for up to 6 hours or use them right away.)

4 In a shallow bowl, stir together the flour, cornstarch, remaining 2 teaspoons salt, remaining 1 teaspoon black pepper, paprika, onion powder, and garlic powder.

5 Working one at a time, remove the pork chops from the buttermilk mixture, shake gently to remove any excess coating, and dredge in the seasonings to coat thoroughly. Gently tap to remove any excess seasonings and then place on a plate. Repeat with the remaining chops.

6 Carefully place two chops in the oil and fry for 4 to 5 minutes per side or until golden brown and the internal temperature reaches 145°F (63°C). (The meat will drop the temperature of the oil initially, so try to keep the temperature of the oil as close to 350°F [175°C] as possible.)

7 Transfer the cooked chops to a plate lined with paper towels and then repeat with the remaining chops. Let the chops rest for 5 minutes before serving.

SCAN TO WATCH

smothered pork chops

4 center-cut bone-in pork chops (1 to 1½-inches thick)

1½ tsp salt

1 tsp black pepper

1 tbsp olive oil

1 large white onion, halved and sliced

8oz (227g) button or crimini mushrooms, sliced

2 tbsp butter

2 garlic cloves, minced

2 tbsp all-purpose flour

2 cups chicken broth

This classic American dish is easy to make and full of flavor. The chops are seared and then finished in the oven while you make a savory, smothering gravy with onions and mushrooms. This recipe is especially delicious served over cooked rice or mashed potatoes.

1 Preheat the oven to 350°F (177°C). Preheat a heavy skillet over medium-high heat. Generously season the pork chops on both sides with salt and black pepper. (The exact amount of salt and black pepper you use can vary depending on the size and thickness of the chops.)

2 Increase the heat to high and place the chops in the skillet. Sear for 3 to 4 minutes per side or until they begin to turn golden brown. Transfer the chops to a 9 x 13-inch (23 x 33cm) baking pan and finish cooking in the oven until the internal temperature reaches 145°F (63°C), about 15 minutes.

3 While the chops are finishing in the oven, reduce the stovetop burner to medium-high and return the skillet to the heat. Add the olive oil, onion, and mushrooms. Sauté for 5 to 7 minutes or until the mushrooms and onion are soft.

4 Add the butter and garlic. Cook for an additional 1 minute and then sprinkle in the flour and stir until the specks disappear, about 1 minute, Pour in the chicken broth and bring to a simmer. Stir continuously until the sauce thickens.

5 When the chops are cooked through, return them to the skillet and spoon the gravy over the top. Serve hot.

························ NOTES ························

For best results, use thick-cut pork chops that are at least 1 inch thick. This recipe is written for thick-cut chops that are 1 to 1½ inches (2.5 to 3.75cm) thick. To make thinner pork chops, cook them in the skillet without transferring them to the oven. Chops that are less than ½ inch (1.25cm) thick can cook as quickly as 4 to 5 minutes per side in a skillet.

SCAN TO WATCH

honey dijon–garlic-roasted pork tenderloin

¼ cup whole-grain Dijon mustard

2 tbsp honey

4 garlic cloves, crushed

½ tsp salt

¼ tsp black pepper

2lb (907g) pork tenderloin

1 tbsp olive oil

This perfectly tender pork tenderloin only requires a few ingredients and a few minutes of preparation to get it roasting in the oven. It's a flavorful, juicy main dish that your family will love!

1 Preheat a large cast-iron skillet or oven-safe skillet over high heat. Preheat the oven to 400°F (204°C).

2 In a small bowl, whisk together the Dijon mustard, honey, garlic, salt, and black pepper. Brush the pork tenderloin with the sauce until thoroughly coated.

3 Pour the olive oil into the preheated skillet. When the oil is hot, place the tenderloin in the skillet and sear on each side. Brush any remaining sauce over the tenderloin to coat again.

4 Once the outside of the tenderloin is seared, transfer the tenderloin to the preheated oven and roast until the internal temperature reaches 145°F (63°C), about 10 to 15 minutes.

5 Allow the tenderloin to rest for 5 minutes before slicing and serving.

······················ NOTES ······················

It's best to cook pork tenderloin by temperature rather than by color; otherwise, you risk drying out the meat. Pork tenderloin is a darker cut of pork, which means it's considered a red meat and will have a rosy hue when cooked to the correct internal temperature of 145°F (63°C). Even at temperatures of 165°F (74°C) and beyond, tenderloin may still have a rosy hue in the center.

SCAN TO WATCH

apple-glazed roasted pork loin

This pork loin is the perfect balance of sweet and savory flavors; it's roasted and then drizzled with a delicious glaze. This roast will impress your guests and they'll have to fight the temptation to lick their plates clean. It's that good!

1 Preheat the oven to 375°F (191°C). Season the pork loin with the salt and black pepper.

2 In a small bowl, whisk together the Dijon mustard and apple cider vinegar. Set aside.

3 Heat the olive oil in a heavy, oven-safe skillet over medium-high heat. Once the oil is hot, place the pork loin in the skillet and sear for 2 to 3 minutes per side or until browned.

4 Brush the mustard and vinegar mixture over the pork roast.

5 Place the skillet in the oven and roast the pork loin until the internal temperature reaches 145°F (63°C), about 30 to 40 minutes depending on the size of the roast.

6 While the pork loin is roasting, make the apple glaze by melting the butter in a medium saucepan over medium-high heat. Whisk in the cornstarch until all the specks are absorbed and then add the apple juice, Dijon mustard, brown sugar, and apple cider vinegar. Continue whisking until the sauce is thickened, about 2 minutes.

7 Remove the pork loin from the oven and set aside to rest about 5 minutes before slicing. Drizzle the apple glaze over the slices. Serve hot.

2–3lb (1–1.5kg) pork loin, trimmed and tied

1½ tsp salt

½ tsp black pepper

2 tbsp Dijon mustard

1 tbsp apple cider vinegar

1 tbsp olive oil

For the glaze

2 tbsp butter

1 tbsp cornstarch

1 cup apple juice

1 tbsp Dijon mustard

1 tbsp light or dark brown sugar

1 tsp apple cider vinegar

.... **NOTES** ....

As with any roast, this one goes great with most traditional side dishes. My family likes it with a garden salad and roasted or mashed potatoes. Cooked veggies, like green beans and asparagus, also go great with it. And don't forget the rolls—they're an easy win!

SCAN TO WATCH

baked pork ribs

2 racks pork ribs
   (baby back, spare, or
   St. Louis style)
1 tbsp smoked paprika
1 tsp salt
1 tsp black pepper
1 tsp onion powder
1 tsp garlic powder
1 tsp ground mustard
1 cup barbecue sauce

Cooked low and slow in the oven, these juicy ribs are fall-off-the-bone tender and packed with flavor. It doesn't matter which type of pork ribs you choose to make with this recipe, it will work with baby back, spare, or St. Louis–style ribs.

1 Preheat the oven to 275°F (135°C). Line a large baking sheet or roasting pan with aluminum foil.

2 Remove the membrane from the back of the ribs by sliding your fingers around the sides to loosen it up and then pulling it off. (If it's slippery, you can use a paper towel to provide a better grip.)

3 In a small bowl, stir together the smoked paprika, salt, black pepper, onion powder, garlic powder, and ground mustard. Rub the mixture generously over the outside of the ribs. Place the seasoned ribs in a single layer onto the prepared baking sheet or roasting pan. Cover the baking sheet or roasting pan tightly with aluminum foil.

4 Bake for 3½ to 4 hours or until the ribs are tender and reach an internal temperature of 195°F to 205°F (91°C to 96°C). Remove the ribs from the oven and then remove the aluminum foil. Brush the ribs with the barbecue sauce.

5 Change the oven setting to broil. Place the ribs 6 inches (15.25cm) beneath the broiler for 3 to 5 minutes or until the barbecue sauce begins to bubble and caramelize. (Watch closely to ensure the sauce doesn't burn.)

6 Allow the ribs to rest for 10 minutes before cutting into individual ribs. Serve warm.

··· NOTES ···

Slow cooker instructions: After removing the membrane and coating the ribs with the dry rub, place them in a slow cooker and then brush with barbecue sauce. Cook on low for 8 to 10 hours and then transfer them to an aluminum foil–lined baking sheet. Brush the tops with more barbecue sauce and then place under the broiler for 3 to 5 minutes or until the barbecue sauce begins to bubble and caramelize.

SCAN TO WATCH

5 don't worry, beef happy

steak bites and gnocchi

1lb (454g) sirloin steak or beef tenderloin, trimmed

2 tbsp lemon juice

1 tbsp olive oil

1 tbsp Worcestershire sauce

1 tbsp apple cider vinegar

1 tsp onion powder

1 tsp garlic powder

1 tsp salt

½ tsp black pepper

2lb (907g) packaged dried gnocchi

2 tbsp butter

2 garlic cloves, crushed

¼ cup freshly grated Parmesan cheese, for serving (optional)

Irresistible marinated steak bites are served with perfectly browned gnocchi in this quick-and-easy meal. This is one of our family's go-to recipes for busy nights; it comes together quickly, has easy cleanup, is a one-dish meal, and most importantly, everyone devours it! Even guests rave about it!

1 Dice the steak into bite-sized pieces. Place the steak bites in a gallon-sized resealable plastic bag or a shallow bowl.

2 Add the lemon juice, olive oil, Worcestershire sauce, apple cider vinegar, onion powder, garlic powder, salt, and black pepper. Toss to coat. Seal the bag or cover the bowl, and place it in the fridge to marinate for 1 to 8 hours.

3 Bring a large pot of water to a boil over high heat. Preheat a large skillet over medium-high heat.

4 Cook the gnocchi in the boiling water according to package directions. Drain and set aside.

5 While the gnocchi is cooking, use tongs to transfer half of the steak to the preheated skillet. Gently shake the steak pieces to remove as much of the marinade as possible. (A little liquid in the pan is okay, but you don't want to steam the steak.) Sauté, stirring occasionally, until the bites are seared and browned. Transfer the cooked bites to a plate and then cook the remaining steak bites, making sure not to crowd the skillet.

6 Return the previously cooked steak to the skillet. Add the butter and crushed garlic. Sauté the garlic for about 1 minute and then add the gnocchi. Sauté 3 to 5 minutes more or until the gnocchi is lightly browned.

7 Serve hot with the grated Parmesan (if using) sprinkled over the top.

.... NOTES ....

If you're short on time, you can skip the marinating. You'll lose a little flavor, but it's still super delicious!

SCAN TO WATCH

READY IN 15 MINUTES · MAKES 4 SANDWICHES

authentic philly cheesesteak

2 beef ribeye steaks or top round (about 3lb [1.35kg])

½ tsp salt

½ tsp black pepper

1 tbsp vegetable oil

1 medium yellow onion, thinly sliced (optional)

4 hoagie rolls*

For the cheese (choose one)

4 slices provolone cheese

4 slices American cheese

½ cup Cheese Whiz

A Philly cheesesteak sandwich is the ultimate comfort food and features thinly sliced steak, cheese, and sautéed onion all served on a soft and delicious hoagie roll. This is one of those recipes that everyone loves!

1 Slice the uncooked steak as thinly as possible. Season with the salt and black pepper. Set aside.

2 Heat the vegetable oil in a large skillet over medium-high heat. Add the sliced onion (if using) and sauté until soft, about 5 to 7 minutes. Remove the onion from the skillet and set aside.

3 Add the steak slices to the skillet in a single layer. Sear 1 to 2 minutes per side and then use a spatula to chop the steak. Add the cooked onion (if using) and any other desired additions.

4 Reduce the heat to low and top the chopped steak with your choice of cheese. Let the cheese melt (if using provolone or American cheese) and then transfer the mixture to the hoagie rolls. Serve immediately.

·· NOTES ··

* If you can find them, use Amoroso's rolls for a truly authentic version!

If you have trouble slicing the uncooked steak, pop it in the freezer for 30 minutes to partially freeze it and make it easier to slice.

Other popular additions might include sautéed bell peppers (sliced or diced), sautéed sliced mushrooms, pickled jalapeño slices, hot cherry peppers, long hot peppers, sweet peppers, lettuce and tomato, marinara sauce (be sure to toast the buns), mayonnaise, mustard, or Tabasco sauce.

SCAN TO WATCH

GF · IG

READY IN 1 HOUR 30 MINUTES • MAKES 3 POUNDS (1.35KG)

classic roast beef

3lb (1.35kg) beef roast (eye of round)*

2 tbsp olive oil

1 tbsp black pepper

1 tsp salt

1 tsp garlic powder

1 tsp onion powder

You'll be amazed at how easy it is to make this amazing roast beef. It's perfect for any holiday meal or a Sunday dinner. The whole family will love it! We love to serve this thinly sliced and topped with gravy or the creamy horseradish sauce from the **Steakhouse-Style Horseradish-Crusted Prime Rib** recipe (p. 87). We also like to serve it with a side of mashed potatoes and our favorite roasted veggies.

1 Position the oven rack in the bottom or second-to-bottom slot. Preheat the oven to 325°F (163°C).

2 Place the roast into a 9 x 13-inch (23 x 33cm) roasting pan or a large cast-iron skillet.

3 In a small bowl, stir together the olive oil, black pepper, salt, garlic powder, and onion powder. Rub the mixture onto the roast, coating all sides.

4 Transfer to the oven and roast for 1 hour or until the internal temperature reaches 135°F (60°C). (Check the roast with a meat thermometer as close to the center as possible after 1 hour.)

5 Remove the roast from the oven and set aside to rest for 10 minutes before carving. (This roast is best served sliced as thinly as possible.)

SCAN TO WATCH

.... NOTES ....

* Eye of round is the ideal cut to use for this recipe, but you can also use top round, sirloin tip, center-cut sirloin, or bottom round.

momma's meatloaf

2 lb (907g) lean ground beef

½ large white onion, diced

1 cup dried breadcrumbs

½ cup milk (whole, 2%, or 1%)

1 large egg

2 tbsp Worcestershire sauce

1 tsp salt

½ tsp black pepper

1 tsp dried basil

1 tsp dried oregano

½ tsp red pepper flakes

FOR THE GLAZE

½ cup ketchup

2 tbsp light or dark brown sugar

1 tbsp Worcestershire sauce

This classic meatloaf features just a hint of heat. It's easy to make, holds together well, and is topped with a simple and delicious glaze! You can easily switch things up by substituting ground turkey for the ground beef or stuffing it with cheese.

1 Preheat the oven to 350°F (177°C). Lightly grease a 9 x 13-inch (23 x 33cm) baking pan.

2 In a large bowl, knead together the ground beef, onion, breadcrumbs, milk, egg, Worcestershire sauce, salt, black pepper, basil, oregano, and red pepper flakes.

3 Shape the mixture into a loaf and transfer it to the prepared baking pan. Bake for 45 minutes.

4 While the meatloaf is baking, make the glaze by whisking together the ketchup, brown sugar, and Worcestershire sauce in a small bowl.

5 After 45 minutes, brush the glaze over the hot meatloaf. Increase the oven temperature to 400°F (204°C) and bake for an additional 15 minutes or until the meatloaf reaches an internal temperature of 165°F (74°C).

·········· VARIATIONS ··········

Turkey Meatloaf: Replace the ground beef with 2 pounds (1kg) ground turkey.

Mozzarella-Stuffed Meatloaf: Make the ground beef mixture as directed and then divide the meat into two halves. Shape one half into the bottom of the prepared pan. Layer 8 ounces (225g) of fresh mozzarella slices down the center of the bottom half, leaving a ½ inch (1.25cm) gap around the ends and sides. Shape the remaining half of the loaf and then place it on top of the bottom layer. Pinch the edges shut and bake the meatloaf as instructed.

SCAN TO WATCH

classic sunday pot roast

3–5lb (1.35–2.25kg) beef chuck or round roast or beef brisket

2 tsp salt, plus more to taste

1 tsp black pepper, plus more to taste

2 tbsp vegetable oil

6 garlic cloves, minced

1–2 cups red wine* (use 2 cups for a larger roast)

2 cups low-sodium beef broth

¼ cup Worcestershire sauce

2 large white onions, cut into 2-inch (5cm) chunks

1lb (454g) baby carrots

1lb (454g) red potatoes, cut into bite-sized chunks

1 sprig fresh rosemary

This classic is an easy-to-make comfort food meal that is hearty, filling, and can easily feed an entire family. This recipe will work for a classic oven braise as well as in a slow cooker or electric pressure cooker.

1 Preheat the oven to 350°F (177°C). Preheat a large oven-safe Dutch oven over high heat.

2 Season both sides of roast with the salt and black pepper. Add the vegetable oil to the pot and sear the roast until browned, about 3 to 4 minutes per side.

3 Remove the roast from the pot and set it aside briefly on a plate or cutting board. Add the garlic to pot and sauté for 1 minute. Deglaze the pan with the red wine and beef broth. Add the roast back to the pot.

4 Pour the Worcestershire sauce over the roast and place the onion, carrots, and potatoes on top of and around the roast. Place the rosemary sprig on top of the roast.

5 Cover and transfer to the preheated oven. Cook for 3 hours or until the internal temperature reaches 202°F (94°C) and the meat shreds easily with a fork. Season the vegetables with additional salt and pepper to taste. Serve hot.

SCAN TO WATCH

* If preferred, you can replace the wine with an equal amount beef broth or grape juice.

Slow cooker instructions: Season the roast with salt and black pepper as directed in step 2. (If desired, sear the roast in oil in a skillet.) Place the meat directly into a slow cooker, add all remaining ingredients, and cook on low for 8 hours.

Electric pressure cooker instructions: Follow the recipe as instructed, using a pressure cooker instead of a Dutch oven. Sear the roast using the "sear" setting. Cook on high pressure for 60 minutes, followed by a 15 minute natural release before switching the release valve to the venting position. Remove the lid once steam has stopped coming out.

· VARIATIONS ·

2 tbsp vegetable oil

3–5lb (1.35–2.25kg) beef chuck or round roast or beef brisket

½ cup beef broth

8 whole pepperoncinis (in juice)

¼ cup pepperoncini juice

2 tbsp powdered ranch dressing seasoning

1 tbsp onion powder

½ cup salted butter

Mississippi Pot Roast

1 Preheat the oven to 350°F (177°C). Preheat an oven-safe Dutch oven over high heat.

2 Add the vegetable oil to the pot and sear the roast until browned, about 3 to 4 minutes per side.

3 Add the beef broth, pepperoncinis, and pepperoncini juice, and then sprinkle the roast with ranch dressing seasoning and onion powder. Add the butter on top of the roast.

4 Cover and transfer to the preheated oven. Cook for 3 hours or until the meat reaches an internal temperature of 202°F (94°C) and shreds easily with a fork.

GF · FF

READY IN 45 MINUTES · MAKES 6 SERVINGS

stuffed bell peppers

6 large bell peppers
(any color)

¾–1 lb (340–454g) lean
ground beef

1 medium white onion,
diced

3 garlic cloves, minced

5oz (142g) can diced
tomatoes, drained

1 cup cooked white rice

1 cup frozen corn kernels

1 tbsp Worcestershire
sauce

1½ tsp salt

½ tsp black pepper

1½ cups shredded pepper
jack cheese, divided

Stuffed bell peppers are an easy way to enjoy one of summer's favorite veggies. These peppers are stuffed with a delicious cheesy ground beef and rice mixture. They're simple and flavorful, but they can also be easily customized with different spices and vegetable additions based on what you have on hand.

1 Preheat the oven to 350°F (177°C). Lightly grease a 9 x 13-inch (23 x 33cm) baking pan.

2 Cut the tops off each bell pepper and then remove the seeds and membranes. Place the peppers in the prepared baking pan. Set aside.

3 In a large skillet over medium-high heat, sauté the ground beef and onion until browned. Drain any excess fat and then add the garlic. Cook for 1 minute more and then remove the skillet from the heat.

4 Stir in the tomatoes, cooked rice, corn, Worcestershire sauce, salt, black pepper, and 1 cup of the pepper jack cheese.

5 Spoon the mixture into the bell peppers until they're full. Sprinkle the remaining cheese over the top of the peppers.

6 Bake for 30 minutes or until the cheese is bubbly and browned.

SCAN TO WATCH

.... NOTES ....

If you prefer your bell peppers be soft instead of tender-crisp, bake for 10 to 15 minutes at 350°F (177°C) in the lightly greased pan before filling.

FF

READY IN 45 MINUTES · MAKES 8 SANDWICHES

sloppy joes

1lb (454g) lean ground beef

1 medium yellow onion, diced

1 medium green bell pepper, diced

2 celery ribs, diced

8oz (227g) canned tomato sauce

6oz (170g) canned tomato paste

2 tbsp Worcestershire sauce

4 garlic cloves, crushed

1 tbsp light or dark brown sugar

1 tsp salt

1 tsp ground mustard

½ tsp red pepper flakes

8 hamburger buns, toasted

These amazing sloppy joes are truly homemade and so delicious that both adults and kids will love them. The entire family will love this delicious easy dinner! It's also a great way to sneak in some extra vegetables for your kids!

1 Place the ground beef and yellow onion in a large skillet over medium-high heat. Cook, stirring occasionally, until the beef is browned and cooked through. Drain any excess fat from the skillet and return the skillet to the heat.

2 Add the bell pepper, celery, tomato sauce, tomato paste, Worcestershire sauce, garlic, brown sugar, salt, ground mustard, and red pepper flakes. Stir to combine.

3 Bring to a simmer and then reduce the heat to medium low. Simmer for 15 to 30 minutes, depending on how soft you prefer the vegetables.

4 Serve the filling hot on the toasted buns.

························· NOTES ·························

You can adjust the amount of vegetables to suit your personal taste. However, the vegetables add extra flavor and an amazing texture to this historically mushy sandwich, so I recommend sticking to the recipe as closely as possible.

SCAN TO WATCH

baked meatballs

1–1½lb (454–680g) lean ground beef

¾ cup plain dried breadcrumbs

½ cup freshly grated Parmesan cheese

2 tsp dried basil

1 tsp salt

½ tsp red pepper flakes

2 garlic cloves, minced

⅓ cup milk (whole, 2%, or 1%)

2 tbsp Worcestershire sauce

1 large egg (optional)

These are the best baked meatballs you'll ever taste! They feature a crispy crust and a juicy, flavorful center. Whenever I make these, I always make a double batch. A second batch is handy to freeze for future meals, and it doesn't take much additional effort to make it.

1 Preheat the oven to 400°F (204°C). Lightly coat a 9 x 13-inch (23 x 33cm) pan or large baking sheet with nonstick cooking spray.

2 Combine all the ingredients in a medium bowl. (You can include the egg as an additional binder or leave it out, as the cheese will also bind the meatballs). Mix thoroughly until the ingredients are fairly evenly distributed.

3 Shape the mixture into 1 to 1½-inch (2.5 to 4cm) meatballs, making sure they are all roughly the same size to ensure even baking.

4 Bake for 25 to 30 minutes or until the internal temperature reaches 165°F (74°C). Serve hot. Store in the fridge in an airtight container for up to 5 days.

················ **NOTES** ················

Freezing and reheating instructions: Place the uncooked meatballs on a baking sheet and freeze for at least 2 hours or until solid. Once frozen, transfer the frozen meatballs to a resealable plastic freezer bag and freeze for up to 3 months. When ready to bake, simply add 10 minutes to the baking time.

SCAN TO WATCH

braised beef short ribs

These short ribs are cooked low and slow until they reach fall-off-the-bone deliciousness. This simple dish is a classic and full of comfort food flavor. These are great served over mashed potatoes, cooked rice, or even couscous.

1 Preheat the oven to 350°F (177°C). Season all sides of the short ribs with the salt and black pepper.

2 Preheat a large, heavy oven-safe pot over high heat. Add the olive oil and allow to heat briefly before adding the short ribs. Sear the ribs for about 1 minute per side to render the fat and then remove the ribs from the pot. Set aside.

3 Add the onion and sauté for 3 to 5 minutes or until softened. Add the garlic and sauté for 1 minute more.

4 Pour in the beef broth, red wine (if using), and Worcestershire sauce. Bring to a simmer and then return the ribs to the pot. Place the rosemary sprig on top of the ribs.

5 Cover the pot and transfer to the preheated oven. Bake for about 2½ hours or until the meat reaches an internal temperature of 202°F (94°C) and shreds easily with a fork. Serve whole.

8 bone-in short ribs (about 4 lb [1.75kg])

½ tsp salt

½ tsp black pepper

3 tbsp extra virgin olive oil

½ cup diced white onion (or 1 tsp onion powder)

2 to 3 garlic cloves, minced (or 1 tsp garlic powder)

1 cup beef broth

1 cup red wine (optional)

¼ cup Worcestershire sauce

1 sprig fresh rosemary

······································ **NOTES** ································

If you're using onion powder and garlic powder in place of the fresh onion and garlic, simply sprinkle the seasoning over the short ribs once the ribs are seared and then proceed with adding the liquids to the pot, slow cooker, or pressure cooker.

Slow cooker instructions: Season the short ribs with salt and black pepper and sear in olive oil in a skillet over high heat. Transfer the seared ribs to a 6-quart slow cooker. Season with the garlic powder and onion powder and then pour in the beef broth, red wine, and Worcestershire sauce. Place the rosemary sprig on top of the ribs, cover, and cook on low for 8 hours or until the meat is fork-tender.

Electric pressure cooker instructions: Use the "sear" feature on the electric pressure cooker to sear the seasoned ribs. Sauté the onion until tender and then add the garlic and sauté for 1 minute more. Pour in the beef broth, red wine, and Worcestershire sauce. Place the rosemary sprig on top of the ribs and cook on high pressure for 50 minutes followed by a 10 to 15 minute natural release.

SCAN TO WATCH

GF · IG

READY IN 45 MINUTES · MAKES 8 TO 10 SERVINGS

garlic–brown butter beef tenderloin

5–6 lb (2.25–2.75kg)
 beef tenderloin

2 tsp salt

2 tsp black pepper

1 tsp white pepper

½ cup unsalted butter

4 garlic cloves

This roasted beef tenderloin is dressed with a simple garlic and brown butter sauce and will melt in your mouth. Yes, tenderloin is the most expensive cut of beef, but all the more reason to keep it simple to ensure it turns out perfectly every time. It's an absolute showstopper!

1 Preheat the oven to 450°F (232°C). Preheat a heavy 12-inch (30.5cm) skillet over medium-high heat.

2 Remove any silver skin from the tenderloin. One half of the roast should have a thinner end that tapers off. Fold the thin end up against the rest of the roast and use kitchen twine to tie it together to create an even thickness in the roast. Season generously with salt, black pepper, and white pepper. (If necessary, cut the tenderloin in half to ensure it fits in the skillet.)

3 Sear the tenderloin in the preheated skillet on all sides until browned, about 3 to 4 minutes per side.

4 Transfer the tenderloin to a large roasting pan or a 9 x 13-inch (23 x 33cm) baking pan. Roast until the internal temperature reaches 120°F to 125°F (50°C to 55°C) for medium-rare, about 30 minutes. Remove the tenderloin from the oven and cover loosely with aluminum foil. Set aside to rest for about 10 minutes.

5 While the tenderloin is resting, melt the butter in a small saucepan over medium heat. Add the garlic cloves and cook, stirring continuously, until the butter turns a dark golden brown. Remove the pan from the heat and discard the garlic cloves.

6 Slice the roast into ½- to ¾-inch (1.25 to 2cm) slices and then drizzle the slices with the browned butter. Serve immediately.

SCAN TO WATCH

perfectly cooked steak

2 beef steaks, cut at least
  1-inch (2.5cm) thick

2 tsp olive oil

1 tsp salt

½ tsp black pepper

½ tsp white pepper

2 tbsp butter, softened

1 to 2 garlic cloves, minced

This easy-to-follow recipe will enable you to cook any kind of steak perfectly every single time. The steak is seared in a skillet before being finished in the oven. This recipe will work with any of your favorite cuts of beef steak, including ribeye, T-bone, strip steak, porterhouse, top sirloin, or tenderloin filet. For best results, only use choice or prime grades of steak.

1 Remove the steaks from the refrigerator and discard any packaging. Let the steaks sit at room temperature for at least 30 minutes. Preheat the oven to 375°F (191°C).

2 Coat both sides of the steaks with the olive oil. Combine the salt, black pepper, and white pepper in a small bowl. Rub both sides of the steaks with the rub mixture.

3 Preheat a heavy oven-safe skillet over high heat. Once the skillet is hot, sear the steaks for 2 to 3 minutes per side. (If the steaks have sides of fat, use tongs to turn the steaks onto their sides and render the fat by searing them for 2 to 3 minutes more.)

4 Transfer the skillet to the oven. Cook the steaks until they reach five degrees less than the temperature for the desired level of doneness. (The internal temperature of the steaks will continue to rise after they are removed from the oven.)

5 While the steaks are cooking, use a fork to mash together the butter and garlic in a small bowl.

6 When the steaks reach the desired temperature, remove them from the oven and immediately top each steak with 1 tablespoon of the garlic-butter mixture. Allow the steaks to rest for 10 minutes before cutting.

Cooking Temperatures for Doneness

RARE	MEDIUM-RARE	MEDIUM	MEDIUM-WELL	WELL
120°F	130°F	135°F	140°F	150°F
(49°C)	(54°C)	(57°C)	(60°C)	(66°C)

SCAN TO WATCH

swedish meatballs and gravy

1lb (454g) 84–93% lean ground beef

1lb (454g) ground pork sausage

½ cup panko breadcrumbs

2 tbsp Worcestershire sauce

1 large egg

½ tsp ground allspice

½ tsp ground nutmeg

½ tsp salt

½ tsp black pepper

1 tbsp olive oil

FOR THE GRAVY

¼ cup salted butter

½ cup all-purpose flour

¼ tsp ground nutmeg

¼ tsp ground allspice

4 cups beef broth

2 tbsp Worcestershire sauce (optional)

Salt, to taste

Black pepper, to taste

⅔ cup sour cream

1 tbsp chopped fresh parsley for garnishing (optional)

These meatballs are made with a combination of ground pork and beef, spiced to perfection, and served with a rich and flavorful gravy. They're served traditionally over mashed potatoes, but you can also serve them over egg noodles or even rice.

1 Make the meatballs by stirring together the ground beef, ground pork, breadcrumbs, Worcestershire sauce, egg, allspice, nutmeg, salt, and black pepper in a medium bowl. Form the mixture into 1-inch (2.5cm) meatballs.

2 Heat the olive oil in a large skillet over medium-high heat. Working in batches, fry the meatballs in the oil until browned on all sides and cooked through. (Be sure not to crowd the pan.) Transfer the cooked meatballs to a paper towel–lined plate to drain.

3 Make the gravy by melting the butter in the same skillet used to cook the meatballs. Once the butter is melted, stir in the flour, nutmeg, and allspice. Continue stirring until it forms a paste.

4 Slowly pour in the beef broth and Worcestershire sauce (if using). Heat over medium-high heat until thickened. Taste the gravy and season with salt and black pepper to taste. Stir in the sour cream until well combined.

5 Return the cooked meatballs to the skillet and stir to coat with the gravy. Serve hot over 6 cups mashed potatoes or cooked egg noodles. Garnish with the chopped parsley, if desired.

·· NOTES ··

Baking instructions: Place the meatballs on a lightly greased baking sheet and bake in a 400°F (204°C) oven for approximately 30 minutes.

SCAN TO WATCH

easy chinese pepper steak

4 tbsp vegetable oil, divided

1 lb (454g) sirloin steak, cut into ¼-inch (.65cm) strips

2 large green bell peppers, cut into 1-inch (2.5cm) squares

1 large red bell pepper, cut into 1-inch (2.5cm) squares

1 large white onion, sliced

¼ cup sliced green onions (optional)

FOR THE SAUCE

¼ cup soy sauce

1 tbsp rice vinegar

1 tbsp sesame oil

2 tbsp cornstarch

½ cup beef broth

1 tbsp granulated sugar

1 to 3 tsp black pepper (adjust according to how peppery you prefer the dish to be)

2 tsp minced fresh ginger

4 garlic cloves, crushed

This easy stir-fry dinner is ready in just 15 minutes! While it's not a traditional or truly authentic dish in Chinese cuisine, this recipe has become an American Chinese–takeout favorite. You can serve it alone or over cooked rice.

1 In a small bowl, make the sauce by whisking together the soy sauce, rice vinegar, sesame oil, cornstarch, beef broth, sugar, black pepper, ginger, and garlic. Set aside.

2 Heat 2 tablespoons of the vegetable oil in a wok or large skillet over high heat. Add the beef and toss until seared, about 2 to 3 minutes. Remove the meat from wok or skillet. Set aside.

3 Add the remaining 2 tablespoons of vegetable oil to the wok or skillet. Add the peppers and onion, and cook until the vegetables are tender-crisp, about 3 minutes.

4 Add the meat back to the wok or skillet and then add the ginger-garlic sauce. Stir and cook about 1 minute more.

5 Transfer to a plate and garnish with the sliced green onions (if using). Serve hot.

SCAN TO WATCH

steakhouse-style horseradish-crusted prime rib

4–5lb (1.75–2.25kg) prime rib roast

½ cup prepared horseradish

10 garlic cloves, crushed

1 tbsp salt

1 tbsp freshly ground black pepper

1 tbsp olive oil

FOR THE SAUCE

⅔ cup sour cream

¼ cup prepared horseradish

2 tbsp lemon juice

½ tsp salt, plus more to taste

¼ tsp black pepper, plus more to taste

1 dash Tabasco sauce (optional)

1 to 2 dashes Worcestershire sauce (optional)

There's no need to be intimidated by cooking this expensive roast—perfect prime rib doesn't get much easier than this! This roast is crusted with horseradish and garlic—a classic combination for prime rib that will impress everyone. This recipe is simple and comes out perfectly every time.

1 Remove the roast from the fridge and let it sit on the counter for 1 to 2 hours to come to room temperature. (This will ensure even cooking.)

2 Preheat the oven to 500°F (260°C).

3 In a small bowl, combine the horseradish, garlic, salt, black pepper, and olive oil. Spread the mixture over the entire roast.

4 Place the roast in a large roasting pan, fat side up. Roast for 15 minutes and then reduce the heat to 325°F (163°C) and continue roasting until the internal temperature reaches 120°F (49°C) on a meat thermometer. (The roasting time will vary depending on the size of the roast, but you should plan for about 15 minutes per pound.)

5 Remove the roast from the oven and set aside to rest in the roasting pan for 20 minutes. (As it sits, the internal temperature will rise to 130°F [54°C], which will be medium-rare.)

6 While the roast is resting, make the creamy horseradish sauce by combining all of the ingredients in a medium bowl. Season with additional salt and black pepper to taste.

7 Cut the prime rib against the grain and into slices. Serve with the creamy horseradish sauce on the side.

SCAN TO WATCH

6 winner winner chicken dinners

baked chicken drumsticks
(four ways)

CLASSIC SEASONED DRUMSTICKS:

10 chicken drumsticks

5 tbsp butter

2 tsp paprika

2 tsp granulated sugar

1 tsp garlic powder

1 tsp onion powder

1 tsp dried oregano

1 tsp dried basil

1 tsp salt

1 tsp black pepper

CAJUN-SPICED DRUMSTICKS:

10 chicken drumsticks

5 tbsp butter

1 tsp paprika

½ tsp salt

½ tsp onion powder

½ tsp garlic powder

½ tsp dried oregano

½ tsp dried basil

¼ tsp dried thyme

¼ tsp black pepper

¼ tsp white pepper

¼ tsp cayenne pepper

ZESTY TEX-MEX DRUMSTICKS:

10 chicken drumsticks

5 tbsp butter

Juice of 2 limes (about ¼ cup), drizzled over the drumsticks prior to coating with the rub

2 tsp ground cumin

1 tsp chili powder

½ tsp cayenne

½ tsp garlic powder

⅛ tsp ground cloves

½ tsp salt

FLAVORS OF INDIA DRUMSTICKS:

10 chicken drumsticks

5 tbsp butter

Juice of 1 large lemon (about ¼ cup), drizzled over the drumsticks prior to coating with the rub

2 tsp ground cumin

2 tsp paprika

1 tsp salt

1 tsp garlic powder

1 tsp ground ginger

1 tsp garam masala

¼ tsp cayenne

These baked chicken drumsticks are so easy to make and feature juicy meat and crispy skin. I've perfected four flavor options to ensure there's something to please everyone. And at only 45 minutes or less from prep to dinner time, this recipe is both kid- and adult-approved!

1 Preheat the oven to 400°F (204°C). Lightly coat a large baking sheet with nonstick cooking spray.

2 Place the drumsticks in a single layer on the prepared baking sheet.

3 Combine the dry rub ingredients in a small mixing bowl. Sprinkle the rub in an even layer over all sides of the drumsticks. (If desired, apply the rub both on and underneath the skin.)

4 Place ½ tablespoon of butter on the top of the meatiest part of each drumstick. (The butter will melt over the meat and skin, keeping the meat juicy and making the skin crispy.)

5 Bake for 25 to 30 minutes or until the internal temperature reaches 165°F (74°C) on a meat thermometer. (Actual cooking time will depend on the size of the drumsticks.)

SCAN TO WATCH

mom's chicken pot pie

4 medium carrots, peeled and sliced

2 celery stalks, sliced

½ cup frozen peas

2 tbsp salted butter

1 small white onion, diced

¼ cup all-purpose flour

2 cups chicken broth

1½ cups cooked diced chicken

½ tsp salt

½ tsp black pepper

2 prepared pie crusts

This chicken pot pie is a comfort food favorite in our house! You can mix and match whatever vegetables you'd like in this recipe to create your own custom homemade pot pie. Your family will love this recipe!

1 Preheat the oven to 425°F (218°C).

2 Add the carrots and celery to a medium saucepan. Fill the pan with enough water to cover the vegetables and then bring to a boil over high heat. Once boiling, reduce the heat to medium and simmer for 8 minutes. Add the peas and continue simmering for another 2 minutes. Drain and set aside.

3 In a medium saucepan, melt the butter over medium heat. Add the onion and sauté for about 5 minutes or until softened. Add the flour and stir until well combined and then whisk in the chicken broth. Cook until thickened, about 5 minutes.

4 Add the vegetable mixture to the sauce along with the cooked chicken. Season with the salt and black pepper.

5 Line a deep-dish pie plate with the prepared bottom crust, letting it hang over the edge by ½ inch (1.25cm).

6 Pour the pot pie filling into the bottom crust. Cover with the top crust and then crimp the edges of the crusts together. Using a sharp knife, make several small slits in the top crust to allow steam to escape during baking.

7 Bake for 30 to 35 minutes or until the top crust is golden brown. Allow to cool for 10 minutes before serving.

······················ **NOTES** ······················

Make-ahead instructions: Cook the filling and prepare the pie crusts. Store separately in the fridge until you're ready to assemble and bake.

Freezing instructions: Assemble the pot pie as directed and freeze immediately. When ready to bake, remove the pot pie from the freezer and preheat the oven to 425°F (218°C). Bake, uncovered, for 15 minutes and then cover with aluminum foil to prevent the crust from burning. Continue baking for 30 to 35 minutes more or until the center is hot.

SCAN TO WATCH

garlic–lime skillet chicken

1 tsp garlic powder

¾ tsp salt

¼ tsp black pepper

½ tsp paprika

¼ tsp cayenne

½ tsp dried parsley

6 boneless, skinless chicken thighs

2 tbsp butter

1 tbsp olive oil

4 garlic cloves, minced

3 tbsp lime juice

Chopped fresh parsley, for garnishing (optional)

1 small lime, cut into wedges, for serving (optional)

This is a simple and easy dinner recipe that will get a tasty dinner on the table fast! This recipe is great served with **Spanish Rice** (p. 230) or **Cilantro–Lime Rice** (p. 233).

1 In a small bowl, mix together the garlic powder, salt, black pepper, paprika, cayenne, and dried parsley. Liberally sprinkle the mixture over the chicken thighs.

2 Heat the butter and olive oil in a heavy skillet over medium-high heat. Add the chicken thighs and sear until golden brown, about 3 to 4 minutes per side.

3 Add the garlic and lime juice. Continue cooking, spooning the juices over the chicken, until the chicken is cooked through and the internal temperature reaches 165°F (74°C).

4 Garnish with the chopped fresh parsley (if using) and lime wedges on the side (if using). Serve hot.

····················· **NOTES** ·····················

Boneless, skinless chicken breasts will also work great in this recipe. The cooking time will likely change slightly depending on the size and thickness of the chicken breasts. Chicken should always be cooked to an internal temperature of 165°F (74°C).

SCAN TO WATCH

READY IN 50 MINUTES • MAKES 6 SERVINGS

crispy baked chicken thighs

6 bone-in, skin-on
  chicken thighs

2 tbsp olive oil

2 tsp ground paprika

1 tsp dried basil

1 tsp dried oregano

½ tsp garlic powder

½ tsp onion powder

½ tsp salt

¼ tsp black pepper

These baked chicken thighs are tender and juicy with perfectly crisp skin. This is such a family favorite, we can't get enough of it! If you want to change up the flavors, try using one of the rub recipes included with the **Baked Chicken Drumsticks** recipe (p. 90).

1 Preheat the oven to 450°F (232°C). Lightly grease a 9 x 13-inch (22 x 33cm) baking dish or 3-quart baking dish.

2 Trim the thighs of any excess fat or skin and then place them skin side up in the prepared baking dish. Drizzle the olive oil over the skin and then rub to coat.

3 In a small bowl, stir together the paprika, basil, oregano, garlic powder, onion powder, salt, and black pepper. Sprinkle the mixture evenly over the chicken thighs.

4 Transfer the thighs to the oven and roast for 35 to 40 minutes or until the chicken reaches an internal temperature of 165°F (74°C) on a meat thermometer.

5 Remove the thighs from the oven and brush the tops with the juices from the pan. Change the oven setting to "broil" and place the thighs under the broiler for 1 to 2 minutes to add extra crispiness to the skin.

SCAN TO WATCH

.... NOTES ....

Potatoes require approximately the same roasting time as these chicken thighs. You can easily cook these on a baking sheet or in a 9 x 13-inch (22 x 33cm) baking pan accompanied with my **"Garlic Bread" Roasted Potatoes** (p. 214).

lasagna-stuffed chicken breasts

2 large boneless, skinless chicken breasts

1 cup whole milk ricotta cheese

1 large egg

3 tsp Italian seasoning, divided

2 garlic cloves, crushed

¾ tsp salt, divided

2 cups shredded mozzarella, divided

1 cup marinara sauce

¼ tsp black pepper

Lasagna-stuffed chicken? Yes! This recipe has all the lasagna flavors you love, but they're stuffed inside tender, juicy chicken breasts and then smothered in cheesy, saucy goodness. There's no pasta in this recipe, just tons of flavor!

1 Preheat the oven to 400°F (204°C). Butterfly the chicken breasts lengthwise and place them in a lightly greased 9 x 13-inch (22 x 33cm) baking dish.

2 In a small bowl, stir together the ricotta cheese, egg, 2 teaspoons of the Italian seasoning, garlic, ½ teaspoon salt, and 1 cup of the mozzarella.

3 Spoon about ¼ cup of the marinara sauce onto one half of each chicken breast. Spread the ricotta mixture on top of the sauce and then fold the chicken breasts over to close.

4 Drizzle the remaining ½ cup of marinara sauce over the chicken breasts and then top with the remaining cup of shredded mozzarella. Sprinkle the remaining 1 teaspoon of Italian seasoning over the top and then season with the remaining ¼ teaspoon salt and the black pepper.

5 Transfer to the oven and bake for 25 to 30 minutes or until the chicken reaches an internal temperature of 165°F (74°C) on a meat thermometer.

SCAN TO WATCH

································ NOTES ································

For best results, you should use large chicken breasts since they are easier to butterfly. Each large breast can easily serve two people, but the recipe can also easily be doubled or tripled to serve more.

roasted chicken

1 whole fryer chicken
1½ tsp salt
1 tsp dried basil
1 tsp dried oregano
1 tsp paprika
½ tsp white pepper
½ tsp onion powder
¼ cup salted butter,
  softened
1 large lemon
2 sprigs fresh rosemary

Knowing how to roast a whole chicken is an essential cooking skill. This same recipe can be used to cook a whole turkey as well. Feel free to experiment with different seasonings and rubs.

1 Preheat the oven to 450°F (232°C).

2 Remove the chicken from the packaging and discard the neck and any giblets from the inside of the chicken. Pat the chicken dry using paper towels.

3 In a small bowl, stir together the salt, basil, oregano, paprika, white pepper, and onion powder. In a separate small bowl, use a fork to mash the softened butter with 2 teaspoons of the seasoning mixture. Set the remaining seasoning mixture aside.

4 Slide your fingers under the chicken skin at the openings and slide them around to loosen the skin. Spread the seasoned butter mixture underneath the skin.

5 Cut the lemon in half and squeeze the juice directly over the chicken skin. Sprinkle the remaining seasoning mixture over the skin to coat. Place the lemon halves and rosemary sprigs inside the chicken cavity.

6 Place the chicken breast side up in a large roasting pan. Roast for 20 minutes and then reduce the temperature to 350°F (177°C) and continue roasting for about another 40 minutes. (Actual cooking time will depend on the size of the chicken. 20 minutes per pound is a good estimate.)

7 Remove the chicken from the oven when the internal temperature reaches 165°F (74°C). (Use a meat thermometer to check the point where the leg connects to the body.) Set the chicken aside to rest for about 20 minutes before carving.

SCAN TO WATCH

How to Carve a Roasted Chicken

Once the chicken is cooked, you can either carve it when serving or remove the meat from the bones prior to serving. Here's how you do it.

1 Locate the line running down the center of the breast. Place a sharp knife just to one side of that line and press down firmly. (You should hear the ribs crack.) Do the same on the opposite side and then remove the center bone.

2 Pull the chicken open to see exactly where your knife needs to be placed to remove the whole breast in one cut. Remove the breasts and cut into slices.

3 Use your knife to carefully remove the wings, drumsticks, and thighs.

· NOTES ·

Don't throw away the bones! You can put them in the fridge or freezer and use them to make homemade chicken stock.

chicken parmesan

4 thin boneless, skinless chicken breasts

1 cup all-purpose flour

1 tsp salt

¼ tsp black pepper

2 large eggs

1 cup panko breadcrumbs

1 cup Italian-style breadcrumbs

1 tsp garlic powder

¾ cup freshly grated Parmesan cheese, divided

¼ cup olive oil

¼ cup butter

1 cup marinara sauce

8oz (227g) fresh mozzarella, sliced

¼ cup chopped fresh basil

This chicken parmesan has a perfectly fried breaded coating and is then smothered in a rich marinara sauce and topped with fresh mozzarella cheese. It's ooey-gooey classic comfort food perfection!

1 Preheat the oven to 450°F (232°C). Lightly grease a 9 x 13-inch (22 x 33cm) baking dish.

2 Place three shallow dishes side by side on a flat surface. Fill the first dish with the flour, salt, black pepper, and then stir to combine. In the second dish, whisk the eggs together, and in the third dish stir together the panko breadcrumbs, Italian-style breadcrumbs, garlic powder, and ½ cup of the grated Parmesan.

3 Coat the chicken breasts in the flour mixture, dip them in the egg to coat, and then roll them in the breadcrumb mixture until well coated. Set aside.

4 Add the olive oil and butter to a heavy skillet over medium-high heat. Once the butter has melted, add the chicken breasts and fry for 2 to 3 minutes per side until the chicken is browned on both sides. Transfer the chicken breasts to the prepared baking dish.

5 Spread the marinara sauce over the top of each chicken breast. Top each breast with two slices of mozzarella and then sprinkle the remaining ¼ cup of Parmesan over the tops.

6 Transfer to the oven and bake until the cheese is bubbly and browned and the chicken reaches an internal temperature of 165°F (74°C) on a meat thermometer, about 15 to 20 minutes. Sprinkle the fresh basil over the top. Serve hot.

.... NOTES ....

If you want to give your chicken parmesan the ultimate crisp, don't add the marinara sauce on top of the breasts until just before serving. Instead, melt the mozzarella and Parmesan directly on the breasts and then warm the marinara sauce on the stovetop just before saucing the chicken.

SCAN TO WATCH

FF

READY IN 35 MINUTES • MAKES 6 SERVINGS

baked chicken nuggets

3 to 4 boneless, skinless chicken breasts, trimmed and cut into bite-sized pieces

1 cup plain breadcrumbs

½ cup freshly grated Parmesan cheese

2 tbsp dried basil

1 tbsp dried oregano

1 tsp salt

½ cup salted butter, melted*

These baked chicken nuggets are so simple to make. They yield a flavorful, moist, baked version of chicken nuggets that grown-ups will love just as much as kids. These will be the best baked chicken nuggets you've ever tasted!

1 Preheat the oven to 400°F (204°C). Lightly grease one to two large baking sheets.

2 In a small bowl, stir together the breadcrumbs, Parmesan, basil, oregano, and salt.

3 Working in small batches, dip the chicken pieces in the melted butter to coat and then transfer them to breadcrumb mixture to coat. Place them on the prepared baking sheet, leaving at least 1 inch (2.5cm) between each nugget.

4 Transfer to the oven and bake for 20 to 25 minutes or until the chicken reaches an internal temperature of 165°F (74°C) on a meat thermometer.

NOTES

* If desired, you can substitute ½ cup buttermilk for the melted butter.

SCAN TO WATCH

VARIATION

Buffalo Chicken Nuggets: Mix ½ cup of buffalo hot sauce in with the butter for a spicy kick. Serve with blue cheese dressing on the side as a dipping sauce.

READY IN 55 MINUTES · MAKES 4 SERVINGS

cajun-style stuffed chicken breasts

These Cajun-spiced chicken breasts are stuffed with bell peppers, mushrooms, onion, and melted zesty pepper jack cheese. This easy dinner is bursting with flavor and is delicious served plain, with rice, or over buttered pasta.

4 large boneless, skinless chicken breasts

1 tbsp olive oil

4 large white or cremini mushrooms, sliced

½ red bell pepper, diced

½ green bell pepper, diced

¼ white onion, diced

½ cup shredded pepper jack cheese

4 tsp Cajun seasoning

4 tbsp salted butter

SCAN TO WATCH

1 Preheat the oven to 400°F (204°C). Lightly grease a 9 x 13-inch (22 x 33cm) baking dish.

2 Heat the olive oil in a heavy skillet over medium-high heat. When the oil is hot, add the mushrooms, bell peppers, and onion. Sauté for 5 minutes or until the vegetables are parcooked.

3 Using a meat tenderizer, pound the chicken breasts until they're about ¼-inch (.65cm) thick. (If you are using thicker-cut chicken breasts, you can butterfly them instead.)

4 Place a large spoonful of the mushroom and bell pepper mixture on top of each chicken breast and then top each with a generous pinch of the pepper jack cheese.

5 Carefully fold the chicken breasts so the filling is completely inside and then secure each with a toothpick. Place in the prepared baking dish and then season generously with the Cajun seasoning. Place a tablespoon of butter on top of each chicken breast.

6 Transfer to the oven and bake until the chicken reaches an internal temperature of 165°F (74°C) on a meat thermometer, about 30 to 40 minutes.

7 Remove the toothpicks. Serve the chicken whole, sliced in half, or sliced into 1-inch (2.5cm) slices.

·········· NOTES ··········

You can use a store-bought Cajun seasoning mix or make your own using the recipe included with my **Baked Chicken Drumsticks** recipe (p. 90).

crispy fried chicken

3 cups buttermilk

½ cup Buffalo hot sauce (optional)

2 tsp salt

1 tsp black pepper

6 skin-on chicken thighs

6 skin-on chicken drumsticks

1qt (946ml) vegetable oil (for frying), divided

FOR THE DREDGING MIXTURE

3 cups all-purpose flour

½ cup cornstarch

1 tbsp salt

1 tbsp paprika

2 tsp onion powder

2 tsp garlic powder

1 tsp dried oregano

1 tsp dried basil

1 tsp white pepper

1 tsp cayenne

This recipe makes perfect fried chicken with a crispy, flavorful crunchy coating and moist and juicy meat on the inside. The key is soaking the chicken in buttermilk prior to breading and frying. The optional hot sauce in this recipe does not make the chicken spicy, but it does add a lot of flavor.

1 In a large bowl, whisk together the buttermilk, hot sauce (if using), salt, and black pepper. Add the chicken pieces to the bowl, toss to coat, cover the bowl with plastic wrap, and refrigerate for 4 hours.

2 While the chicken is soaking, make the dredging mixture by combining the flour, cornstarch, salt, paprika, onion powder, garlic powder, oregano, basil, white pepper, and cayenne in a gallon-sized resealable plastic bag or in a shallow dish. Shake or stir to combine the ingredients.

3 When ready to cook, pour enough vegetable oil in a large, deep skillet until the oil is about ¾ inch (1.90cm) deep. Heat the oil to 350°F (177°C). (Watch the oil closely and adjust the heat as needed to maintain the correct temperature.)

4 Working one piece at a time, remove the chicken pieces from the buttermilk mixture, shake gently to remove any excess buttermilk, and then place each piece in the dredging mixture to coat thoroughly. Tap off any excess mixture.

5 Place the breaded chicken pieces into the hot oil 3 to 4 pieces at a time. (The chicken will drop the temperature of the oil, so try to keep it as close to 350°F (175°C) as possible.) Fry for 14 minutes, turning each piece about halfway through the cooking time, until the chicken reaches an internal temperature of 165°F (74°C) on a meat thermometer.

6 Remove the pieces from the oil and place them on a paper towel–lined plate to drain to rest for at least 10 minutes before serving.

SCAN TO WATCH

classic chicken à la king

½ cup salted butter

8oz (227g) button or crimini mushrooms, sliced

2 egg yolks

⅓ cup heavy cream

½ cup all-purpose flour

2 cups chicken broth

1½ cups milk (whole or 2%)

1 cup frozen peas

1 cup chopped, drained pimientos

4 cups chopped precooked chicken (white or dark meat)

Salt and black pepper to taste

This classic American dish originated in a famous New York City restaurant and instantly became a favorite with patrons. It's rich and creamy and so easy to make. Feel free to experiment and add different vegetables to the sauce.

1 In a large saucepan, melt the butter over medium-high heat. Add the mushrooms and cook until soft, about 5 minutes.

2 While the mushrooms are cooking, whisk together the egg yolks and heavy cream in a small bowl. Set aside.

3 Add the flour to the saucepan and stir until there are no more specks. Pour in the chicken broth and milk. Bring to a boil and then reduce the heat to low and simmer until the sauce is thickened, about 3 minutes.

4 Working quickly, slowly pour ½ cup of the hot broth mixture into the egg mixture while whisking vigorously. Immediately pour the egg mixture back into the saucepan while continuing to whisk. Cook for 2 minutes more.

5 Stir in the peas, pimientos, and cooked chicken. Let it heat through, about 2 to 3 minutes.

6 Season to taste with salt and black pepper. Serve hot over cooked rice, pasta, toast, or biscuits.

··· NOTES ···

There are several great options for any recipe that calls for precooked chicken.

Rotisserie chicken. Many American grocery stores sell precooked rotisserie chickens that you can shred. Many stores also offer preshredded and packaged rotisserie chicken.

Frozen cooked chicken. Check out the freezer section of your grocery store for precooked chicken strips and chunks.

Baked chicken. Place the chicken breasts in a lightly greased 9 × 13-inch (22 x 33cm) baking pan. Season with salt and black pepper. Bake at 350°F (177°C) for 25 to 30 minutes until cooked through. Chop into chunks and use right away or freeze for later use.

Boiled chicken. Place the chicken breasts in a large pot of boiling water or chicken broth. Boil for 15 minutes or until the chicken is cooked through. Shred or chop.

Quick skillet chicken. Preheat a large heavy skillet over medium-high heat. Add 1 tablespoon of vegetable oil and place the chicken breasts in the skillet. Season with salt and black pepper. Cook 5 to 7 minutes per side or until cooked through.

SCAN TO WATCH

READY IN 40 MINUTES • MAKES 4 SERVINGS

mom's chicken cacciatore

2 tbsp extra virgin olive oil

1 tbsp salted butter

6 boneless, skinless chicken thighs

½ tsp salt, plus more to taste

½ tsp black pepper, plus more to taste

¼ cup all-purpose flour

1 small white onion, diced

1 red bell pepper, sliced

1 yellow bell pepper, sliced

8oz (170g) button or crimini mushrooms, sliced

6oz (227g) tomato paste

2 tsp minced garlic

1 tbsp Italian seasoning

¼ tsp red pepper flakes (optional)

½ cup red cooking wine

¼ cup heavy cream

15oz (425g) crushed tomatoes

8oz (226g) tomato sauce

2 tbsp fresh or 2 tsp dried parsley, for garnishing

2 tbsp grated Parmesan cheese (optional)

Chicken cacciatore is an easy skillet dinner that is full of rich herb and tomato flavors. It's traditionally served over either pasta or rice, and it's ready in only 40 minutes!

1 Add the olive oil and butter to a large skillet over medium-high heat.

2 Season the chicken thighs with the salt and black pepper. Sprinkle the flour over the chicken and gently rub to coat. Place the chicken in the skillet and brown for 3 minutes per side or until just browned. Transfer to a plate. Set aside.

3 Add the onion, peppers, and mushrooms to the skillet. Cook until softened, about 7 to 10 minutes, stirring occasionally. Add the tomato paste, garlic, Italian seasoning, and red pepper flakes (if using). Cook 1 to 2 minutes more and then pour in the cooking wine, heavy cream, crushed tomatoes, and tomato sauce. Stir to combine.

4 Return the chicken to the pan and simmer over medium heat until the chicken is cooked to an internal temperature of 165°F (74°C), about 15 minutes. Season to taste with additional salt and black pepper, if desired.

5 Garnish with chopped parsley and Parmesan (if using). Serve hot.

SCAN TO WATCH

baked bbq chicken

3 lb (1.35kg) skin-on,
bone-in chicken pieces

FOR THE SAUCE
1 cup tomato sauce
¼ cup molasses
2 tbsp Worcestershire
sauce
1 tbsp hot sauce
¼ cup light brown sugar
2 tsp cornstarch
1 tsp salt
2½ tsp Cajun seasoning
1 tsp smoked paprika
3 garlic cloves

This baked BBQ chicken is easy to make and includes a homemade
no-cook barbecue sauce. It's finger lickin' good! You can use any bone-in,
skin-on part of the chicken. This recipe uses every part!

1 Preheat the oven to 400°F (204°C). Lightly grease a baking sheet or
9 x 13-inch (22 x 33cm) baking pan.

2 In a blender, make the sauce by combining the tomato sauce,
molasses, Worcestershire sauce, hot sauce, brown sugar, cornstarch, salt,
Cajun seasoning, smoked paprika, and garlic cloves. Purée until smooth.

3 Transfer half of the sauce to a medium bowl and reserve for later.
Brush the remaining sauce onto the chicken pieces.

4 Place the chicken pieces in the prepared baking pan. Bake for 20
minutes and then flip the pieces and baste with the reserved sauce.
Continue baking for another 20 minutes or until the chicken reaches an
internal temperature of 165°F (74°C).

5 Switch the oven to the "broil" setting and broil for another 2 to 3
minutes or until the sauce caramelizes. Serve hot.

·· NOTES ··

Be careful about cross contamination. If you touch the chicken with a brush or spoon and
then stick that utensil back into the bowl, the sauce will become contaminated, meaning
the unused sauce cannot be consumed.

SCAN TO WATCH

quick-and-easy lemon chicken

4 boneless, skinless
chicken breasts

FOR THE MARINADE

Juice of 2 lemons
(about ½ cup)

2 tbsp extra virgin olive oil

2 tsp lemon pepper

1 tsp dried basil

1 tsp dried oregano

¼ tsp salt

Chopped fresh parsley,
for garnishing (optional)

1 lemon, sliced, for serving
(optional)

This recipe requires only a handful of pantry ingredients, but don't let the simplicity fool you—it's outrageously delicious!

1 Combine the lemon juice, olive oil, lemon pepper, basil, oregano, and salt in a gallon-sized resealable plastic bag. Seal and gently shake to combine. Add the chicken breasts, reseal the bag, and gently shake again until the chicken is coated in the marinade.

2 Transfer the chicken to the fridge to marinate for 30 minutes or up to 8 hours.

3 Preheat a heavy skillet over medium-high heat.

4 Remove the chicken from the marinade and place it directly into the hot skillet. Discard any remaining marinade.

5 Cook the chicken 6 to 7 minutes per side, flipping halfway through until the chicken reaches an internal temperature of 165°F (74°C).

6 Garnish with freshly chopped parsley (if using) and top with lemon slices (if using). Serve hot.

·· NOTES ··

Marinating in a resealable plastic bag helps ensure that the marinade covers the meat completely. If you prefer not to marinate the meat in a plastic bag, you can also marinate it in a small glass mixing bowl or shallow baking dish that has been covered with plastic wrap.

SCAN TO WATCH

baked buffalo chicken wings

2–3lb (907–1361g)
  chicken wings
1 tbsp aluminum-free
  baking powder
½ tsp salt
½ tsp black pepper
½ tsp paprika

FOR THE SAUCE
¼ cup Buffalo hot sauce
¼ cup melted butter
1 tbsp honey

Make perfectly crispy oven-baked chicken wings with this easy method, which includes seven different flavor options for a variety of wings that will please everyone at the table. These do require some preparation a day ahead for best results, but it will be worth the effort! You'll get perfectly crispy wings without frying.

1 Place a wire rack on a baking sheet.

2 Pat the chicken wings as dry as possible with paper towels and place the wings in a large bowl.

3 In a small bowl, stir together the baking powder, salt, black pepper, and paprika. Sprinkle the mixture over the chicken wings and toss until the wings are evenly coated.

4 Place the wings in a single layer on the prepared baking sheet. Refrigerate uncovered for 12 to 24 hours.

5 Preheat the oven to 425°F (218°C). Transfer the wings directly from refrigerator to the preheated oven. Bake for 30 minutes or until the wings are brown and crispy and the internal temperature reaches 165°F (74°C). (The actual cooking time will vary based on the size of the wings.)

6 While the wings are baking, make the Buffalo sauce by whisking together the Buffalo hot sauce, melted butter, and honey.

7 When the wings are done baking, transfer them to a large bowl. Pour the sauce over the wings and toss to coat. (You can also serve them plain.) Serve hot.

···································· NOTES ····································

You can substitute the Buffalo sauce with any of the flavorings on the following pages!

SCAN TO WATCH

baked chicken wings (alternative flavors)

LEMON PEPPER SAUCE

2 tbsp extra virgin olive oil

1 tbsp lemon pepper

SIMPLE BBQ SAUCE

¼ cup light brown sugar

2 tsp cornstarch

1 tsp salt

2½ tsp Cajun seasoning

1 tsp smoked paprika

1 cup tomato sauce

¼ cup molasses

2 tbsp Worcestershire
sauce

1 tbsp hot sauce

3 garlic cloves, minced

HONEY GARLIC SAUCE

1 tsp olive oil

5 garlic cloves, minced

⅓ cup honey

¼ cup water

2 tbsp apple cider vinegar

1 tbsp soy sauce

TERIYAKI SAUCE

⅓ cup light brown sugar

2 tbsp cornstarch

½ tsp ground ginger

1 cup water

¼ cup soy sauce

1 tbsp honey

1 garlic clove, minced

GARLIC PARMESAN SAUCE

¼ cup melted butter

⅓ cup grated Parmesan
cheese

½ tsp garlic powder

¼ tsp salt

¼ tsp black pepper

SALT AND VINEGAR SAUCE

2 cups distilled white
vinegar

1 cup water

3 tbsp salt

½ tsp black pepper

Lemon Pepper Wings

1 In a small bowl, whisk together the olive oil and lemon pepper.

2 Add the cooked chicken wings to a large mixing bowl. Pour the sauce over the wings and then toss to coat.

Simple BBQ Wings

1 In a medium saucepan, whisk together the brown sugar, cornstarch, salt, Cajun seasoning, and paprika.

2 Whisk in the tomato sauce, molasses, Worcestershire sauce, hot sauce, and garlic.

3 Bring to a simmer over medium-high heat and then reduce the heat to medium-low. Simmer, stirring occasionally, for 15 minutes.

4 Add the cooked chicken wings to a large mixing bowl. Pour the sauce over the wings and then toss to coat.

Honey Garlic Wings

1 Heat the olive oil in a small saucepan over medium-high heat. Add the garlic and sauté for 90 seconds.

2 Add the honey, water, apple cider vinegar, and soy sauce. Bring to a simmer and then remove from the heat.

3 Add the cooked chicken wings to a large mixing bowl. Pour the sauce over the wings and then toss to coat.

Teriyaki Wings

1 In a medium saucepan, whisk together the brown sugar, cornstarch, and ginger.

2 Stir in the water, soy sauce, honey, and garlic. Bring to a simmer over medium-high heat.

3 Let simmer until thickened, about 2 minutes, then remove the pan from the heat.

4 Add the cooked chicken wings to a large mixing bowl. Pour the sauce over the wings and then toss to coat.

Garlic Parmesan Wings

1 In a small mixing bowl, whisk together the melted butter, Parmesan cheese, garlic powder, salt, and black pepper.

2 Add the cooked chicken wings to a large mixing bowl. Pour the sauce over the wings and then toss to coat.

Salt and Vinegar Wings

1 In a large bowl, stir together the vinegar, water, salt, and black pepper until dissolved. Add the uncooked chicken wings to the bowl, ensuring sure they are completely submerged in the liquid. Cover and transfer to the fridge. Soak for 2 hours.

2 Pat the wings completely dry with paper towels and then proceed with the baked chicken wings instructions.

chicken salad

12oz (340g) cooked chicken breast, chopped or shredded

1 celery rib, minced

2 tbsp minced sweet onion

¼ cup halved red grapes

¼ cup slivered almonds

½ cup mayonnaise

1 tsp lemon juice

2 tsp whole-grain mustard

¼ tsp salt

¼ tsp black pepper

Pinch of garlic powder

This chicken salad is a tried-and-true favorite and perfect for almost any kind of gathering. It's easy to make and tasty all by itself or served atop lettuce or on sandwiches. My family's personal favorite is serving this on flaky croissants.

1 In a large bowl, toss together the chicken, celery, onion, grapes, and almonds.

2 Add the mayonnaise, lemon juice, mustard, salt, black pepper, and garlic powder. Stir until well combined.

3 Serve atop lettuce leaves, sliced tomatoes, avocado halves, or on top of bread.

SCAN TO WATCH

30-minute chicken lo mein

12oz (340g) uncooked lo mein noodles

1 tbsp sesame oil

1–1½lb (454–680g) boneless, skinless chicken breasts, cut into 1-inch (2.5cm) cubes

½ tsp salt

3 large carrots, shredded or cut into matchsticks

½ head green cabbage, shredded or thinly sliced

½ cup sliced green onion

FOR THE SAUCE

¼ cup oyster sauce

3 tbsp soy sauce

1 tsp sesame oil

1 tbsp cornstarch

¼ cup chicken broth

2 garlic cloves, minced

2 tsp freshly minced ginger

This chicken lo mein is so easy to put together and has the most incredible flavor. You can use refrigerated or dried lo mein noodles or even spaghetti. Or you can turn it into a chow mein by using crunchy chow mein noodles.

1 In a small bowl, make the sauce by whisking together the oyster sauce, soy sauce, sesame oil, and cornstarch. Stir in the chicken broth, garlic, and ginger. Set aside.

2 Cook the lo mein noodles according to package directions.

3 Heat the sesame oil in a large skillet over medium-high heat. Add the chicken to the skillet and season with the salt. Cook until the chicken is browned, about 5 minutes.

4 Add the carrots and cabbage and cook until the vegetables are tender and the chicken is completely cooked through, about 5 to 7 minutes.

5 Pour the sauce over the vegetables and chicken. Cook 2 to 3 minutes more, stirring constantly.

6 Add the cooked noodles and toss to combine. Garnish with the green onion.

SCAN TO WATCH

classic chicken marsala

4 thin boneless, skinless chicken breasts or 2 thick chicken breasts sliced in half lengthwise

½ tsp salt

½ tsp black pepper

½ cup all-purpose flour

4 tsp olive oil, divided

8oz (227g) button mushrooms, sliced

4 garlic cloves, minced

1 cup Marsala wine

½ cup chicken broth

2 tbsp finely chopped fresh parsley

12oz (340g) cooked spaghetti, for serving (optional)

Satisfy your inner Italian with this classic chicken Marsala, featuring panfried chicken in a Marsala wine reduction. This is yet another amazing 30-minute meal. Along with any vegetable, this dish pairs well with **The Creamiest Mashed Potatoes** (p. 213), **"Garlic Bread" Roasted Potatoes** (p. 214), or **Easy Couscous** (p. 142).

1 Season the chicken breasts with the salt and black pepper. Spread the flour onto a plate or in shallow bowl. Dip the chicken breasts into the flour to coat and then shake off the excess flour.

2 Heat 2 teaspoons of the olive oil in a large skillet over medium-high heat. Add the chicken breasts and sear on each side until golden brown and cooked through, about 7 minutes per side. Remove from the skillet and set aside.

3 In the same skillet, heat the remaining 2 teaspoons olive oil over medium-high heat. Add the mushrooms and sauté until soft, about 3 to 4 minutes.

4 Add the garlic and cook 1 minute more. Pour in the Marsala wine and chicken broth. Bring to a simmer and cook until the liquid is reduced by half, about 6 to 7 minutes, and then reduce the heat to low.

5 Add the chicken breasts back to the pan to heat through, about 3 to 5 minutes. Spoon the sauce and mushrooms over the top of the chicken. Garnish with the chopped parsley.

6 Serve the chicken over cooked spaghetti (if using) and then top with the mushroom Marsala sauce. Serve warm.

SCAN TO WATCH

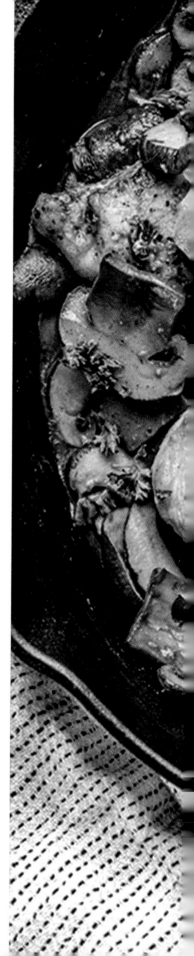

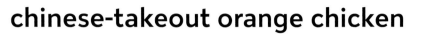
chinese-takeout orange chicken

4 egg whites

2 tbsp cornstarch

1 tsp salt

½ tsp white pepper

4 boneless, skinless chicken breasts, cut into bite-sized pieces

Vegetable oil, for frying

¼ cup sliced green onion, for garnishing (optional)

FOR THE SAUCE

1 cup orange juice

Zest of 1 orange

¼ cup rice vinegar

2 tbsp soy sauce

⅓ cup light brown sugar

1 tsp ground ginger

½ tsp red pepper flakes

¼ cup water

1 tbsp cornstarch

This orange chicken is breaded, fried, and coated with the most amazing sweet and spicy orange sauce. Despite the name, this has never been a traditional Chinese dish. Instead, it was invented by an American takeout restaurant chain that's popular for American-style Chinese takeout. This is so quick and easy to make—you'll never go back to takeout!

1 In a medium bowl, whisk together the egg whites, cornstarch, salt, and white pepper. Submerge the chicken pieces in the mixture. Set aside.

2 Make the orange sauce by stirring together the orange juice, orange zest, rice vinegar, soy sauce, brown sugar, ginger, and red pepper flakes in a small saucepan over medium-high heat. Bring to a simmer.

3 In a small bowl, whisk together the water and cornstarch to make a slurry. Pour the slurry into the sauce mixture. Stir until thickened and then remove from the pan from the heat. Set aside.

4 Add 2 inches of vegetable oil to a large, heavy-bottomed pot. Heat the oil to 350°F (177°C). Working in small batches, fry the chicken pieces until they're cooked through and golden brown, about 3 to 4 minutes per batch, and then transfer the pieces to a paper towel–lined plate to drain.

5 Transfer the fried chicken pieces to a large bowl. Pour the sauce over the chicken and gently toss to coat. Garnish with the green onions (if using) and serve hot with steamed white rice on the side, if desired.

SCAN TO WATCH

READY IN 40 MINUTES • MAKES ABOUT 18 MEATBALLS

baked chicken meatballs

1–1½lb (454–680g) ground chicken

¾ cup plain breadcrumbs

½ cup freshly grated Parmesan cheese

2 garlic cloves, minced

2 tsp dried basil

1 tsp salt

¼ tsp red pepper flakes

2 tbsp milk (whole or 2%)

1 large egg

2 tbsp Worcestershire sauce

1 tbsp extra virgin olive oil

These savory chicken meatballs are always a winner—for kids and adults alike! You'll love how easily they come together. They can be eaten plain or served up in classics like spaghetti and meatballs or on chicken meatball subs.

1 Preheat the oven to 400°F (204°C). Lightly coat a 9 x 13-inch (22 x 33cm) baking pan or large baking sheet with nonstick cooking spray.

2 In a large bowl, combine the ground chicken, breadcrumbs, Parmesan, garlic, basil, salt, and red pepper flakes. Add the milk, egg, Worcestershire sauce, and olive oil. Mix until the ingredients are well combined.

3 Shape the mixture into 1 to 1½-inch (2.5 to 3.8cm) meatballs. (Whatever size you choose to make, they should all be roughly the same size to ensure even cooking.)

4 Bake for 25 to 30 minutes or until the internal temperature reaches 165°F (74°C). (For extra crispy meatballs, add another 15 minutes of baking time.) Store the cooked meatballs in an airtight container in the fridge for up to 5 days.

·· NOTES ··

Freezing and reheating instructions: Place the uncooked meatballs on a baking sheet after forming them into meatballs. Transfer the baking sheet to the freezer. Once the meatballs are frozen, transfer them to a resealable plastic bag. Freeze for up to 3 months. When ready to bake, place the frozen meatballs on a baking pan and add an additional 10 minutes to the baking time.

SCAN TO WATCH

GF

READY IN 1 HOUR 40 MINUTES • MAKES 5 SERVINGS

chicken and rice casserole

- 2 cups long-grain white rice*
- 1 medium white onion, diced
- 6 tbsp salted butter, melted and divided
- 2 tbsp all-purpose flour
- 5 cups chicken broth
- 1 cup heavy cream
- 1 tsp salt
- ½ tsp black pepper
- 4 to 6 bone-in, skin-on chicken thighs
- 2 tsp Italian seasoning
- ½ tsp garlic powder
- ½ tsp paprika

This savory and simple one-pan recipe is made completely from scratch. The rice is creamy and delicious, and the chicken is moist and juicy. It may sound simple, but the mild flavor is just the kind of deliciousness that defines comfort food.

1 Preheat the oven to 350°F (177°C). Lightly grease a 9 x 13-inch (22 x 33cm) baking pan.

2 Combine the rice, onion, 3 tablespoons of the melted butter, and the flour directly in the prepared baking pan. Stir until well combined and no flour specks remain.

3 Add the chicken broth, heavy cream, salt, and black pepper. Stir to combine and then spread the mixture evenly across the bottom of the baking pan.

4 Place the chicken thighs on top of rice mixture. Brush the remaining melted butter over the thighs and then sprinkle the Italian seasoning, garlic powder, and paprika over the chicken. Cover with aluminum foil and bake for 1 hour.

5 After 1 hour, remove the foil and bake for another 30 minutes or until the rice and chicken are cooked through and the chicken skin crisps up. (For even crispier skin, place the chicken under the broiler for 2 to 3 minutes before serving.) Serve hot.

SCAN TO WATCH

.... NOTES ....

* The cooking time and ratios in this recipe rely on using a long-grain white rice. For best results, use jasmine or basmati varieties. Other types of rice require several adjustments to the amount of liquids and baking time, which could result in dry or undercooked chicken.

30-minute butter chicken

½ cup plain Greek yogurt

2 tbsp lemon juice

2 tsp ground cumin

1 tsp garam masala

1 tsp salt

1 tsp ground ginger

2 lb (907g) boneless, skinless chicken breasts, cubed

FOR THE SAUCE

6 tbsp butter or ghee

1 medium white onion, diced

2 garlic cloves, minced

1 jalapeño, minced

1 tsp ground cumin

2 tsp paprika

1 tsp garam masala

1 cup tomato sauce

1 cup heavy cream

½ tsp salt

¼ cup chopped fresh cilantro, for garnishing

Butter chicken originated in Northern India in the late 1950s and quickly became a global favorite. The makhani sauce and chicken come together with the most incredible spice and flavor. Serve over rice for a quick and delicious meal.

1 In a medium bowl, combine the Greek yogurt, lemon juice, cumin, garam masala, salt, ginger, and cubed chicken. Stir until well combined and the chicken is completely coated. Transfer to the fridge to marinate for 10 to 15 minutes.

2 Preheat a large skillet over medium-high heat. Add the marinated chicken and cook, stirring occasionally, until cooked through, about 5 to 7 minutes. Remove the chicken from the pan and set aside.

3 Wipe the skillet clean and return to medium-high heat. Add the butter or ghee and then add the onion. Sauté for 5 minutes or until the onion begins to soften.

4 Add the garlic, jalapeño, cumin, paprika, and garam masala. Toast in the skillet for 1 to 2 minutes.

5 Add the tomato sauce, heavy cream, and salt. Bring to a simmer and then add the chicken back to the skillet. Stir to combine and then remove from the heat and serve hot over cooked rice. Garnish with the chopped cilantro.

SCAN TO WATCH

moroccan chicken gyros

2 lemons, thinly sliced and divided

2 lb (907g) boneless, skinless chicken breasts

¼ cup butter, softened

2 tsp paprika

1 tsp ground cumin

½ tsp turmeric

½ tsp cayenne

½ tsp salt

¼ tsp ground cinnamon

¼ tsp ground ginger

8 pitas or Arabic flatbreads, for serving

Prepared vegetables of your choice (see notes)

FOR THE SAUCE

1 cup plain Greek yogurt

¼ cup lemon juice

2 tbsp tahini paste

2 garlic cloves, minced

¼ tsp salt

Pinch of black pepper

FOR SERVING (OPTIONAL)

Shredded purple or green cabbage

Sliced cucumber

Diced tomato

Thinly sliced red onion

Roughly chopped cilantro

Moroccan-spiced chicken breasts are sliced and served gyro-style with loads of vegetables and then topped with a zingy tahini sauce. People always want to know what my very favorite recipe is, and this one right here is it! I can eat it every day for weeks on end!

1 Preheat the oven to 350°F (177°C). Spray a 9 x 13-inch (22 x 33cm) baking pan with nonstick cooking spray.

2 Place half the lemon slices in the bottom of the pan to create a bed for the chicken. Place the chicken breasts on top of the lemon slices.

3 In a small bowl, stir together the butter, paprika, cumin, turmeric, cayenne, salt, cinnamon, and ginger. Spread the mixture over the top of the chicken breasts. Place the remaining lemon slices on top of the chicken breasts.

4 Bake for 30 to 35 minutes or until the chicken reaches an internal temperature of 165°F (74°C).

5 While the chicken is baking, make the tahini sauce by whisking together the Greek yogurt, lemon juice, tahini paste, garlic, salt, and black pepper.

6 Thinly slice the chicken breasts. Stuff the pitas or flatbreads with the chicken. Serve hot or cold, topped with the tahini sauce and any desired vegetable toppings (if using).

·· NOTES ··

You can serve these with just the meat and tahini sauce or mix and match different vegetables to create whatever combinations you prefer. I recommend serving these gyros with shredded purple or green cabbage, sliced bell pepper, sliced cucumber, sliced tomato, thinly sliced red onion, and roughly chopped cilantro.

SCAN TO WATCH

7 pasta la vista, baby!

old-fashioned beef stroganoff

2 lb (907g) sirloin steak

¼ cup all-purpose flour

1 lb (454g) egg noodles

1 tbsp olive oil

1 medium white onion, sliced

8 oz (227g) button or crimini mushrooms, sliced

¼ cup salted butter

3 cups beef broth

2 tbsp Worcestershire sauce

1 cup sour cream

1 tbsp Dijon mustard

Salt and black pepper to taste

Beef stroganoff is the original family favorite skillet meal. This recipe is so decadent and savory, you won't believe it's a 30-minute meal! The sauce is creamy, with a bite of mustard and a slight zing from the Worcestershire sauce.

1 Slice the sirloin against the grain and into thin strips. Dust with the flour to coat. Set aside.

2 Cook the egg noodles according to package directions. Drain well and set aside.

3 Heat the olive oil in a large heavy skillet over medium-high heat. When the oil is hot, add the onion and mushrooms. Sauté until tender, about 7 minutes, and then remove from the skillet and set aside.

4 Without cleaning the skillet, add the butter and let it melt over medium-high heat. Add the steak slices and cook until browned, about 4 to 5 minutes.

5 Return the onion and mushrooms to the skillet. Pour in the beef broth and Worcestershire sauce. Simmer until thickened, about 2 to 3 minutes.

6 Add the sour cream and Dijon mustard, and stir until incorporated. Add the cooked egg noodles, stir to combine, and then season to taste with salt and black pepper. Serve hot.

SCAN TO WATCH

pasta carbonara

1 tbsp salt

1 lb (454g) spaghetti

1 lb (454g) diced pancetta or diced thick-cut bacon

4 egg yolks

2 whole eggs

1½ cups grated Pecorino Romano cheese, divided

½ tsp freshly ground black pepper

Pasta carbonara is a classic Italian pasta dish that features an egg and cheese sauce. Pancetta is used in the authentic preparation, but you can also use bacon, which is less expensive and easier to find. The eggs in this dish are cooked by the residual heat from the spaghetti and pasta water, but I like to cook the eggs a bit longer in the pan, just to be safe.

1 Add the salt to a large pot of water. Bring the salted water to a boil over high heat. Cook the spaghetti according to package directions, reserving 1½ cups of the pasta water before draining the spaghetti.

2 In a large skillet, cook the pancetta or bacon over medium heat until crisp, about 7 to 10 minutes. Reserve 2 tablespoons of the rendered fat and then drain the remaining fat from the skillet.

3 In a medium bowl, whisk together the egg yolks, eggs, and 1 cup of the Pecorino Romano cheese.

4 Toss the drained spaghetti with the cooked pancetta or bacon and reserved fat in the skillet. Add the egg mixture along with 1 cup of the reserved pasta water. Toss for 2 minutes to cook the eggs. (If desired, add additional reserved pasta water to thin out the sauce.)

5 Sprinkle the remaining cheese and the freshly ground black pepper over the pasta. Serve hot.

---------------- **NOTES** ----------------

For an eggless, faux carbonara sauce, substitute ½ cup heavy cream for the egg yolks and eggs.

SCAN TO WATCH

stovetop macaroni and cheese

1lb (453g) elbow macaroni

½ cup salted butter

½ cup all-purpose flour

1 tsp salt

½ tsp white pepper

1½ tsp onion powder

1½ tsp ground mustard

3 cups milk (whole,
2%, or 1%)

2 tbsp cayenne pepper
hot sauce (optional)

8oz (227g) shredded sharp
cheddar cheese

Say goodbye to the boxed stuff forever! This easy, creamy homemade mac and cheese is ready in just 15 minutes. The hot sauce does not add heat, but it's an old chef's secret for enhancing the flavor of the cheese. Experiment with combinations of other types of melting cheeses including Gruyère, Gouda, mozzarella, fontina, Monterey Jack, or Brie.

1 Fill a large saucepan with water and bring to a boil over high heat. Stir in the elbow macaroni and cook until al dente, about 7 to 8 minutes. Drain well.

2 While the elbow macaroni are cooking, melt the butter in another large saucepan over medium heat. Stir in the flour, salt, white pepper, onion powder, and ground mustard. Cook 1 to 2 minutes.

3 Pour in the milk and hot sauce (if using). Whisk until smooth. Cook over medium-high heat, stirring constantly, for 3 to 5 minutes or until the sauce begins to thicken. Turn off the heat and add the cheese. Whisk until melted.

4 Add the cooked macaroni to the cheese sauce and stir well to combine. Serve hot.

·········· VARIATIONS ··········

Baked Mac and Cheese: Increase the milk to 4 cups. Place the cooked pasta and sauce into a lightly greased 9 x 13-inch (22 x 33cm) baking pan and stir to combine. If desired, add a crunchy topping by stirring together 1½ cups panko breadcrumbs, ½ cup freshly grated Parmesan cheese, and 3 tablespoons olive oil in a small bowl. Sprinkle the topping over the pasta. Bake, uncovered, in a 400°F (204°C) oven for 10 minutes.

SCAN TO WATCH

baked ziti

2 tbsp olive oil

1lb (454g) ground beef

1 white onion, diced

8oz (227g) button or crimini mushrooms, sliced (optional)

5 garlic cloves, minced

6oz (170g) can tomato paste

28oz (794g) canned crushed tomatoes

15oz (425g) canned tomato sauce

1 tbsp dried basil

1 tbsp dried oregano

½ tsp salt

¼ tsp black pepper

1lb (454g) ziti

8oz (227g) cream cheese, softened

8oz (227g) ricotta cheese

1 cup freshly grated Parmesan cheese

SCAN TO WATCH

This is seriously the best baked ziti ever! Your family is going to love the homemade meat sauce, and the ricotta and cream cheese topping takes it to the next level. It's hearty and filling, and the creamy topping is rich and decadent, making this a comfort food meal your family will request again and again.

1 Preheat the oven to 350°F (177°C). Lightly grease a 9 x 13-inch (22 x 33cm) baking pan.

2 Heat the olive oil in a large deep skillet over medium-high heat. Add the ground beef and brown, about 5 minutes, and then add the onion and mushrooms (if using). Sauté for 5 to 7 minutes or until the onion is soft and translucent and the ground beef is cooked through. Drain any excess grease from the pan.

3 Add the garlic and tomato paste to the skillet and toast for 2 minutes. Pour in the crushed tomatoes and tomato sauce. Stir in the basil, oregano, salt, and black pepper. Bring to a simmer and then reduce the heat to low. Simmer about 8 to 10 minutes and then remove from the heat and set aside.

4 Cook the ziti according to package directions.

5 While the ziti is cooking, combine the cream cheese, ricotta, and Parmesan in a small bowl. Mix until smooth.

6 Once the ziti is cooked, add it to the meat sauce and stir to combine. Pour the mixture into the prepared baking pan. Spread the cheese mixture over the top of the pasta.

7 Bake, uncovered, for 20 minutes or until the cheese is melted and bubbly. Serve hot.

the most amazing lasagna

This lasagna is one of the most highly rated recipes I've ever published. The balance between layers of cheese, noodles, and homemade Bolognese sauce is perfection. The sauce is a particular favorite, with the secret ingredient being the fennel seeds, which enhance the meat flavors.

1lb (454g) sweet Italian sausage

1lb (454g) lean ground beef

1 large white onion, diced

5 garlic cloves, minced

2 tbsp granulated sugar

½ cup chopped fresh basil

1 tsp fennel seeds

1 tsp ground oregano

1 tsp salt, divided

¼ tsp black pepper

¼ cup plus 2 tbsp chopped fresh parsley

28oz (794g) canned crushed tomatoes

12oz (227g) canned tomato paste

15oz (425g) can of tomato sauce

½ cup white wine* (optional)

1lb (454g) lasagna noodles

30oz (850g) ricotta cheese

1 large egg

⅛ tsp ground nutmeg

1lb (454g) thinly sliced mozzarella cheese (about 24 slices)

1 cup freshly grated Parmesan cheese

SCAN TO WATCH

1 Add the ground sausage and ground beef to a large pot over medium heat. Use a spoon to break the meat into small pieces.

2 Add the onion and garlic. Cook, stirring constantly, until the meat is browned.

3 Add the sugar, basil, fennel, oregano, ½ teaspoon salt, black pepper, and ¼ cup parsley. Pour in the crushed tomatoes, tomato paste, tomato sauce, and wine (if using). Stir well. Bring just to a simmer and then reduce the heat to low and simmer, covered, 1 to 4 hours, stirring occasionally. (The longer you simmer the sauce, the more developed the flavor will be.)

4 While the sauce is cooking, place the lasagna noodles in the bottom of a large pan. Pour hot tap water directly over the noodles, making sure the pasta is completely immersed in the water. Soak for 30 minutes and then drain and discard the water. Set the noodles aside.

5 In a medium bowl, combine the ricotta cheese with the egg, remaining 2 tablespoons parsley, remaining ½ teaspoon salt, and nutmeg. Cover and refrigerate until you're ready to assemble the lasagna.

6 Preheat the oven to 375°F (191°C). Lightly grease a deep 9 x 13-inch (22 x 33cm) baking pan.

7 To assemble the lasagna, spread about 1 cup of the meat sauce in the bottom of the prepared pan. Place 4 noodles on top, spread ⅓ of the ricotta cheese mixture on top of the noodles, and then top with ¼ of the mozzarella cheese slices. For the next layer, spoon 1½ cups of the meat sauce over the mozzarella, then sprinkle ¼ cup Parmesan cheese over the mozzarella. Repeat the same layering twice more to create three complete meat layers. To finish, add a final layer of pasta noodles topped with 1 cup of the meat sauce to cover the pasta. Top with the remaining mozzarella and Parmesan. Cover loosely with aluminum foil.

8 Bake for 25 minutes, then remove the foil and bake for an additional 25 minutes to allow the cheese to brown. Serve hot.

·········· **NOTES** ··········

* The white wine can be replaced with an equal amount of red wine, chicken broth, or beef broth.

Make-ahead instructions: After preparing and assembling the lasagna, cover and refrigerate for up to 48 hours before baking. (Freezing a lasagna of this size is possible, but once frozen it will require a very long baking time in order to heat it all the way through.)

GF · FF · VG · VE
READY IN 1 HOUR 10 MINUTES · MAKES 8 SERVINGS

marinara sauce

2 tbsp olive oil

1 large white onion, minced

5 garlic cloves, crushed

½ cup white wine or chicken broth

28oz (794g) canned crushed tomatoes

15oz (425g) canned tomato sauce

6oz (170g) canned tomato paste

1 tbsp granulated sugar

1 tbsp fennel seeds

1 tbsp ground oregano

½ tsp salt

¼ tsp black pepper

½ cup chopped fresh basil

¼ cup chopped fresh parsley

This marinara sauce is so full of flavor and is perfect served over any shape of pasta. It's easy to make in large batches for freezing or canning. You can add cooked ground beef to make a meat sauce or you can add **Baked Meatballs** (p. 78), which is our family's favorite. It's perfect for any recipe calling for a marinara sauce.

1 Heat the olive oil in a large pot over medium-high heat. Add the onion and sauté for 5 minutes or until softened. Add the garlic and sauté for another 30 to 60 seconds.

2 Add the wine or chicken broth, crushed tomatoes, tomato sauce, tomato paste, sugar, fennel, oregano, salt, black pepper, basil, and parsley. Stir to combine.

3 Bring just to a simmer and then reduce the heat to low and simmer, covered, for 30 to 60 minutes. (30 minutes is sufficient, but 60 minutes will develop more flavor.)

4 Using an immersion blender, purée the mixture until smooth. (Alternatively, you can transfer the sauce to a blender and blend until smooth. Just be sure to properly vent the blender jar to ensure the hot sauce doesn't explode.)

.... NOTES ....

For easy long-term storage, allow the sauce to cool and then transfer it to several gallon-sized resealable freezer bags. Lay the bags flat on a baking pan, place them in the freezer, and freeze until solid. Allow the sauce to thaw before removing it from the bags. After removing the sauce from the bags, reheat in the microwave or on the stovetop.

SCAN TO WATCH

Q+E · VG

READY IN 15 MINUTES · MAKES 6 SERVINGS

penne rosa

1lb (454g) penne

1 tbsp olive oil

8oz (227g) button or crimini mushrooms, sliced

2 garlic cloves, crushed

1½ cups store-bought marinara sauce or **Marinara Sauce** (p. 138)

¼ to ½ tsp red pepper flakes

4 Roma tomatoes, diced

3 cups fresh baby spinach leaves

½ cup heavy cream

Salt and black pepper to taste

½ cup shredded Parmesan cheese

Penne rosa is a creamy tomato pasta dish with a delightful kick. It's a 15-minute, one-dish pasta meal that everyone will love. This is a copycat recipe from a popular restaurant chain, but boy, is it easy (and less expensive) to make at home!

1 Cook the penne according to package directions. Drain well and set aside.

2 While the penne is cooking, heat the olive oil in a large skillet over medium-high heat. Add the mushrooms and sauté for 3 minutes or until the mushrooms are tender. Add the garlic and sauté for 1 minute more.

3 Stir in the cooked penne, marinara sauce, and red pepper flakes.

4 Add the tomatoes and baby spinach. Stir to combine and then stir in the heavy cream. Season to taste with salt and black pepper.

5 Sprinkle the Parmesan over the top. Serve hot.

SCAN TO WATCH

cacio e pepe

1 tbsp salt

1 lb (454g) tonnarelli or thick spaghetti

1 tbsp freshly ground black pepper*

1½ cups freshly grated Pecorino Romano cheese, divided

Cacio e pepe is a simple Roman pasta dish that translates to "cheese and pepper." It's so easy to make and it tastes absolutely heavenly! This cheesy, peppery Italian pasta has survived since the Roman Empire for a reason!

1 Bring a large pot of water to a boil over high heat. Add the salt and tonnarelli or spaghetti. Cook until the pasta is al dente.

2 Add the black pepper to a small skillet over medium heat. Toast for 1 to 2 minutes and then remove from the heat and set aside.

3 Using tongs, transfer the cooked pasta from the water to a large bowl. Reserve about 1 cup of the pasta water and discard the remaining water.

4 Working quickly, add 1¼ cups of the Pecorino Romano cheese along with ½ cup of the pasta water and the black pepper to the bowl with the pasta. Stir rapidly with the tongs to allow the heat from the pasta and water to melt the cheese. Continue adding the reserved pasta water until you have a thick, creamy sauce coating the pasta.

5 Sprinkle the remaining ¼ cup of the cheese over the pasta. Serve hot.

····················· **NOTES** ·····················

* How much black pepper you add is a matter of personal preference and can vary based on how strong your pepper is. Some may prefer up to 2 tablespoons of black pepper while others may only enjoy 1 or 2 teaspoons.

Freshly grated cheese melts better than pregrated or preshredded cheese since it doesn't contain any additives. Use the fine shredding side of your cheese grater to produce the best results.

The original technique used to make this dish calls for melting the cheese in the skillet over low heat along with the toasted black pepper and pasta water. However, if the cheese melts too quickly it can clump up, making this technique tricky for some people to master. Using a mixing bowl is a simplified method, but if you are feeling brave, you can learn to master the original technique, as well.

SCAN TO WATCH

easy couscous
(five ways)

2 ½ cups water or chicken broth

½ tsp salt

1 tbsp olive oil or butter

2 cups Moroccan couscous*

Couscous is super easy to make and is an excellent side dish for so many different recipes. Once you learn how to make it, you'll want to serve it weekly—at least!

1 In a medium saucepan, bring the water or chicken broth, salt, and olive oil or butter to a boil over high heat.

2 Stir in the couscous, cover the pan with a lid, and remove from the heat. Let stand 5 minutes.

3 Fluff the couscous with a fork. Serve hot.

.... NOTES ....

* If you're using Israeli couscous (also known as *pearl* couscous), increase the amount of water or broth to 3 cups. This type of couscous needs to simmer uncovered for 10 minutes before being covered and sitting an additional 5 minutes.

.... VARIATIONS ....

Garlic and Olive Oil Couscous: Heat 2 tablespoons of olive oil in a saucepan. Sauté 1 tablespoon freshly minced garlic in the oil for 60 to 90 seconds before adding the water and bringing it to a boil.

Parmesan Couscous: Use 2 ½ cups chicken broth instead of water and 1 tablespoon butter in place of the olive oil. While fluffing the cooked couscous with a fork, slowly sprinkle in ¾ cup of freshly grated Parmesan cheese.

Herbed Chicken Couscous: Use 2 ½ cups chicken broth instead of water. In addition to the salt, add ½ teaspoon onion powder along with ⅛ teaspoon dried sage and ¼ teaspoon each of garlic powder, dried parsley, dried rosemary, and dried thyme.

Mediterranean Couscous: In addition to the salt, add ½ teaspoon each of ground cumin, onion powder, and dried rosemary, along with ¼ teaspoon each of dried oregano, garlic powder, and ground turmeric, along with a generous pinch of ground cinnamon.

SCAN TO WATCH

brown butter–garlic angel hair pasta

2 tbsp salt

1lb (454g) angel hair pasta

½ cup unsalted butter

2 garlic cloves, peeled and halved

½ cup freshly grated Parmesan cheese

Minced fresh chives or fresh parsley, for garnishing (optional)

A nutty brown butter is infused with garlic in this incredibly easy pasta side dish. This is a quick and versatile side that you'll use again and again.

1 Add the salt to a large pot of water. Bring to a boil over high heat. Add the pasta and cook until it's al dente. Drain and transfer to a large bowl.

2 While the pasta is cooking, melt the butter in a small saucepan over medium heat. Add the garlic cloves and continue cooking until the butter begins to foam, giving the pan a good occasional swirl. (Keep a close eye on the butter, as the color will change from yellow to tan and then brown fairly quickly.)

3 Once the butter reaches a brown color, immediately remove it from the heat, discard the garlic cloves, and pour the browned butter over the cooked pasta.

4 Stir in the Parmesan until melted and then sprinkle the minced chives or parsley over the top (if using). Serve hot.

·· **NOTES** ··

Try garnishing the pasta with a little tarragon. I absolutely love tarragon, it's fun to use to switch up the flavors a bit and add a little gourmet feel to such a simple dish. And, of course, you should feel free to use any other pasta shape for this dish.

SCAN TO WATCH

Q+E · VG · VE

READY IN 15 MINUTES · MAKES 6 SERVINGS

easy olive oil pasta

2 tbsp salt

1 lb (454g) spaghetti

¼ cup plus 2 tbsp extra virgin olive oil

8 garlic cloves, minced

½ tsp red pepper flakes

2 tsp lemon juice

3 tbsp finely chopped fresh parsley

This super easy olive oil pasta is a simple side dish that is quick to make and easily customizable to become a full meal—all you need to add is meat and veggies! Or you can serve it as a quick-and-easy side dish as part of a weeknight quick comfort food dinner.

1 Add the salt to a large pot of water. Bring to a boil over high heat. Add the pasta and cook until it's al dente. Drain and transfer to a large bowl.

2 In a small saucepan, add ¼ cup of the olive oil and heat over low heat for 1 minute. Add the garlic and red pepper flakes. Stir and cook for 1 more minute and then remove the pan from the heat.

3 Pour the olive oil mixture over the cooked pasta. Add the remaining 2 tablespoons of olive oil, lemon juice, and parsley. Toss until the pasta is coated in the sauce. Serve hot.

SCAN TO WATCH

pasta pomodoro

28oz (794g) canned whole peeled tomatoes*

3 tbsp extra virgin olive oil

1 medium white onion, finely diced

5 garlic cloves, minced

¼ tsp red pepper flakes

1 tbsp plus ½ tsp salt

1lb (454g) spaghetti

2 tbsp butter

¼ cup freshly grated Parmesan cheese

2 tbsp chopped fresh basil

Pasta pomodoro is a quick-and-easy pasta dish that will quickly become a family favorite. This quick pasta sauce is full of tomato flavor. It's simple, tasty, and total comfort food.

1 Add the tomatoes to a blender or food processor. Purée until smooth. Set aside.

2 Heat the olive oil in a large skillet over medium-high heat. Add the onion and sauté 5 to 7 minutes or until soft. Add the garlic and red pepper flakes. Sauté for 1 minute more.

3 Add the tomato purée and ½ teaspoon salt. Bring just to a simmer and then reduce the heat to medium. Simmer for 10 minutes and then transfer to a large bowl.

4 While the sauce is simmering, add the remaining 1 tablespoon salt to a large pot of water. Bring to a boil over high heat. Cook the pasta until it's al dente and then drain.

5 Add the cooked pasta to the bowl with the sauce. Toss to coat and then add the butter and Parmesan. Toss until the butter is melted.

6 Sprinkle the fresh basil over the top of the pasta. Serve hot.

.... **NOTES** ....

* For best results, use San Marzano canned tomatoes. San Marzano is a variety of tomato that comes from a specific region of Italy. These preserved tomatoes are the best for sauce making.

SCAN TO WATCH

15-minute shrimp scampi

1 tbsp plus 1 tsp salt

1lb (454g) linguine

4 tbsp salted butter

2 tbsp olive oil

1 tbsp minced garlic

1lb (454g) peeled and deveined shrimp

½ tsp red pepper flakes

½ cup white wine

¼ cup lemon juice

1 tsp Italian seasoning

2 tbsp grated Parmesan cheese

2 tbsp chopped fresh parsley

This shrimp scampi is a family favorite weeknight meal for busy families and is ready in just 15 minutes! It is quick and easy to make, and everyone always raves about it. Trust me, you'll be licking your plate clean when you make this!

1 Add 1 tablespoon salt to a large pot of water. Bring to a boil over high heat. Add the pasta and cook until it's al dente and then drain. Set aside.

2 While the pasta is cooking, add the butter and olive oil to a large skillet over medium-high heat. When the butter is melted, add the garlic and shrimp and then season with the remaining 1 teaspoon salt and the red pepper flakes. Stir continuously until the shrimp just turns pink, about 2 minutes.

3 Pour in the white wine to deglaze pan. Stir in the lemon juice and Italian seasoning. Simmer for another 3 to 5 minutes.

4 Add the cooked pasta to the skillet and toss to coat with the sauce. Top with the Parmesan and then garnish with the parsley. Serve hot.

SCAN TO WATCH

creamy cajun chicken pasta

1 tablespoon salt

1lb (454g) linguine

4 boneless, skinless chicken breasts

6 tsp Cajun seasoning, divided

6 tbsp butter, divided

3 bell peppers (various colors), sliced

1 red onion, sliced

8oz (227g) button or crimini mushrooms, sliced

2 cups heavy cream

This creamy Cajun chicken pasta is the perfect family meal. Juicy Cajun-spiced chicken is served over a bed of creamy linguine that's packed full of sautéed veggies. This is the first dish I ever made for my husband when we were dating, so it will always hold a special place in my heart.

1 Add the salt to a large pot of water. Bring to a boil over high heat. Add the linguine and cook until it's al dente and then drain. Set aside.

2 While the pasta is cooking, rub each chicken breast with 1 teaspoon of the Cajun seasoning. Preheat a large skillet over medium-high heat. Add 3 tablespoons of the butter.

3 Sear the chicken breasts in the butter until browned on each side. Reduce the heat to medium-low and continue cooking until the chicken reaches an internal temperature of 165°F (74°C), about 5 to 7 minutes per side, depending on the thickness of the breasts. Remove the chicken from the skillet and set aside to rest.

4 Without cleaning the skillet, melt the remaining 3 tablespoons of butter over medium-high heat. Add the bell peppers, onion, and mushrooms. Sauté until the veggies are tender. Sprinkle the remaining 2 teaspoons of Cajun seasoning over the veggies and cook for 1 minute more.

5 Pour in the heavy cream and bring the sauce to a simmer. Continue simmering until the sauce thickens.

6 Stir in the cooked linguine and toss until it is coated in the sauce and the veggies are evenly distributed. Slice the chicken breasts and serve them over the hot pasta.

SCAN TO WATCH

········· **NOTES** ·········

You can use a store-bought Cajun seasoning mix or make your own using the recipe included with my **Baked Chicken Drumsticks** (p. 90).

READY IN 35 MINUTES • MAKES 6 SERVINGS

creamy chicken casserole

12oz (340g) egg noodles

¼ cup butter

½ medium white onion, diced

3 garlic cloves, minced

¼ cup all-purpose flour

2 cups chicken broth

2 cups milk (whole, 2%, or 1%)

¼ tsp salt

¼ tsp black pepper

2 cups frozen peas

1lb (454g) diced cooked chicken

2 cups shredded cheddar cheese

1 cup crushed Ritz snack crackers

¼ cup grated Parmesan cheese

1 tbsp olive oil

This creamy chicken casserole has a made-from-scratch sauce and a crunchy parmesan–cracker topping that takes it over the top. Feel free to mix and match other frozen vegetables for a mild flavored one-dish meal that's ready in about 35 minutes.

1 Preheat the oven to 400°F (204°C). Lightly grease a 9 x 13-inch (22 x 33cm) baking pan.

2 Cook the egg noodles according to the package directions. Drain and then add the noodles to the prepared baking pan.

3 While the noodles are cooking, melt the butter in a medium saucepan over medium heat. Add the onion and sauté 5 to 7 minutes or until softened. Stir in the garlic and flour and cook for 1 minute more. Slowly pour in the chicken broth and milk and then season with the salt and black pepper. Bring to a simmer and continue cooking, stirring constantly, until the mixture thickens.

4 Stir in the peas, chicken, and cheddar cheese. Turn off the heat and stir continuously until the cheese is melted. Pour the sauce over the noodles.

5 In a small bowl, use a fork to mix together the crushed crackers, Parmesan, and olive oil. Sprinkle the topping over the pasta.

6 Bake, uncovered, for 15 to 20 minutes or until the crackers are lightly browned. Serve hot.

SCAN TO WATCH

8 seafood (and eat it)

baked salmon
(four ways)

2–3 lb (907–1360g) salmon fillet, deboned

½ cup soy sauce

¼ cup honey

¼ cup orange juice

4 garlic cloves, minced

1 tsp ground ginger

¼ tsp red pepper flakes

1 thinly sliced orange (optional)

1 tbsp minced fresh parsley, for garnishing (optional)

Baking salmon is the perfect way to prepare a simple, delicious, and nutritious meal. This recipe can be used for an entire salmon fillet or for partial fillets. I've included a basic salmon marinade as well as three additional seasoning options so you can easily switch things up.

1 Place the salmon fillet in a shallow dish or gallon-sized resealable plastic bag.

2 In a small bowl, whisk together the soy sauce, honey, orange juice, garlic, ginger, and red pepper flakes. Pour the marinade over the salmon. Cover or seal and transfer to the fridge to marinate for 30 minutes.

3 Preheat the oven to 375°F (191°C). Line a large baking sheet with aluminum foil.

4 Place the salmon fillet in the center of the baking sheet. Place the orange slices (if using) on top of the fillet and then loosely wrap aluminum foil around the fillet to trap the steam. Bake for 15 to 20 minutes or until the salmon flakes easily with a fork. Top with the minced parsley (if using).

· VARIATIONS ·

Lemon–Garlic Salmon: For the marinade, use 2 tablespoons olive oil, 2 tablespoons lemon juice, 3 minced garlic cloves, ½ teaspoon salt, ½ teaspoon dried basil, ½ teaspoon dried oregano, and ¼ teaspoon black pepper. Top with thinly sliced lemon and bake as instructed. Garnish with fresh parsley.

Garlic Dill Butter Salmon: Skip the marinating and simply whisk together ½ cup melted salted butter, ¼ cup lemon juice, 8 crushed garlic cloves, and 2 tablespoons finely minced dill. Drizzle the sauce over the salmon fillet and bake as instructed.

Chili–Lime Salmon: Skip the marinating and whisk together ¼ cup lime juice, 2 teaspoons chili powder, and ¼ teaspoon salt. Brush the liquid over the top of the salmon fillet and top with thinly sliced lime. Bake as instructed and garnish with chopped fresh cilantro.

SCAN TO WATCH

easy broiled lobster tails

2 lobster tails

½ cup salted butter, melted

1 tsp minced garlic

¼ tsp salt

¼ tsp black pepper

1 large lemon, cut into wedges

No need to be intimidated by cooking lobster tails! This is the easiest method ever and it will help you cook perfect restaurant-quality broiled lobster tails every time. The tender sweet lobster meat is smothered in garlic butter for the ultimate luxurious lobster experience.

1 Preheat the oven on the "broil" setting.

2 Using kitchen shears or a sharp knife, carefully cut the lobster tails open lengthwise on the tops sides to expose the meat. Place the lobster tails on a small ungreased baking sheet.

3 In a small bowl, whisk together the melted butter, garlic, salt, and black pepper. Drizzle the mixture directly over the exposed lobster meat.

4 Place the baking sheet 6 inches (15cm) beneath the broiler flame. Broil the lobster tails until the meat is no longer translucent, about 5 to 10 minutes, depending on the size of the lobster tails. Watch them closely and remove them immediately once they are white and no longer translucent.

5 Serve immediately with the lemon wedges on the side. (The lemon juice should be squeezed over the lobster meat just before eating.)

.... NOTES ....

You can remove the lobster meat and place it on top of the shell for a pretty presentation,, but I prefer to keep the meat inside the shells to better contain the butter and seasonings.

SCAN TO WATCH

how to cook crab legs

2 clusters snow crab legs
½ cup melted butter
1 tbsp Old Bay® seasoning
1 lemon, cut into wedges.

Crab legs are easy to make, so skip the expensive restaurant markup and enjoy this gourmet treat at home!

Boiled Crab Legs

1 Add 1 tablespoon salt (optional) to a large pot of water. Bring to a boil over high heat.

2 Reduce the heat to medium. Submerge the crab legs in the water and simmer for 5 minutes before removing to drain.

3 Serve with the melted butter and Old Bay® seasoning for dipping, with lemon wedges on the side. (Squeeze the lemon juice over the crab meat after you've removed it from the shells.)

Steamed Crab Legs

1 Bring a large pot to a boil over high heat. Place a steamer basket over the boiling water. (The basket should not touch the water.)

2 Place the crab legs in the steamer basket, cover, and steam for 5 to 7 minutes. Remove the crab legs from the basket.

3 Serve with the melted butter and Old Bay® seasoning for dipping, with lemon wedges on the side. (Squeeze the lemon juice over the crab meat after you've removed it from the shells.)

Broiled Crab Legs

1 Preheat the oven on the "broil" setting.

2 Place the crab legs on a baking sheet. Brush with melted butter or olive oil, if desired.

3 Place the sheet 6 to 8 inches beneath the broiler flame. Broil 3 to 4 minutes per side, flipping the legs halfway through the process.

4 Serve with the melted butter and Old Bay® seasoning for dipping, with lemon wedges on the side. (Squeeze the lemon juice over the crab meat after you've removed it from the shells.)

SCAN TO WATCH

GF · Q+E

READY IN 10 MINUTES · MAKES 2 SERVINGS

tuna-stuffed avocado

1 medium avocado, halved and pitted

5oz (142g) canned tuna, drained

¼ cup diced red bell pepper

1 tbsp minced jalapeño

¼ cup roughly chopped fresh cilantro

1 tbsp lime juice

Salt and black pepper to taste

This tuna-stuffed avocado is loaded with a flavorful southwest combination of tuna, bell pepper, jalapeño, and fresh cilantro. No mayo necessary here! It's the perfect healthy lunch.

1 Using a spoon, scoop out some of the avocado from the avocado halves to create "bowls."

2 Place the scooped avocado into a medium bowl and mash it with a fork. Add the tuna, bell pepper, jalapeño, and cilantro. Pour in the lime juice and stir until everything is well combined. Season to taste with salt and black pepper.

3 Scoop the tuna mixture into the avocado bowls. Serve promptly.

SCAN TO WATCH

how to cook shrimp

1 lb (454g) raw large shrimp

FOR SAUTÉED SHRIMP
1 tbsp salted butter
1 tbsp olive oil

FOR ROASTED SHRIMP
1 tbsp olive oil
¼ tsp salt
¼ tsp black pepper

FOR BOILED SHRIMP
1 large lemon, halved
1 tbsp salt
1 tsp whole black peppercorns

FOR STEAMED SHRIMP
½ cup water
½ cup white vinegar

Cook shrimp in five different and delicious ways! Each cooking method will lend a different texture and flavor to your shrimp. Use the flavors as listed or serve the shrimp with the sauces included with the **Seared Scallops** (p. 162) on the side.

Preparation

1 Rinse the shrimp thoroughly.

2 Using a sharp knife, carefully cut about ¼ inch (.65cm) into the back of the shells, following the outer edge of the curves. (This will cut into the shells and make it easier to slip them off and expose the vein.)

3 If there is a visible black vein, use the sharp tip of the knife to gently lift the vein out of the shrimp. Discard the vein.

4 Once the vein is removed, you can either peel the shrimp or leave the shells on for cooking, which will add more flavor. If you choose to peel the shrimp prior to cooking, it should easily slip off when given a little tug. (You can discard the shells or save and freeze them for making seafood stock.)

Sautéed Shrimp

1 Add the butter and olive to a medium saucepan over medium-high heat.

2 When the butter is melted, add the shrimp and season as desired. Stir continuously until the shrimp just turn pink, about 2 minutes.

Roasted Shrimp

1 Preheat the oven to 400°F (204°C).

2 Combine the olive oil, salt, and black pepper in a medium bowl. Add the shrimp and toss to coat.

3 Spread the seasoned shrimp out into a single layer on a baking sheet. Roast just until the shrimp turn pink, about 6 to 8 minutes.

Boiled Shrimp

1 Fill a small pot or large saucepan with water. Fill a large bowl with ice water. Set aside.

2 Squeeze the lemon juice into the water and then add the lemon halves to the water. Add the salt and black peppercorns. Bring to a boil over high heat.

3 Once boiling, add the shrimp. Cook 2 to 2½ minutes or until the shrimp turn pink and are no longer translucent.

4 Drain the shrimp and immediately transfer to the ice water to stop the cooking process. Drain the shrimp once they have cooled completely.

SCAN TO WATCH

Steamed Shrimp

1   Add the water and white vinegar to a saucepan fitted with a steamer basket. Bring to a boil.

2   Season the shrimp as desired and place them in the steamer basket. Cover the pan and steam until the shrimp just turn pink, about 4 to 6 minutes.

Grilled Shrimp

1   Preheat an outdoor grill to high heat, about 500°F (260°C).

2   Season the shrimp as desired. Soak wooden skewers (if using) in water for 10 minutes.

3   Thread the shrimp onto the skewers and then place them on the grill grates. (Alternatively, you can skip the skewers and place the individual shrimp directly on the grill grates. Just make sure the shrimp are large enough to not fall through the grates.)

4   Grill for 2 to 3 minutes per side or until the shrimp are pink and no longer translucent.

seared scallops
(four ways)

1 lb (454g) scallops, fresh or frozen and completely thawed

¼ tsp salt

¼ tsp black pepper

2 tbsp olive oil

FOR LEMON–GARLIC SAUCE

2 tbsp salted butter

5 garlic cloves, minced

¼ cup white wine or chicken broth

2 tbsp lemon juice

FOR CILANTRO–LIME SAUCE

¼ cup chopped fresh cilantro

¼ cup lime juice

2 tbsp olive oil

½ tsp salt

¼ tsp black pepper

FOR ORANGE–GINGER SAUCE

¼ cup orange juice

1½ tbsp soy sauce

1 tbsp olive oil

½ tsp ground ginger

½ tsp brown sugar

FOR BALSAMIC SAUCE

1 tbsp olive oil

2 garlic cloves, minced

2 tbsp balsamic vinegar

2 tsp Dijon mustard

¼ tsp salt

¼ tsp black pepper

Scallops are an extremely versatile and flavorful seafood dish. Ready in just 10 minutes, they're one of the easiest and quickest seafood dinners you'll ever make. Here I give you four different sauce options, so you can easily switch up the flavors to find your family's favorite.

1 Choose the preferred sauce and follow the instructions for making the sauce. Set aside.

2 Pat the scallops dry with a clean towel or paper towel. Season with the salt and black pepper.

3 Heat the olive oil in a large skillet over medium-high heat.

4 Sear the scallops in the hot oil for about 2 minutes per side or until they're cooked through and have a golden brown crust.

5 Remove the scallops from the skillet and top with the sauce.

Lemon–Garlic Sauce
1 Add the butter to a large skillet over medium-high heat.

2 Once the butter is melted, add the garlic and sauté for 1 minute. Pour in the white wine and simmer for 2 to 3 minutes and then stir in the lemon juice.

3 Pour the sauce over the cooked scallops.

Cilantro–Lime Sauce
1 Whisk all the ingredients together in a small bowl.

2 Pour the sauce over the cooked scallops.

Orange–Ginger Sauce
1 Whisk all the ingredients together in a small bowl.

2 Pour the sauce over the scallops during the last 30 seconds of cooking so the sauce heats briefly.

Balsamic Sauce
1 Heat the olive oil in a large skillet over medium-high heat. Add the garlic and sauté for 1 minute and then whisk in the balsamic vinegar, Dijon mustard, salt, and black pepper.

2 Pour the sauce over the cooked scallops.

SCAN TO WATCH

GF · Q+E

READY IN 35 MINUTES · MAKES 6 SERVINGS

no-mayo tuna salad

10oz (284g) canned tuna, drained

1 celery rib, minced

2 tbsp minced red or sweet onion

⅓ cup plain Greek yogurt

½ medium avocado, diced

1 tsp lemon juice

2 tsp whole-grain mustard

¼ tsp salt

¼ tsp black pepper

Pinch of garlic powder

Tuna salad is a simple and satisfying comfort food favorite. This recipe has been lightened up by replacing mayonnaise with Greek yogurt for a healthier tuna salad that not only tastes great but is also good for you!

1 In a medium bowl, stir together the tuna, celery, and onion.

2 Gently stir in the Greek yogurt, avocado, lemon juice, mustard, salt, black pepper, and garlic powder. Gently stir until well combined.

3 Serve alone, as a sandwich, as a dip, or over toast.

SCAN TO WATCH

READY IN 35 MINUTES · MAKES 6 SERVINGS

pan-seared white fish

4 white fish fillets or portions, 6oz (170g) each

2 tbsp olive oil

¼ cup lemon juice (about 1 lemon)

FOR THE SEASONING MIX

½ tsp dried dill

½ tsp lemon pepper

¼ tsp dried basil

¼ tsp dried oregano

¼ tsp onion powder

¼ tsp garlic powder

Don't be intimidated by cooking fish! Pan searing is a quick-and-easy way to get a delicious seafood dinner on the table in minutes. This recipe can be used with any white fish variety, including halibut, sea bass, cod, tilapia, sole, and more!

1 Using a sharp knife, trim the fish of any undesired skin. (Most fish can be eaten with the skin intact, so this is a matter of personal preference. If you do choose to cook your fish with the skin on, you'll want to sear the skin side first.)

2 In a small bowl, make the seasoning mix by stirring together the dill, lemon pepper, basil, oregano, onion powder, and garlic powder. Season both sides of the fillets with the seasoning mix. (Alternatively, you can marinate the fish in one of the other seafood flavorings in this book for 15 minutes.)

3 Preheat a heavy skillet over high heat. Once the skillet is hot, add the olive oil and heat until shimmering, about 1 minute.

4 Carefully, lay the fillets into the skillet. Cook the fish two thirds of the way through and then flip the fillets.

5 Continue cooking until the fish is cooked through. (Actual cooking time will depend on how thick the fillets are.) The fish should no longer be translucent and should flake easily with a fork. If it needs additional time, reduce the heat to medium and continue cooking until done.

6 Drizzle the lemon juice over the fish. Serve hot.

SCAN TO WATCH

beer-battered fish and chips

1 qt (946ml) vegetable oil

4 large russet potatoes, peeled

1 cup all-purpose flour

¼ cup cornstarch

1 tsp baking powder

1 tsp salt, plus more to taste

¼ tsp black pepper

1 to 1½ cups light beer*

2 lb (907g) cod fish, sliced into strips

This classic beer-battered fish and chips recipe is salty, savory, and full of flavor! For a truly authentic fish and chips experience, serve it up with tartar sauce, lemon wedges, and malt vinegar.

1 Heat the vegetable oil to 350°F (177°C) in a large pot over medium heat. (Monitor the temperature closely and adjust the heat as needed to ensure the oil doesn't get too hot.)

2 While the oil is heating, cut the potatoes into wedges or strips (fries). Pat them dry with paper towels. Set aside.

3 In a medium bowl, make the beer batter by whisking together the flour, cornstarch, baking powder, salt, and black pepper. Slowly whisk in the beer until the ingredients are well combined and smooth. Set aside.

4 Working in 2 to 3 batches, carefully add the potatoes to the hot oil and fry until soft, about 3 to 4 minutes per batch. Use a skimmer spoon or slotted metal spoon to transfer the potatoes from the oil to a paper towel–lined plate to drain. (Monitor the oil temperature and adjust the heat as needed to maintain the proper cooking temperature.)

5 Dip the cod pieces in the beer batter to coat and then place them directly into the hot oil. Fry until golden brown and flaky, about 3 to 4 minutes per side, flipping them halfway through the cooking time. Carefully transfer the cod pieces to a paper towel–lined plate to drain.

6 Return the potatoes to the oil to fry a second time for 2 to 3 minutes per batch or until crisp. Again transfer the potatoes to a paper towel–lined plate to drain. Season the potatoes to taste with salt. Serve hot.

.... **NOTES** ....

* If desired, you can substitute equal amounts of milk, buttermilk, or a dark soda like Coca Cola for the beer.

SCAN TO WATCH

9 south of the border

beef enchiladas

1½lb (680g) lean ground beef

1 medium white onion, diced

½ tsp salt

¼ tsp black pepper

7oz (198g) canned diced green chiles, drained

12 corn tortillas

2 tbsp vegetable oil (for frying), divided

3 cups shredded Monterey Jack cheese, divided

¼ cup chopped fresh cilantro

FOR THE SAUCE

2 tbsp vegetable oil

1 tbsp cornstarch

¼ cup chili powder

½ tsp garlic powder

½ tsp salt

¼ tsp ground cumin

¼ tsp dried Mexican oregano

2 cups vegetable broth

These simple homemade enchiladas are filled with savory ground beef and feature classic Mexican comfort food flavors. This recipe includes a quick homemade red enchilada sauce and an easy ground beef filling that's all oven-ready in 30 minutes.

1 Preheat the oven to 350°F (177°C). Lightly grease a 9 x 13-inch (22 x 33cm) baking pan with nonstick cooking spray.

2 Make the red sauce by heating the vegetable oil in a medium saucepan over medium heat. Whisk in the cornstarch, chili powder, garlic powder, salt, cumin, and oregano. Pour in the vegetable broth and simmer until thickened, about 2 to 3 minutes. Remove the pan from the heat and set aside.

3 Preheat a large skillet over medium-high heat. Add the ground beef and onion and then season with the salt and black pepper. Sauté until the ground beef is browned and cooked through, about 7 to 10 minutes. Drain any excess fat and then stir in the green chiles.

4 Spread ½ cup of the red enchilada sauce into the bottom of the prepared baking pan. Set aside.

5 Heat 1 tablespoon of the vegetable oil in a small skillet over medium heat. Working one at a time, fry the tortillas in the oil until soft, but do not let them crisp. Add the remaining 1 tablespoon of oil as needed to fry the remaining tortillas.

6 Dip each tortilla in the enchilada sauce to coat and then transfer the to a plate. Fill the tortilla with a scoop of the ground beef filling and then top with a generous pinch of the cheese. Roll up the enchilada and then place it in the prepared pan. Repeat with the remaining tortillas.

7 Drizzle the remaining sauce over the enchiladas and top with the remaining shredded cheese. Bake, uncovered, for 20 to 25 minutes or until the cheese is warm and bubbly. Top with the chopped cilantro and serve hot.

SCAN TO WATCH

beer-braised carnitas

3–5lb (1.35–2.25kg) pork butt or shoulder roast

1 tbsp ground cumin

1½ tsp chili powder

1 tsp cayenne

1 tsp garlic powder

½ tsp ground cloves

1½ tsp salt

4 tbsp vegetable oil, divided

12fl oz (355ml) Mexican lager or pilsner beer

1 large naval orange, sliced

It's very possible these will be the best carnitas you'll ever taste! This recipe is super easy to make in the oven or in the slow cooker. The combination of warm spices adds a flavor to the meat that you'll be craving again and again.

1 Preheat the oven to 350°F (177°C). Trim and slice the roast into ¼-inch-thick (.60cm-thick) pieces.

2 In a small bowl, combine the cumin, chili powder, cayenne, garlic powder, ground cloves, and salt. Set aside.

3 Heat 1 tablespoon vegetable oil in a large Dutch oven or oven-safe pot over high heat. Add the meat slices and sear for 5 to 7 minutes, stirring occasionally.

4 Sprinkle the seasoning mixture over the meat and toss to coat. Pour the beer over the meat and then top with the orange slices.

5 Cover and transfer to the oven. Braise 2–2½ hours or until the meat can be easily shredded with a fork. Remove the orange slices and then use two forks to shred the meat.

6 Heat 1 tablespoon of the vegetable oil in a large skillet over medium-high heat. Working in 3 batches, use tongs to place the meat into the hot oil. Sauté until crisp, about 3 to 5 minutes. (Add 1 tablespoon of the oil for each new batch.) Serve hot.

·· **NOTES** ··

For a crispy texture without frying, spread the shredded carnitas out onto a baking sheet in an even layer. Drizzle with the remaining 3 tablespoons of vegetable oil and then place under the broiler for 3 to 5 minutes or until crisp.

Slow cooker instructions: Sear the meat, add the spices as instructed, and then transfer the meat to a slow cooker. (Alternatively, if you are short on time, you can simply add all the ingredients to the slow cooker without searing.) Cook on low for 8 hours or on high for 5 to 6 hours.

SCAN TO WATCH

grilled carne asada

Juice of 2 limes

4 garlic cloves, crushed

½ cup orange juice

1 cup chopped fresh cilantro

½ tsp salt

¼ tsp black pepper

¼ cup vegetable oil

1 jalapeño, minced

2 tbsp white vinegar

2 lb (907g) flank or skirt steak

Carne asada translates to "roast meat." In this version of the classic recipe, marinated flank or skirt steak is grilled to perfection. This tender grilled meat is zingy with a mild spice from the jalapeño. You can cook this on the stovetop (see notes), but for best results use a grill to add that smoky flavor that only a grill can provide.

1 In a gallon-sized resealable bag, combine the lime juice, garlic, orange juice, cilantro, salt, black pepper, vegetable oil, jalapeño, and white vinegar. Seal the bag and turn gently to combine the ingredients.

2 Place the flank steak in the bag and seal it tightly. Gently turn the bag to coat all sides of the meat in the marinade. Refrigerate for at least 2 hours or overnight.

3 Preheat an outdoor grill to high heat. Remove the flank steak from the bag and discard the marinade.

4 Grill the steak for 7 to 10 minutes per side or until the steak reaches an internal temperature of 130°F to 135°F (54°C to 57°C) for medium-rare.

5 Transfer the carne asada to a cutting board to rest for 10 minutes before slicing thinly against the grain. Serve warm.

·················· NOTES ··················

Indoor cooking instructions: Heat a large heavy skillet over high heat. Sear the flank steak for 3 to 4 minutes per side. Reduce the heat to medium and continue cooking for another 8 to 10 minutes, flipping the steak halfway through, until the steak reaches 130°F to 135°F (54°C to 57°C) for medium-rare.

SCAN TO WATCH

green chile chicken enchiladas

8oz (227g) cream cheese, softened

7oz (198g) canned diced green chiles

1 tbsp lime juice

¼ tsp salt

½ tsp ground cumin

½ tsp chili powder

½ cup chopped fresh cilantro, plus more for garnishing

3 cups diced cooked chicken

1 cup sour cream

16oz (454g) salsa verde

10 8-inch (20cm) flour tortillas or 12 6-inch (15cm) corn tortillas

2 cups shredded Monterey Jack cheese

A classic American family favorite! This recipe is ready for the oven in less than 15 minutes. My mom always made this dish using flour tortillas, which is a common choice in the American West, but enchiladas in Mexican cuisine always use corn tortillas. Feel free to use either!

1 Preheat the oven to 375°F (191°C). Lightly grease a 9 x 13-inch (22 x33cm) baking pan.

2 In a medium bowl, beat the cream cheese with a hand mixer until it's light and fluffy, about 60 seconds. Using a spoon or rubber spatula, stir in the green chiles, lime juice, salt, cumin, chili powder, and cilantro. Stir until well combined and then fold in the cooked chicken.

3 In a separate medium bowl, whisk together the sour cream and salsa verde until combined. Place a large spoonful of the salsa verde mixture in the bottom of the prepared baking pan and spread it out into a thin, even layer. (Just enough to wet the bottom of the pan.)

4 Assemble the enchiladas by placing a large scoop of the chicken filling onto the center of a tortilla. Roll up the tortilla, tucking in the ends as you go, and then lay it in the pan. Repeat with the remaining filling and tortillas.

5 Pour the remainder of the salsa verde mixture over the top of the assembled enchiladas. Sprinkle the Monterey Jack cheese over the top of the enchiladas.

6 Bake for about 30 minutes or until the cheese is bubbly and lightly browned and then place the enchiladas under the broiler setting for 2 to 3 minutes for additional browning. Garnish with more freshly chopped cilantro, if desired.

SCAN TO WATCH

fish tacos

¼ cup extra virgin olive oil

2 tbsp lime juice

1 tbsp chili powder

¼ tsp salt

¼ tsp black pepper

1 lb (454g) white fish (mahi mahi, flounder, tilapia, or grouper), sliced into 2- x 1-inch (5x2.5cm) strips

1 tbsp minced jalapeño

1 tbsp chopped fresh cilantro

8 8-inch (20cm) flour tortillas or 10 6-inch (15cm) corn tortillas, warmed

FOR THE SLAW

2 cups shredded cabbage

2 tbsp red wine vinegar

Salt and black pepper to taste

FOR SERVING

½ red onion, diced

2 Roma tomatoes, diced

¼ cup chopped fresh cilantro

½ cup guacamole (optional)

2 medium limes, quartered

These amazing fish tacos are healthy, full of flavor, and super easy to make. The fish is spicy, with a hit of lime and cilantro, and the cabbage slaw adds all of the acidity you want in a good fish taco. If you really want to take your fish tacos to the next level, be sure to make the sauce included in the notes.

1 Combine the olive oil, lime juice, chili powder, salt, and black pepper in a small bowl. Whisk to combine.

2 Place the fish in a baking shallow dish. Pour the marinade over the top of the fish and sprinkle the jalapeño and cilantro over the top. Place the fish in the fridge to marinate for 15 minutes.

3 While the fish is marinating, prepare the slaw by tossing the shredded cabbage and red wine vinegar in a small bowl. Season to taste with salt and black pepper. Set aside.

4 Preheat a large heavy skillet over medium-high heat. Add the fish and cook for about 5 minutes per side. The fish is done when it can easily be flaked with a fork.

5 Assemble each taco by topping a warm tortilla with two or three pieces of fish, a heaping spoonful of slaw, sprinklings of diced onion, tomato, cilantro, and a dollop of guacamole (if using). Serve with a lime wedge on the side for squeezing.

.... NOTES ....

If you're looking for a great sauce for your fish tacos, try this one! Combine the following ingredients in a food processor or blender. Blend on low until smooth

1 cup fresh cilantro
½ white onion
2 jalapeños, stems and seeds removed
1 tsp salt
1 cup heavy cream
2 tbsp sour cream
1 tbsp lime juice

SCAN TO WATCH

shrimp ceviche

1lb (454g) fully cooked, peeled, and deveined large shrimp

¼ cup lime juice

¼ cup lemon juice

¼ cup chopped fresh cilantro

¼ cup diced red onion

2 Roma tomatoes, diced

1 large avocado, diced

Pinch of salt

This simple shrimp ceviche is super easy to make. It uses precooked shrimp that's marinated in citrus juices and then combined with fresh cilantro, red onion, tomato, and avocado. Even ceviche newbies will love this recipe!

1 Cut the shrimp into ¼-inch (.60cm) pieces and place in a large bowl.

2 Pour in the lime juice and lemon juice. Toss to coat. Cover and transfer to the fridge to marinate for 30 minutes.

3 Gently stir in the cilantro, red onion, tomato, and avocado. Season with a pinch of salt, adding more to taste, if desired. Serve chilled.

················ **NOTES** ················

If desired, you can add 1 cup diced cucumber to this recipe to add some extra crunch.

SCAN TO WATCH

tacos al pastor

2–3lb (905–1360g) boneless pork butt or pork loin

FOR THE MARINADE

1 large pineapple, peeled and cored

1 medium white onion, roughly chopped

½ cup orange juice

¼ cup distilled white vinegar

1 chipotle pepper in adobo sauce (pepper only)

2 tbsp ancho chili powder

4 garlic cloves, minced

1½ tsp salt

1 tsp dried Mexican oregano

FOR SERVING

12 6-inch (15.25cm) corn or flour tortillas, warmed

½ cup chopped fresh cilantro

1 small red onion, diced

2 large limes, cut into wedges

Al pastor means "shepherd style" in Spanish, as the dish was originally made by roasting lamb over a spit. While you can still use lamb, it's most often made today using pork. These tacos feature thinly sliced and marinated pork that is topped with diced onion, grilled pineapple, and fresh cilantro. It makes for an incredible taco and a fantastic dinner for your Taco Tuesday!

1 Using a sharp knife, cut the pork into thin slices. Transfer the slices to a large bowl or gallon-sized resealable plastic bag. Set aside.

2 Cut the pineapple into 2-inch (5cm) wide spears. Dice approximately 1 cup of the pineapple and set the remaining spears aside.

3 Make the marinade by combining the onion, diced pineapple, orange juice, white vinegar, chipotle pepper, chili powder, garlic, salt, and oregano in a blender. Purée until smooth.

4 Pour the marinade over the pork, cover or seal and transfer to the fridge to marinate for at least 4 hours. After 4 hours, remove the pork from the bowl or bag and discard the marinade.

5 Preheat an outdoor grill to high heat. Working in small batches, sear the pork slices until cooked through, about 2 to 4 minutes per piece, while simultaneously grilling the pineapple spears until lightly charred. Transfer the cooked pork and grilled pineapple spears to a cutting board. Roughly chop the pork slices and then roughly chop the pineapple spears.

6 To serve, add the meat to a warmed tortilla and then top with cilantro, diced grilled pineapple, a little diced red onion. Serve with a lime wedge on the side for squeezing.

SCAN TO WATCH

beef barbacoa

This easy beef barbacoa is full of authentic flavors and can be easily made in the oven, a slow cooker, or an electric pressure cooker. It's smoky and spicy, with just a hint of sweetness from the brown sugar and cinnamon.

1 Place the dried guajillo peppers and ancho peppers in a bowl or jar. Fill the container with water until the peppers are covered. Soak 1 to 4 hours or until softened.

2 Preheat the oven to 300°F (149°C).

3 Season the beef with the black pepper and 2 teaspoons salt. Heat 2 tablespoons olive oil in a large cast iron pot over high heat. Sear the meat on all sides. Once the meat is seared, remove the pot from the heat and set aside.

4 Combine the guajillo peppers, ancho peppers, chipotle pepper, garlic, apple cider vinegar, brown sugar, remaining 1 teaspoon salt, oregano, cinnamon, remaining 2 tablespoons olive oil, and water in a blender. Blend until smooth, adding more water if necessary to thin the sauce out enough to blend.

5 Pour the sauce over the meat in the pot. Cover and place in the oven. Braise for 3 hours or until the meat is tender and easily shreds with a fork.

6 Use two forks to shred the beef. Serve warm.

2 dried guajillo peppers, stemmed and seeded

2 dried ancho peppers, stemmed and seeded

3–5lb (1.35–2.25kg) beef chuck roast or beef cheeks

1 tsp black pepper

3 tsp salt, divided

4 tbsp olive oil, divided

1 chipotle pepper in adobo sauce (pepper only)

3 garlic cloves, minced

1 tbsp apple cider vinegar

1 tbsp light brown sugar

1 tsp dried oregano

½ tsp ground cinnamon

¼ cup water

······················ NOTES ······················

Serving suggestion: Serve on warmed corn tortillas with some diced red onion, chopped cilantro, and diced jalapeño.

Slow cooker instructions: Place the seasoned and seared roast in a slow cooker. Make the sauce according to directions and then pour it over the meat. Cook on high for 6 hours or on low for 8 to 10 hours.

Electric pressure cooker instructions: Use the "sear" setting to sear the seasoned roast. Make the sauce and pour it over meat. Cook on the "beef/stew" setting for about 70 minutes.

SCAN TO WATCH

GF

READY IN 1 HOUR 20 MINUTES · MAKES 12 SERVINGS

easy weeknight chicken tacos

4 boneless, skinless chicken breasts*

FOR THE MARINADE

1 tsp garlic powder

¾ tsp salt

½ tsp paprika

½ tsp dried parsley

¼ tsp black pepper

¼ tsp cayenne

3 tbsp lime juice

3 tbsp olive oil

FOR SERVING

½ cup chopped fresh cilantro

2 medium Roma tomatoes, diced

½ medium red onion, diced

½ cup crumbled queso fresco

12 8-inch (20cm) corn or flour tortillas, warmed

If you're looking for an easy weeknight meal, you've found it! These chicken tacos are simple to prepare and extremely delicious! A simple marinade brings a ton of flavor to the chicken, and you can fill the tacos with whatever toppings your family loves.

1 Place the chicken breasts in a shallow dish or gallon-sized resealable plastic bag.

2 Make the marinade by whisking together the garlic powder, salt, paprika, parsley, black pepper, cayenne, lime juice, and olive oil. Pour the marinade over the chicken breasts and then gently toss or turn to coat. Transfer to the fridge to marinate for 1 hour.

3 Preheat a large skillet over medium-high heat. Cook the chicken breasts for 5 to 6 minutes per side or until the chicken reaches an internal temperature of 165°F (74°C).

4 Transfer the chicken to a cutting board and chop into small bite-sized pieces.

5 To serve, top a warm tortilla with the chicken, cilantro, tomato, onion, and queso fresco.

· **NOTES** ·

* If desired, you can substitute 6 to 8 boneless, skinless chicken thighs for the chicken breasts. (The cooking time will need to be increased slightly.)

SCAN TO WATCH

fajitas (steak or chicken)

3 large bell peppers
(multiple colors), sliced

1 medium red onion, sliced

8oz (227g) button or
crimini mushrooms,
sliced

2 garlic cloves, minced

¼ cup lime juice
(about 2 limes)

10 6-inch (15cm) flour
tortillas, warmed

sour cream (optional)

cilantro (optional)

guacamole (optional)

salsa (optional)

FOR STEAK FAJITAS

2 tbsp olive oil

1½lb (680g) flank steak,
thinly sliced against
the grain

1 tbsp Worcestershire
sauce

FOR CHICKEN FAJITAS

3 tbsp olive oil, divided

4 boneless skinless
chicken breasts

FOR THE SEASONING MIX

2 tsp ground cumin

2 tsp chili powder

1 tsp onion powder

1 tsp salt

1 tsp red pepper flakes

Fajitas are an easy one-dish meal that's ready in under 30 minutes. These are made with a quick homemade fajita seasoning with all the traditional bell pepper and onion filling. Our family likes to add mushrooms into the mix too! I've included instructions for both steak and chicken fajitas.

Steak Fajitas

1 In a small bowl, make the seasoning mix by stirring together the cumin, chili powder, onion powder, salt, and red pepper flakes. Set aside.

2 Add the olive oil to a large skillet over high heat. When the oil is hot, add the bell peppers, onion, and mushrooms. Sauté the vegetables for about 7 to 8 minutes and then add half the seasoning mix and the garlic. Cook an additional 1 to 2 minutes until the vegetables are tender-crisp and then transfer the vegetables to a serving dish.

3 Return the skillet to high heat. Add the flank steak and sprinkle in the remaining seasoning mixture and then pour in the Worcestershire sauce. Cook the steak, tossing continuously, until browned, about 2 to 3 minutes for medium-rare. (Flank steak is best eaten medium-rare. For well-done flank steak, add an additional 3 to 4 minutes cooking time.)

4 Once the meat is cooked, add the vegetables back to the skillet. Drizzle in the lime juice and toss the ingredients together.

5 To serve, top the warm tortillas with the meat and vegetables. Serve plain or top with sour cream, cilantro, guacamole, or salsa (if using).

Chicken Fajitas

1 In a small bowl, make the seasoning mix by stirring together the cumin, chili powder, onion powder, salt, and red pepper flakes. Season both sides of the chicken breasts with half of the seasoning mix.

2 Add 1 tablespoon of the olive oil to a large skillet over medium-high heat. Add the chicken breasts and sauté for 5 to 6 minutes per side or until the chicken reaches an internal temperature of 165°F (74°C). Transfer the chicken breasts to a cutting board. Return the skillet to the stovetop and increase the heat to high.

3 Add the remaining 2 tablespoons of olive oil to the hot skillet. Add the bell peppers, onion, and mushrooms. Sauté the vegetables for about 7 to 8 minutes and then add the remaining seasoning mix and the garlic. Cook an additional 1 to 2 minutes or until the vegetables are tender-crisp.

4 Slice the chicken breasts into thin strips and return the strips to the skillet. Drizzle in the lime juice and toss the ingredients together.

5 To serve, top the warm tortillas with the meat and vegetables. Serve plain or top with sour cream, cilantro, guacamole, or salsa (if using).

SCAN TO WATCH

ultimate nachos

1lb (454g) ground beef

16oz (454g) tortilla chips

2 tbsp taco seasoning

¼ cup water

16oz (425g) canned refried beans

4 cups shredded cheddar cheese, divided

FOR THE SEASONING

2 tsp chili powder

1 tsp paprika

¾ tsp ground cumin

¾ tsp onion powder

½ tsp garlic powder

½ tsp salt

¼ tsp black pepper

¼ tsp cayenne

FOR THE TOPPINGS

½ cup sour cream

½ cup guacamole

⅓ cup sliced olives

½ cup fresh salsa

⅓ cup roughly chopped fresh cilantro

¼ cup sliced or pickled jalapeños

¼ cup diced red onion

¼ cup sliced green onion

This truly is the ultimate nacho recipe! Crispy chips are topped with melted cheese, seasoned ground beef and refried beans, and all of your favorite nacho toppings.

1 Preheat the oven to 350°F (177°C).

2 Make the taco seasoning by combining all of the seasoning ingredients in a small bowl. Stir to combine. (Alternatively, you can use a store-bought taco seasoning mix.)

3 Preheat a large skillet over medium-high heat. Add the ground beef and use a spoon to break up the meat. Cook 8 to 10 minutes or until the meat is fully cooked through. Drain, add the taco seasoning, stir, and cook 60 to 90 seconds more.

4 Pour in the water and add the refried beans. Stir to combine and cook until heated through. Remove the skillet from the heat.

5 Spread the chips out onto a baking sheet or a large oven-safe baking dish. Sprinkle 2 cups of the cheese over the chips. Dot with the beef and bean mixture and then top with the remaining 2 cups of cheese.

6 Bake for 5 to 7 minutes or until the cheese is melted.

7 Remove the pan from the oven and evenly distribute the toppings over the top of the chips. Serve warm.

SCAN TO WATCH

10 no-lettuce salads

avocado caprese salad

1 pint (454g) red cherry or grape tomatoes, halved

1 pint (454g) yellow cherry or grape tomatoes, halved

2 large avocados, diced

8oz (227g) mini mozzarella balls

½ cup sliced fresh basil

3 tbsp honey

3 tbsp white balsamic vinegar

3 tbsp extra virgin olive oil

¼ tsp salt

¼ tsp black pepper

This salad is light, refreshing, and super easy to make, with all of the flavors of traditional caprese plus avocado for creaminess. This will be a huge hit wherever you serve it—a picnic, potluck, backyard barbecue, or just at home.

1 In a large bowl, gently toss together the red tomatoes, yellow tomatoes, diced avocado, mini mozzarella balls, and basil.

2 In a small microwave-safe bowl, heat the honey for 15 to 20 seconds to thin. Whisk in the vinegar and olive oil.

3 Pour the dressing over the tomato-mozzarella mixture. Season with the salt and black pepper and then toss to combine.

SCAN TO WATCH

GF · VG · PL

READY IN ABOUT 2 HOURS · MAKES 8 SERVINGS

cucumber salad
(two ways)

This recipe is a family favorite that people in my circle have been enjoying for ages. Here I give you a classic vinaigrette version as well as a creamy version. Whichever version you prefer, I promise both will be absolutely delicious!

FOR A CLASSIC VINAIGRETTE VERSION

2 English cucumbers, thinly sliced

1 tsp salt

1 medium red onion, thinly sliced

1 cup distilled white vinegar

½ cup water

½ cup granulated sugar

2 tbsp fresh dill, minced

FOR A CREAMY VERSION

½ cup sour cream

2 tbsp distilled white vinegar

4 garlic cloves, minced

2 tbsp freshly chopped dill

2 tsp granulated sugar

¼ tsp salt

2 English cucumbers, thinly sliced

1 medium red onion, thinly sliced

SCAN TO WATCH

Classic Vinaigrette Cucumber Salad

1 Add the cucumbers to a large bowl and season with the salt. Set aside to sweat for 1 hour and then drain. Toss the cucumber slices with the onion slices.

2 In a small saucepan over high heat, combine the white vinegar, water, and sugar. Stir continuously until the sugar is dissolved, about 3 to 5 minutes.

3 Pour the vinegar-sugar mixture over the cucumbers and onions and then add the dill. Toss to combine, cover with plastic wrap, and refrigerate for 1 hour before serving. Serve chilled or at room temperature.

Creamy Cucumber Salad

1 In a large bowl, whisk together the sour cream, white vinegar, garlic, dill, sugar, and salt.

2 Add the cucumbers and onions to the bowl. Stir until well combined.

3 Cover the bowl with plastic wrap and refrigerate for a minimum of 1 hour before serving. Serve chilled.

mom's macaroni salad

4 tsp salt, divided

1 lb (454g) elbow noodles

4oz (114g) cheddar cheese, cubed or shredded

½ small red onion, minced

4 celery ribs, diced

1 red bell pepper, minced

1 cup frozen peas, thawed

½ cup mayonnaise

¼ cup apple cider vinegar

¼ cup minced fresh dill

2 tbsp granulated sugar

2 tbsp sweet pickle relish

1 tbsp Dijon mustard

½ tsp black pepper

Macaroni salad is a classic picnic, barbecue, or cookout side dish. Filled with tender pasta, crunchy veggies, and a creamy mayonnaise-based dressing, this recipe is easy to put together and even easier to scarf down! My mom always added cheddar cheese to her macaroni salad, so to me, it's just not macaroni salad without the cheese!

1 Add 3 teaspoons salt to a large pot water. Bring to a boil over high heat. Cook the elbow noodles until al dente and then transfer to a colander. Rinse with cold water until the pasta is cooled. Drain well.

2 In a large bowl, toss together the cooked noodles, cheese, onion, celery, bell pepper, and peas.

3 In a small bowl, whisk together the mayonnaise, apple cider vinegar, dill, sugar, relish, Dijon mustard, remaining 1 teaspoon salt, and black pepper.

4 Pour the dressing over the pasta and then toss gently until the ingredients are well coated. Cover the bowl with plastic wrap and refrigerate for at least 1 hour before serving.

·········· **VARIATIONS** ··········

Tuna Macaroni Salad: For a tuna twist, add three 5oz (142g) cans solid white albacore tuna that have been drained and five large hard-boiled eggs that have been diced.

SCAN TO WATCH

german potato salad

2 lb (907g) red potatoes, diced

1 lb (454g) bacon, diced

1 medium red onion, diced

¼ cup white vinegar

¼ cup olive oil

2 tbsp granulated sugar

1 tbsp Dijon mustard

1 tsp salt

½ tsp black pepper

¼ cup chopped fresh parsley

This potato salad has perfectly crispy bacon and red onion, and it is dressed with a Dijon vinegar dressing. It can be served either hot or cold, but I personally prefer it warm. German potato salad is much more savory than standard American potato salad. It has a strong bacon flavor with the German flavor influences of vinegar, onion, and mustard. This is the kind of potato salad people will pile onto their plates!

1 Bring a large pot of water to a boil over high heat. Add the potatoes and boil until tender, about 10 to 12 minutes. Drain and transfer the potatoes to a large bowl.

2 While the potatoes are cooking, add the bacon to a cold large skillet. Cook over medium heat until crisp, about 8 to 10 minutes. Use a slotted spoon to transfer the bacon to a plate lined with a paper towel. Set aside. (Leave the grease in the pan.)

3 Add the red onion to the skillet with the grease. Cook 5 minutes or until the onions are soft. Whisk in the white vinegar, olive oil, sugar, Dijon mustard, salt, and black pepper. Cook until heated through, about 1 to 2 minutes.

4 Pour the dressing over the cooked potatoes and then add the bacon and parsley. Toss until well combined. Serve hot or chill to serve cold.

SCAN TO WATCH

GF · PL

READY IN 1 HOUR 25 MINUTES · MAKES 8 SERVINGS

creamy american potato salad

2 lb (907g) red potatoes, diced

1 lb (454g) bacon, cooked and crumbled (optional)

½ small red onion, diced

4 celery ribs celery, diced

4 hard-boiled eggs, roughly chopped

¾ cup mayonnaise

¼ cup apple cider vinegar

¼ cup minced fresh dill

2 tbsp granulated sugar

1 tbsp Dijon mustard

1 tbsp sweet pickle relish

1 tsp salt

½ tsp black pepper

The best creamy potato salad recipe needs to have the perfect balance of flavors, with just the right amount of mayo and a variety of delicious ingredients. That's all that's necessary to create a potato salad that everyone will love. And this is that recipe!

1 Bring a large pot of water to a boil over high heat. Add the diced potatoes and cook until tender, about 10 to 15 minutes. Drain and then rinse with cold water to cool.

2 In a large bowl, gently combine the cooled potatoes with the bacon (if using), onion, celery, and eggs. Set aside.

3 In a small bowl, whisk together the mayonnaise, apple cider vinegar, dill, sugar, Dijon mustard, pickle relish, salt, and black pepper.

4 Pour the dressing over the potatoes and toss until the ingredients are well coated with the dressing. Cover and refrigerate at least 2 hours before serving.

SCAN TO WATCH

GF · VG
READY IN 22 MINUTES · MAKES 6 SERVINGS

rachel's infamous egg salad

1 dozen large eggs

¼ cup mayonnaise

2 tbsp Dijon mustard

1 tbsp prepared horseradish

1 tbsp sweet pickle relish

¼ cup minced dill

¼ cup minced chives

This recipe will knock your socks off! It's the perfect balance of flavors, and the horseradish is the secret ingredient that makes people come back to this egg salad again and again. This recipe goes viral almost every time I share it online and has become infamous amongst my fans. It wouldn't be *The Stay At Home Chef Family Favorites Cookbook* without my infamous egg salad recipe!

1 Place the eggs in the bottom of a medium saucepan. Fill the pan with enough water to cover the eggs by 1 inch (2.5cm). Place the saucepan over high heat and bring to a boil. Once the water comes to a boil, turn off the heat, place a lid on the pan, and let the eggs sit for 8 minutes. While the eggs are resting, fill a large bowl with ice and water.

2 After 8 minutes, plunge the cooked eggs into the ice water to stop the cooking process. Peel the eggs and chop into bite-sized pieces.

3 Place the chopped eggs into a large mixing bowl. Add the mayonnaise, Dijon mustard, horseradish, pickle relish, dill, and chives. Gently fold until well combined. Chill until ready to serve.

SCAN TO WATCH

street corn salad

6 ears corn, shucked

¼ cup mayonnaise

¼ cup Mexican crema or sour cream

½ cup grated cotija cheese, divided

½ tsp ancho chili powder

¼ tsp salt

¼ cup chopped fresh cilantro

1 tbsp Mexican hot sauce

This recipe packs all the yumminess of street corn into a simple-to-prepare salad that can be served right away or served chilled.

1 Preheat the oven or an outdoor grill to 400°F (204°C).

2 Individually wrap the corn ears in aluminum foil and place in the oven or on the grill for 15 minutes. Unwrap the ears and set aside to cool.

3 While the corn ears are roasting, whisk together the mayonnaise, Mexican crema or sour cream, ¼ cup of the cotija cheese, ancho chili powder, and salt in a small bowl.

4 Cut the kernels from the cobs and stir into the mayonnaise mixture.

5 Sprinkle the remaining ¼ cup of Cotija cheese and cilantro over the salad and then drizzle the hot sauce over the top. Serve immediately or chill and serve cold.

·· NOTES ··

If desired, add 1 to 2 diced red bell peppers and/or 1 to 2 diced avocados for a fun flavor twist! For a splash of citrus flavor, squeeze in the juice from one lime (about 2 tablespoons) over the top of the salad.

SCAN TO WATCH

GF · VG · VE · PL

READY IN 20 MINUTES · MAKES 8 SERVINGS

simple black bean and corn salad

2 cups frozen corn kernels

30oz (850g) canned black beans, drained and rinsed

2 medium Roma tomatoes, diced

1 medium red bell pepper, diced

2 medium avocados, diced

½ small red onion, minced

½ cup chopped fresh cilantro

¼ cup lime juice

¼ cup extra virgin olive oil

2 garlic cloves, minced

½ tsp salt

½ tsp red pepper flakes

This simple salad is a fresh, colorful combination of black beans, corn, bell pepper, avocado, and onions. It's tossed in a light and tangy dressing that is both healthy and delicious.

1 Thaw the corn kernels in a microwave-safe bowl for 3 to 4 minutes, stirring every 90 seconds.

2 Toss the thawed corn kernels with the black beans, tomatoes, bell pepper, avocado, onions, and cilantro. Set aside.

3 In a small bowl, whisk together the lime juice, olive oil, garlic, salt, and red pepper flakes.

4 Pour the dressing over the salad and gently toss to combine. Serve at room temperature or chill for serving later.

········· NOTES ·········

This recipe is best enjoyed within 1 day due to the avocados, which will begin to brown after 24 hours. If you'd like this salad to last longer, omit the avocado.

SCAN TO WATCH

READY IN 20 MINUTES • MAKES 8 SERVINGS

italian pasta salad

1 lb (454g) rotini

1 pint (454g) cherry tomatoes, halved

8 oz (227g) fresh mini mozzarella cheese balls, halved

½ cup to 1 cup sliced black olives (depending on your preferences)

1 cup mini pepperoni slices

½ cup pepperoncinis, roughly chopped

½ small red onion, diced

FOR THE DRESSING

½ cup extra virgin olive oil

¼ cup red wine vinegar

1 tsp lemon juice

2 tsp Italian seasoning

1 tsp granulated sugar

½ tsp garlic powder

Pinch of red pepper flakes

This classic cold Italian pasta salad features a homemade Italian dressing that's also delicious served over a green salad. It's the perfect potluck or summer side dish, and despite the name, it isn't an Italian dish at all but rather a beloved American classic. One fan of my website calls it "pizza salad," and I have to say it's a fitting name!

1 Bring a large pot of water to a boil over high heat. Cook the rotini until al dente. Transfer the cooked pasta to a colander and rinse with cold water until cooled. Drain and set aside.

2 In a large bowl, make the dressing by whisking together the olive oil, red wine vinegar, lemon juice, Italian seasoning, sugar, garlic powder, and red pepper flakes.

3 Add the cooked pasta, tomatoes, mozzarella, olives, mini pepperoni slices, pepperoncinis, and onion to the bowl with the dressing. Toss to coat.

4 Tightly cover the bowl with plastic wrap and refrigerate for at least 1 hour before serving.

SCAN TO WATCH

cucumber–tomato salad

2 English cucumbers, sliced and quartered

1 pint (454g) cherry or grape tomatoes, halved

1 small red onion, diced

2 tbsp extra virgin olive oil

2 tbsp lemon juice

1 tbsp apple cider vinegar

1 tsp granulated sugar or honey

1 tsp salt

½ tsp black pepper

2 tbsp minced fresh dill

This cucumber tomato salad is super simple and healthy, and it packs a punch of flavor! You'll love the delicious lemon dill dressing with it's zingy bite and hint of sweetness. You'll want to balance the acidity of the dressing with some sweetness, so don't skip using either the sugar or honey as instructed. Or you can use another similar sweetener of your choice.

1 In a large bowl, toss together the cucumbers, tomatoes, and onions.

2 Make the dressing by whisking together the olive oil, lemon juice, apple cider vinegar, sugar or honey, salt, black pepper, and dill in a small bowl.

3 Pour the dressing over the vegetables and then toss to combine.

4 Tightly cover the bowl with plastic wrap and refrigerate at least 1 hour before serving.

SCAN TO WATCH

11 eat your veggies

steakhouse-style garlic mashed potatoes

6 cups chicken broth

5 lb (2.25kg) red potatoes (unpeeled), cut into 1-inch (2.5cm) cubes

5 garlic cloves

½ cup salted butter

4oz (113g) cream cheese

½ cup buttermilk

1 tsp salt

These potatoes are a classic steakhouse side. They're perfectly creamy, with a punch of garlic. Serve these alongside a juicy steak and you'll feel like you are eating in a steakhouse for sure! Unlike traditional mashed potatoes, this recipe uses red potatoes with the edible skins getting mashed right along with the potato and garlic cloves. These mashed potatoes have both texture and flavor!

1 Bring the chicken broth to a boil in a large pot over high heat.

2 Place the potatoes and garlic cloves into the boiling chicken broth. Boil until the potatoes are tender, about 15 minutes.

3 Use a slotted spoon to transfer the cooked potatoes and garlic cloves to a large bowl.

4 Add the butter, cream cheese, buttermilk, and salt. Use a potato masher to mash the ingredients until the butter and cream cheese are melted and everything is completely mashed together.

SCAN TO WATCH

yellow squash casserole

1 tbsp cooking oil (canola, vegetable, or olive)

3 lb (1.35kg) yellow squash, sliced

1 medium white onion, diced

1 tsp salt

8oz (227g) sour cream

1 cup shredded cheddar cheese

¾ cup grated Parmesan cheese, divided

1 large egg

1 sleeve Ritz crackers, crushed

2 tbsp salted butter, melted

This is a classic Southern side dish! Sliced squash is baked in a cheesy cream sauce and topped with a buttery cracker crumble. It's decadent and turns simple squash into something totally craveable. Who would have thought squash could be this good?

1 Preheat the oven to 350°F (177°C). Lightly grease a 9 x 9-inch (23 x 23cm) baking pan or casserole dish.

2 Heat the cooking oil in a large skillet over medium-high heat. Add the squash and onion and then season with the salt. Cook, stirring frequently, until the squash just begins to soften and the liquids have been released, about 7 to 10 minutes. Drain well.

3 In a large bowl, combine the sour cream, cheddar cheese, ½ cup of the Parmesan, and the egg. Stir until well combined. Gently fold in the squash until well coated. Pour the mixture into the prepared baking pan.

4 In a small bowl, toss together the crushed crackers, melted butter, and remaining ¼ cup of Parmesan. Sprinkle the mixture over the top of the squash.

5 Bake, uncovered, for 20 to 25 minutes or until the topping is lightly browned. Serve hot.

SCAN TO WATCH

READY IN 1 HOUR · MAKES 4 SERVINGS

roasted butternut squash
(four ways)

1 large butternut squash
2 tbsp olive oil
2 garlic cloves, minced
1 tsp salt
1 tsp black pepper

Enjoy the aromatic, sweet flavor of roasted butternut squash with this simple recipe that features four different flavor options. You really can't go wrong with any of the options, they are all equally delicious. Simply choose whichever option pairs best with the rest of your meal.

1 Preheat the oven to 400°F (204°C).

2 Use a fork to prick holes in the skin over the entire surface of the squash. Microwave the squash for 3 minutes on high and then let it cool to a point where you can easily handle it.

3 Use a vegetable peeler to remove the skin and then cut the squash in half lengthwise. Use a spoon to scrape out the seeds and then cut the neck portion from each half. Dice both ends of the squash into 1-inch (2.5cm) cubes.

4 Place the squash in a large bowl and toss with the olive oil, garlic, salt, and black pepper. Spread the squash in an even layer onto a large baking sheet.

5 Roast for 40 to 50 minutes or until the squash is tender. Serve hot.

.... VARIATIONS ....

Brown Sugar–Roasted Butternut Squash: Toss the cubed squash with 3 tablespoons melted butter, 3 tablespoons light brown sugar, and ¼ teaspoon salt.

Maple-Roasted Butternut Squash: Toss the cubed squash with 1 tablespoon olive oil, 3 tablespoons maple syrup, and ¼ teaspoon salt.

Rosemary-Roasted Butternut Squash: Add 2 tablespoons minced fresh rosemary or 2 teaspoons dried rosemary in step 4.

SCAN TO WATCH

parmesan roasted broccoli

2 medium heads broccoli, cut into florets

3 garlic cloves, thinly sliced

2 tbsp olive oil

¼ tsp salt

¼ tsp black pepper

1 medium lemon, zested and juiced

½ cup grated Parmesan cheese

This roasted broccoli is one of the most delicious side dishes ever! A few extra ingredients like garlic and Parmesan make this green veggie shine. You'll be surprised at just how simple this is to prepare and also how quickly your family will scarf it down.

1 Preheat the oven to 425°F (218°C).

2 Spread the broccoli florets onto a large baking sheet. Toss with the garlic slices, drizzle with the olive oil, and then season with the salt and black pepper.

3 Roast until the broccoli is tender-crisp, about 15 to 20 minutes.

4 Remove the broccoli from the oven. Drizzle the lemon juice over the top and then sprinkle the lemon zest and Parmesan over the top. Serve hot.

SCAN TO WATCH

cheesy scalloped potatoes

4 large russet potatoes, peeled

1 cup heavy cream

½ cup grated Parmesan cheese

2 garlic cloves, minced

½ tsp salt

½ tsp ground nutmeg

¼ tsp black pepper

½ cup shredded sharp cheddar cheese

These amazing scalloped potatoes are easier to make than you might think! They feature a classic creamy sauce and are topped with gooey cheese. Technically, these potatoes are *au gratin* due to the addition of the cheese (original scalloped potatoes don't contain cheese), but no matter what you call it, these potatoes will be devoured!

1 Preheat the oven to 350°F (177°C). Lightly grease a 9 x 9-inch (23 x 23cm) or 2-quart baking dish.

2 Use a mandoline slicer, sharp knife, or food processor to thinly slice the potatoes. Transfer the slices to a large bowl.

3 Pour the heavy cream over the potatoes and then add the Parmesan, garlic, salt, nutmeg, and black pepper. Toss until the potatoes are well coated and the cheese and seasonings are evenly dispersed.

4 Layer the potato slices into the prepared baking dish. Sprinkle the cheddar cheese over the top.

5 Bake for about 1 hour or until the potatoes are fork-tender and the cheese is melted and bubbly. Serve hot.

.... NOTES ....

The baking time ultimately depends on how thinly you slice the potatoes. If you slice the potatoes thicker, they may take 15 to 30 minutes longer to bake. If you slice the potatoes paper thin, they may be done after only 40 minutes. Adjust the cooking time accordingly.

SCAN TO WATCH

GF · MA · VG

READY IN 40 MINUTES · MAKES 8 SERVINGS

the creamiest mashed potatoes

5 lb (2.25kg) russet potatoes, washed, peeled, and cut into 1-inch (2.5cm) cubes or chunks

8 cups chicken broth

½ cup salted butter

8 oz (227g) cream cheese

¾ cup buttermilk

1 tsp salt, plus more to taste

This is *the* perfect mashed potatoes recipe! The potatoes are infused with the herbaceous flavors of chicken broth while they cook, adding a whole new level of flavor. I once heard a chef state that the secret to the best mashed potatoes is allowing the potatoes to carry the maximum amount of butter and fat. This recipe does just that with the combination of butter, cream cheese, and buttermilk. These are the mashed potatoes that people won't be able to stop eating.

1 Place the potatoes in a large pot. Pour in the chicken broth. (The potatoes should be just covered with the liquid.)

2 Place the pot over high heat and bring to a boil. Once boiling, reduce the heat to medium and simmer until the potatoes are tender, about 15 minutes.

3 Strain the potatoes from the broth and transfer the still hot potatoes to a large bowl.

4 Add the butter, cream cheese, buttermilk, and salt. Using a hand mixer, whip the potatoes until light, fluffy, and creamy, about 3 to 5 minutes. (Alternatively, you can use a potato masher or a potato ricer to mash the potatoes.) Season to taste with additional salt, if desired. Serve hot.

.... NOTES ....

Make-ahead instructions: The cooked mashed potatoes can be kept in a slow cooker on the "low" or "warm" settings for up to 4 hours before serving. This can be quite convenient for large gatherings or demanding holiday meals.

SCAN TO WATCH

"garlic bread" roasted potatoes

8 medium Yukon Gold or red potatoes, scrubbed and cut into bite-sized chunks

2 tbsp olive oil

½ tsp salt, plus more to taste

¼ tsp black pepper, plus more to taste

4 tbsp salted butter

5 garlic cloves

1 tsp dried basil

½ tsp dried oregano

½ cup shredded Parmesan cheese

These roasted potatoes feature all the flavors of garlic bread that you love in an easy roasted potato dish! Seriously, it will taste like you are eating garlic bread instead of roasted potatoes! My kids can never get enough of these potatoes. If you love garlic bread, you'll love this recipe too.

1 Preheat the oven to 400°F (204°C).

2 Spread the potatoes out onto a large baking sheet. Drizzle them with the olive oil and season with salt and black pepper. Transfer to the oven and bake for 30 minutes.

3 While the potatoes are baking, combine the butter, garlic cloves, basil, and oregano in a food processor. Process until everything is puréed and slightly whipped.

4 Remove the potatoes from the oven and top with the garlic butter compound. Toss until the potatoes are well coated and then place them back in the oven for another 15 minutes.

5 After 15 minutes, sprinkle the Parmesan over the potatoes and then put them back in the oven for 5 minutes more to let the cheese melt a bit. (Actual total cooking time will depend on the potato variety and how big the chunks are cut.) Season to taste with additional salt and black pepper, if desired. Serve hot.

SCAN TO WATCH

GF · VG

READY IN 30 MINUTES · MAKES 8 SERVINGS

cinnamon–honey butter mashed sweet potatoes

3–4 lb (1.35–1.80kg) sweet potatoes, peeled and cubed

½ cup salted butter

¼ cup honey

½ tsp ground cinnamon

⅓ cup milk (whole, 2%, or 1%)

¼ tsp salt, plus more to taste (optional)

These deliciously easy mashed sweet potatoes are a delightful side dish that will add some sweet flavor to your dinner. Serve them up on a regular weeknight or use this as a special recipe for holiday meals.

1 Place the cubed sweet potatoes in a large pot. Fill the pot with water to cover. Bring to a boil over high heat.

2 Once boiling, reduce the heat to low and simmer until the sweet potatoes are tender, about 15 to 20 minutes. Drain well.

3 Transfer the still-hot sweet potatoes to a large bowl. Add the butter, honey, cinnamon, milk, and salt (if using).

4 Using a hand mixer, whip the potatoes until light, fluffy, and creamy, about 3 to 5 minutes. (Alternatively, you can use a potato masher or a potato ricer to mash the potatoes.) Add more salt to taste, if desired. Serve hot.

SCAN TO WATCH

easy green bean casserole

½ lb (227g) bacon, diced

2 tbsp all-purpose flour

2 garlic cloves, minced

1 cup chicken broth

1 cup half-and-half

½ tsp black pepper

¼ tsp ground nutmeg

45oz (1275g) canned green beans, drained

1½ cups french fried onions

This simple green bean casserole is so easy to make and doesn't require using canned cream of mushroom soup! Instead, you'll get amazing flavor by using only scratch ingredients.

1 Preheat the oven to 450°F (232°C). Lightly grease 9 x 13-inch (23 x 33cm) baking pan.

2 Preheat a large skillet over medium heat. Add the bacon and cook until crispy, about 12 minutes. (Do not drain the grease from the skillet.)

3 Add the flour to the skillet and stir until completely incorporated, about 3 minutes. Add the garlic and sauté for 1 minute and then pour in the chicken broth and half-and-half. Sprinkle in the black pepper and nutmeg. Bring to a boil and then reduce the heat to medium. Let simmer until thickened, about 3 minutes.

4 Place the green beans in the prepared baking pan. Pour the bacon mixture over the green beans and then toss to coat.

5 Bake for 15 minutes. Remove from the oven, sprinkle the french fried onions over the top, and then return to the oven for 5 minutes more. Serve hot.

.... **NOTES** ....

It you'd like to reduce the amount of fat in this recipe, reserve two tablespoons of the bacon fat after cooking the bacon and then drain the rest from the skillet. Add the reserved fat back to the skillet in step 2.

SCAN TO WATCH

easy fried cabbage

5 to 6 thick bacon strips, diced

⅓ cup diced white or yellow onion

½ head green cabbage, shredded or roughly chopped

1 tbsp light brown sugar (optional)

¼ tsp salt, plus more to taste

¼ tsp black pepper, plus more to taste

¼ tsp smoked paprika

This fried cabbage comes together in less than 30 minutes. It's delicious and super easy to make, with just a few ingredients. You can also switch up the flavors by replacing the bacon with a half pound of ground pork sausage or a sliced whole sausage, like kielbasa.

1 Add the bacon to a large nonstick pan over medium heat. Cook until crisp, about 7 to 10 minutes, and then use a slotted spoon to transfer the bacon to a paper towel–lined plate to drain. (Do not drain the grease from the pan.)

2 To the same pan, add the onion. Cook until translucent, about 5 minutes.

3 Add the cabbage, brown sugar (if using), salt, black pepper, smoked paprika to the pan. Stir to combine. Cook until the cabbage is tender, about 7 minutes.

4 Add the bacon back to the pan and stir to combine with the cabbage. Serve warm.

.... **NOTES** ....

You can make this dish vegetarian by omitting the bacon and substituting 2 to 3 tablespoons unsalted butter for sautéing the onions and cabbage.

SCAN TO WATCH

GF · **VG**

READY IN 35 MINUTES · MAKES 6 SERVINGS

garlic butter–roasted brussels sprouts

2 lb (907g) Brussels
sprouts, trimmed and
halved

4 garlic cloves

¼ cup salted butter,
melted

2 tbsp olive oil

¼ tsp salt

½ tsp black pepper

¼ cup freshly grated
Parmesan cheese

These savory and delicious Brussels sprouts are seasoned and roasted to absolute perfection—they're the perfect side dish for any occasion. This is the recipe that will turn Brussels sprouts haters into Brussels sprouts lovers!

1 Preheat the oven to 475°F (246°C).

2 Place the sprouts in a large bowl. Roughly chop the garlic cloves into 4 to 5 pieces each and then add them to the bowl with the sprouts. Drizzle with the melted butter and olive oil and then season with the salt and black pepper. Toss to combine.

3 Spread the seasoned Brussels sprouts out in a single layer on a large baking sheet.

4 Roast until the sprouts are tender, about 20 to 25 minutes. (Sprinkle the Parmesan over the sprouts during the last 5 minutes of roasting.) Serve hot.

SCAN TO WATCH

GF · VG

READY IN 35 MINUTES · MAKES 6 SERVINGS

the best green beans ever!

1½ lb (680g) fresh green
beans, ends trimmed

4 tbsp salted butter

1 tsp salt

½ tsp black pepper

These really are the best green beans ever! They are so simple to make, but totally delicious. And they just might become your family's new favorite vegetable side dish. I make a half pound per person whenever I make this recipe for my family. They love it that much!

1 Place a steamer basket in a large pot. Add 2 to 3 inches of water to the pot or enough water to a point just below the bottom of the basket. (The water should not touch the bottom of the basket.) Bring to a boil over high heat.

2 Add the green beans, cover the pot, reduce the heat to medium-low, and steam the beans until tender.

3 Preheat a large skillet over medium-high heat. Add the butter and steamed green beans and then season with the salt and black pepper. Sauté for 3 to 5 minutes. Serve hot.

················· NOTES ·················

Saucepan steaming instructions: This method isn't ideal because the beans can get a little overcooked and soggy, but it does work. Add a ½ inch (1.25cm) of water to the bottom of a large saucepan. Bring the water to a boil, add the beans, cover, and reduce the heat to low. The water will create enough steam to cook the beans.

Microwave steaming instructions: Add just enough water to a microwave-safe bowl to cover the bottom of the bowl. Add the beans to the bowl, cover the bowl with plastic wrap, use a knife to poke a few holes in the plastic wrap to allow some steam to escape. Microwave on high until the desired doneness is reached.

SCAN TO WATCH

honey-roasted carrots

12 medium carrots, tops removed and peeled (peeling is optional)

3 tbsp salted butter, melted

3 tbsp honey

½ tsp salt

¼ tsp black pepper

1 tbsp chopped fresh parsley for garnishing (optional)

Who wouldn't love carrots smothered in honey butter? This recipe is simply divine and an easy and delicious way to enjoy carrots. The carrots are buttery and sweet with the addition of the honey, and the roasting process also caramelizes the natural sugars in the carrots.

1 Preheat the oven to 400°F (204°C). Lightly grease a large baking sheet.

2 Slice the carrots at an angle and into 2 to 3-inch pieces. Transfer the cut carrots to a large bowl.

3 Drizzle the melted butter and honey over the carrots and then season with the salt and black pepper. Toss to coat and then spread the carrots in an even layer onto the prepared baking sheet.

4 Roast for about 20 minutes or until the carrots are caramelized and tender. Garnish with the parsley (if using). Serve warm.

·········· NOTES ··········

For more even cooking, use carrots that are roughly equal in size and try to cut them down to be similar in size.

SCAN TO WATCH

12 we go together like beans and rice

classic baked beans

1 lb (454g) dried navy beans

1 lb (454g) bacon, diced

1 medium yellow onion, diced

2 medium bell peppers (red and green), diced

2 cups ketchup

2 cups beef broth

2 tbsp Worcestershire sauce

1 tbsp apple cider vinegar

¼ cup light or dark brown sugar

2 tbsp ground mustard

1 tbsp smoked paprika

1 tsp garlic powder

1 tsp salt

1 tsp black pepper

Smokey and savory with just a touch of sweetness, these classic baked beans are a filling and satisfying side dish. They are ideal for bringing along to your next family get-together, picnic, or barbecue. I promise you they'll be gobbled right up!

1 Place the navy beans in a large bowl or pot. Fill the bowl or pot with water until the beans are covered. Set the beans aside to soak for 12 hours or overnight.

2 Drain and rinse the soaked beans and then place them in a large oven-safe pot. Fill the pot with enough water to cover the beans. Bring to a boil over high heat. Once boiling, reduce the heat to medium-low and let the beans simmer for 1 hour or until tender. Drain well and return the beans to the pot.

3 Preheat the oven to 300°F (149°C).

4 Add the bacon to the pot along with onion and bell peppers. Stir in the ketchup, beef broth, Worcestershire sauce, apple cider vinegar, brown sugar, ground mustard, smoked paprika, garlic powder, salt, and black pepper.

5 Cover and bake for 3 to 3½ hours or until the sauce is thick and develops a deep reddish-brown color. Serve hot.

.... NOTES ....

If you don't have an oven-safe pot with a lid, transfer the bean mixture to a 9 x 13-inch (22 x33cm) baking pan or 3-quart casserole dish. Cover with aluminum foil and bake as instructed.

SCAN TO WATCH

GF · VG · VE

READY IN 20 MINUTES · MAKES 6 SERVINGS

mexican-style black beans

1 tbsp vegetable oil

1 small yellow onion, diced

3 garlic cloves, minced

½ tsp ground cumin

¼ tsp cayenne (optional)

30oz (850g) canned black beans (undrained)

¼ tsp salt

¼ cup chopped fresh cilantro

These Mexican-style black beans are a treat worth making and the perfect side dish for any type of Mexican dish. They're flavorful and packed with good-for-you nutrients, and they're also so simple to make.

1 Preheat a heavy skillet over medium-high heat. Add the vegetable oil and let it heat briefly.

2 Add the onion. Sauté for 5 to 7 minutes or until soft.

3 Add the garlic, cumin, and cayenne (if using). Sauté for 1 minute more.

4 Add the black beans along with the liquids from the cans. Simmer for 5 minutes. Serve hot topped with the fresh cilantro.

.... NOTES ....

For true restaurant-style black beans, add ¼ cup of lard, shortening, or butter to the bean mixture and let it melt to flavor the beans.

SCAN TO WATCH

READY IN 20 MINUTES • MAKES 6 SERVINGS

cheesy rice pilaf

1 tbsp butter

1 tbsp olive oil

1 small white or yellow onion, finely chopped

2 cups long-grain white rice

4 cups chicken broth

1 cup freshly grated Parmesan cheese

¼ tsp white pepper

¼ tsp salt

This delicious side dish that goes with absolutely everything! Toasted rice is cooked in chicken broth and then topped with Parmesan cheese. My family affectionately just calls it "cheesy rice."

1 In a large saucepan, heat the butter and olive oil over medium-high heat. When the butter is melted, add the onion and sauté for 3 to 4 minutes or until the onion begins to soften.

2 Add the rice to the saucepan and toast for 3 to 4 minutes more.

3 Add the broth, cover, and bring to a boil. Once boiling, reduce the heat to low and simmer until all the broth is absorbed, about 15 minutes.

4 Remove the pan from the heat and stir in the Parmesan, white pepper, and salt. Serve hot.

NOTES

Classic rice pilaf sometimes uses a mixture of half long-grain white rice and half toasted orzo pasta. To make this classic style, add 1 cup of dried orzo pasta in with the onion and toast 3 to 4 minutes before adding 1 cup of long-grain white rice and then proceeding with the recipe as directed.

SCAN TO WATCH

easy spanish rice

2 vine-ripened tomatoes, quartered

1 medium white onion, quartered

4 garlic cloves

1 jalapeño, stem removed and roughly chopped

¼ cup tomato sauce

⅓ cup olive oil

2 cups long-grain white rice

2 cups chicken broth

1 tsp salt

1 lime cut into wedges, for serving

Chopped fresh cilantro, for garnishing (optional)

Spanish rice is an easy and delicious side dish that goes well with any Mexican-inspired meal. The rice gets infused with tomato flavor as it cooks and soaks up the additional flavors of onion, garlic, and jalapeño. You end up with a flavorful rice with a mild heat to it. It's served with lime wedges so people can squeeze on a little acidity, and the fresh cilantro is always a beloved addition in our house.

1 Place the tomatoes, onion, garlic, jalapeño, and tomato sauce in a blender. Blend until smooth. Set aside.

2 Heat the olive oil in a large saucepan over medium-high heat. Once the oil is hot, add the rice and sauté, stirring frequently, until the rice is lightly toasted and golden, about 3 to 4 minutes.

3 Add the tomato purée, chicken broth, and salt to the pan. Bring to a boil and then reduce the heat to low. Cover and simmer for 20 minutes or until all the liquid has been absorbed. Turn off the heat and let the rice sit for 10 minutes before serving. Garnish with the cilantro (if using). Serve hot with a lime wedge on the side for squeezing.

SCAN TO WATCH

cilantro–lime rice

2 tbsp olive oil

1 medium white onion, diced

2 cups long-grain white rice (jasmine or basmati)

4 cups chicken broth

1 tsp salt, plus more to taste

⅓ cup lime juice

2 tbsp butter (optional)

½ cup chopped fresh cilantro

Cilantro lime rice is an easy side dish that's popular in fast-casual Mexican-American restaurants. It goes perfectly with any Mexican-inspired meal and works great as a filler for tacos, burritos, and enchiladas. It's full of zippy lime flavor and fresh cilantro.

1 Heat the olive oil in a large saucepan over medium-high heat. When the oil is hot, add the onion and sauté for 3 minutes, stirring occasionally.

2 Add the rice to the pan and toast for 3 minutes or until the rice is lightly toasted and golden.

3 Pour in the chicken broth and add the salt. Increase the heat to high and bring to a boil. Once boiling, reduce the heat to low, cover, and simmer for 15 minutes or until all the liquid has been absorbed and the rice is tender.

4 Stir in the lime juice, butter (if using), and cilantro. Heat until the butter until melted. Add more salt to taste, if desired. Serve hot.

SCAN TO WATCH

bread is life

best dinner rolls ever

2 cups milk
(whole, 2%, or 1%)

2 tbsp instant dry yeast

¼ cup granulated sugar

2 tsp salt

8 tbsp salted butter,
softened and divided

2 large eggs

6 cups all-purpose flour,
divided

These dinner rolls are so soft and will practically melt in your mouth. The best compliment I ever received on them was from an 87-year-old friend who said she had thought she made the best dinner rolls until she had mine and decided she absolutely needed the recipe. Millions of people have enjoyed these rolls ever since I first posted the recipe!

1 Place the milk in a small saucepan. Heat on low until it reaches a temperature of 105°F to 110°F (41°C to 43°C). (Alternatively, place the milk in a small microwave-safe bowl and heat in 30-second increments, stirring in between, until the milk is heated to the desired temperature.)

2 In the bowl of a stand mixer fitted with a dough hook, combine the warm milk, yeast, sugar, salt, 7 tablespoons of the softened butter, eggs, and 5½ cups of the flour.

3 Turn the mixer on low speed. Once the flour starts to incorporate into the dough, increase the speed to medium. Slowly add the remaining ½ cup of flour until the dough pulls away from the sides of the bowl. (The dough mixture should be slightly sticky and soft. The amount of flour you add in bread making is always an approximation and you should go by feel. Add more flour just until the dough reaches the desired consistency.)

4 Transfer the dough to a large lightly greased bowl. Cover with a tea towel and set aside to rise for 90 minutes.

5 Lightly grease a large baking sheet. Punch down the dough and then form it into 24 rolls. Place the rolls on the prepared baking sheet in six rows of four rolls. Cover again and set aside to rise for 1 hour more.

6 Preheat the oven to 375°F (191°C). Bake the rolls for 12 to 14 minutes or until lightly browned.

7 Place the remaining 1 tablespoon of butter in a small microwave-safe bowl. Heat in the microwave until melted.

8 Remove the rolls from the oven and brush with melted butter. Let the rolls rest on the baking sheet for 15 minutes before transferring them to a wire cooling rack. Serve warm or allow to cool completely. Store the cooled rolls in an airtight container for 3 to 4 days.

SCAN TO WATCH

perfect french bread

2 cups water

1½ tbsp instant dry yeast

1½ tsp salt

4½–5 cups all-purpose flour

1 large egg, beaten

This French bread recipe only requires a handful of simple ingredients for a perfect, bakery-style loaf. Once you fall in love with this recipe, I highly recommend purchasing French bread loaf pans to take your French bread to the next level.

1 Place the water in a small saucepan. Heat on low until it reaches a temperature of 105°F to 110°F (41°C to 43°C). (Alternatively, place the water in a small microwave-safe bowl and heat in 30-second increments, stirring in between, until the water is heated to the desired temperature.)

2 In the bowl of a stand mixer fitted with a dough hook, combine the yeast, warm water, salt, and 4 cups of the flour.

3 Knead on slow speed until the flour starts to combine with the other ingredients, and then increase the speed to medium and gradually add the remaining flour until the dough pulls away from the sides of the bowl. (The exact amount of flour you use will vary. The dough should be soft and tacky, but should not stick to your hands.)

4 Transfer the dough to a large lightly greased mixing bowl. Cover with a tea towel or plastic wrap and set aside to rise until the dough has doubled in size, about 1 hour.

5 Divide the dough into two halves. Roll each half into a large rectangle, rolling the halves up tightly from the long ends. Place the dough halves onto a lightly greased baking sheet or in French bread loaf pans. Cover again and set aside to rise for 30 to 45 minutes more.

6 Preheat the oven to 375°F (191°C). Use a sharp knife to cut diagonal slashes on the top of each bread loaf, cutting about ¼ inch (.60cm) deep. Brush the loaves with the egg wash. Bake for 35 to 40 minutes or until golden brown.

SCAN TO WATCH

irish soda bread

2 tsp salt

1 tsp baking soda

3–3 ½ cups all-purpose flour, divided

1½ cups buttermilk

1 cup raisins

1 tsp caraway seeds (optional)

This traditional Irish soda bread is dense and moist. It requires no rising time and just simple ingredients to make. Even better, it's ready in just 45 minutes from start to finish. You can make a plain loaf or add raisins and caraway seeds for additional flavor.

1 Preheat the oven to 425°F (218°C).

2 In a large bowl, whisk together the salt, baking soda, and 2½ cups of the flour. Add the buttermilk, raisins, and caraway seeds (if using). Stir just until the dough comes together.

3 Turn the dough out onto a lightly floured surface. Knead until it forms a smooth ball, gradually adding additional flour as needed to achieve a dough that is firm but not sticky. Dust the outside of the dough ball with more flour and then place the dough on an ungreased baking sheet. Use a sharp knife to slash a 1-inch-deep (2.5cm) cross on top of the loaf.

4 Bake for 35 minutes or until golden brown.

SCAN TO WATCH

rye bread

2 ¼ cups water, divided

1½ tbsp instant dry yeast

1½ tsp salt

1½ tbsp caraway seeds

1½ cup rye flour

3 cups all-purpose flour, divided

2 tbsp cornmeal

¼ tsp cornstarch

Delicious homemade rye doesn't get much simpler than this bakery-style artisan bread. Caraway and rye flour give the bread its distinct flavor.

1 Add 2 cups of water to a small saucepan. Heat on low until it reaches a temperature of 105°F to 110°F (41°C to 43°C). (Alternatively, place the water in a small microwave-safe bowl and heat in 30-second increments, stirring in between, until the water is heated to the desired temperature.)

2 In the bowl of a stand mixer fitted with a dough hook, combine the yeast, warm water, salt, caraway seeds, and rye flour. Knead on low speed until just combined. Add the all-purpose flour, 1 cup at a time, until the dough forms a ball that doesn't stick to the sides of the bowl. (The dough should be soft, not stiff, and should hold together on its own without being overly sticky.)

3 Transfer the dough to a large lightly greased mixing bowl. Cover the bowl with a tea towel or plastic wrap and set the dough aside to rise until it doubles in size, about 1 hour.

4 Shape the dough into a loaf by using your thumbs to stretch the dough from the top center, over the edges, and then underneath the ball. (It should look and feel like you are holding the loaf with two hands as you are pulling the dough inside out with your thumbs.) Give the dough several pulls until you have a nice-looking loaf.

5 Dust a pizza peel or wooden cutting board with the cornmeal. Put the loaf on the prepared board and let it rise for another 40 minutes.

6 Preheat a pizza or baking stone in the oven to 450°F (232°C). Place a shallow pan on the rack below the baking stone.

7 Dissolve the cornstarch in the remaining ¼ cup water and heat in the microwave for 45 seconds. Brush the cornstarch liquid on top of the loaf and then use a sharp knife to cut several parallel lines that are ¼ to ½ inch deep across the top surface of the loaf.

8 Pour a tall glass of water into the shallow pan below the baking stone. Carefully place the loaf directly on the stone. (When you put the loaf on the stone, it will pop and sizzle and steam, so be careful). Bake for 30 minutes or until the loaf sounds hollow when tapped.

SCAN TO WATCH

.... **VARIATIONS** ....

Dark Rye Bread: Add ¼ cup unsweetened cocoa powder and 3 tablespoon dark bootstrap molasses when mixing the dough.

garlic–parmesan–herb bread

1 cup water

1 tbsp instant dry yeast

1 tbsp granulated sugar

1 tsp salt

2 tsp dried rosemary

1 tsp dried basil

1 tsp dried oregano

6 garlic cloves, minced

2–2½ cups all-purpose flour, divided

⅓ cup grated Parmesan cheese

2 tbsp olive oil

1 tbsp salted butter, divided

Anyone can make this savory artisan-style bread! It's delicious, fragrant, and a wonderful complement to any meal. My older sister was the first to teach me how to make this bread. It's evolved over the years into a garlic-herb wonder in my kitchen and it's now the recipe I use to introduce kids to bread making.

1 Place the water in a small saucepan. Heat on low until it reaches a temperature of 105°F to 110°F (41°C to 43°C). (Alternatively, place the water in a small microwave-safe bowl and heat in 30-second increments, stirring in between, until the water is heated to the desired temperature.)

2 In a large bowl, dissolve the yeast and sugar in the warm water. Stir in the salt, rosemary, basil, oregano, and garlic.

3 Add 2 cups of the flour and the Parmesan. Stir until combined. Gradually add the remaining ½ cup flour (if needed) until you have a smooth and elastic dough that is tacky but doesn't stick to your hands.

4 Transfer the dough to a lightly greased mixing bowl. Cover with a tea towel or plastic wrap and set aside to rise until the dough doubles in size, about 1 hour.

5 Preheat the oven to 375°F (191°C). Drizzle the olive oil onto a large baking sheet.

6 Divide the dough into two halves and shape the halves into two round loaves. Place the loaves on the prepared baking sheet. Set aside to rise uncovered for an additional 15 to 20 minutes.

7 Top each loaf with ½ tablespoon butter. Bake for 18 to 20 minutes or until golden brown.

SCAN TO WATCH

italian-style pizza dough

2 tsp instant dry yeast
1 tbsp granulated sugar
1½ tsp salt
1¾ cups warm water
⅓ cup olive oil
5–6 cups all-purpose
 or 00 flour

You can achieve perfect Italian-style pizzas at home. This recipe works best with 00 flour, but all-purpose flour or bread flour will also work. For best results, I highly recommend using a pizza stone. I've even included my Two-Minute Pizza Sauce for the best homemade pizzas ever!

1 In the bowl of a stand mixer fitted with a dough hook, combine the yeast, sugar, salt, water, olive oil, and 5 cups of the flour.

2 Knead on low until the dough forms a soft ball and the sides of the bowl are clean, adding more flour as needed until the desired texture is achieved.

3 Divide the dough into 4 to 6 equal pieces. Dust with additional flour and place the dough pieces on a large baking sheet or large tray. Cover with a tea towel or plastic wrap and set aside to rest 4 to 5 hours to allow the gluten to rest, which will give a chewier result.

4 When you're ready to bake the pizzas, Preheat the oven to 550°F (288°C). Roll the dough pieces out into large circles. Place the crusts on a pizza pan or cornmeal-dusted pizza peel, top each crust with a thin layer of the **Two-Minute Pizza Sauce,** and then top with any desired toppings. Place the crusts on a pizza pan or transfer to a preheated pizza stone.

5 Bake until the toppings are hot and the cheese is bubbly and brown, about 5 to 10 minutes, depending on the toppings.

·············· **NOTES** ··············

Two-Minute Pizza Sauce: Combine the following ingredients in a small bowl:

8oz (227g) can tomato sauce
8oz (227g) can tomato paste
2 tsp dried basil
1 tsp dried oregano
1 tsp minced garlic
½ tsp paprika
¼ tsp salt

Stir until well combined and thick. Use immediately or transfer to the fridge until ready to use. Store in an airtight container in the fridge for up to 2 weeks.

SCAN TO WATCH

naan
(four ways)

1 cup water

1 tsp instant dry yeast

2 tbsp granulated sugar

2 tbsp yogurt

1 large egg

1 tsp salt

2½–3 cups flour

¼ cup melted butter

It's so easy to make your own delicious homemade naan. This traditional Indian flatbread can easily be made at home and is amazing served alongside curries for dipping or used for wraps or even flatbread pizzas! Enjoy plain or try one of the variations listed below.

1 Place the water in a small saucepan. Heat on low until it reaches a temperature of 105°F to 110°F (41°C to 43°C). (Alternatively, place the water in a small microwave-safe bowl and heat in 30-second increments, stirring in between, until the water is heated to the desired temperature.)

2 In a large bowl or stand mixer bowl fitted with a dough hook, combine the yeast and warm water. Add the sugar, yogurt, egg, salt, and 2 cups of the flour. Stir or mix on low, adding additional flour ¼ cup at a time until you have a soft dough that pulls away from the sides of the bowl. Knead the dough for about 5 minutes by hand or for 2 to 3 minutes in a stand mixer. Cover with a tea towel or plastic wrap and set aside to rise for 1 hour or until the dough doubles in size.

3 Separate the dough into 8 equal-sized balls and then place them on a tray or clean countertop. Cover the balls loosely with a tea towel or plastic wrap and set aside to rise for 30 minutes, After 30 minutes, roll each ball into a thin teardrop shape or oval. (They should be quite thin.)

4 Heat a large heavy skillet over medium-high heat. Working one at a time, brush one side of each dough piece with the melted butter and place the dough pieces butter side down in the skillet. Brush the top sides as the bottom sides cook.

5 Flip the pieces when bubbles appear on the surface, about 1 to 2 minutes. Cook the other side for another 1 to 2 minutes before transferring to a plate. Serve warm.

···················· VARIATIONS ····················

Garlic Naan: Add 2 teaspoons minced garlic to the dough or add ½ teaspoon garlic powder to the melted butter for brushing.

Onion Naan: Add 1 teaspoon onion powder and 2 teaspoons finely diced onion or dried onion.

Cinnamon Naan: Add 2 teaspoons ground cinnamon. After cooking, sprinkle the tops with a 1:1 mixture of brown sugar and ground cinnamon.

SCAN TO WATCH

flaky old-fashioned biscuits

2 cups all-purpose flour

1 tbsp baking powder

1 tbsp granulated sugar

1 tsp salt

⅓ cup very cold butter or very cold shortening*

1 cup milk (whole, 2%, or 1%) or buttermilk

2 tbsp melted butter, for brushing (optional)

Nothing beats warm flaky biscuits straight from the oven! This foolproof homemade biscuit recipe is easy to make and requires just six ingredients.

1 Preheat the oven to 425°F (220°C).

2 In a large bowl, stir together the flour, baking powder, sugar, and salt.

3 Using a cheese grater, grate the cold butter and then stir it into the flour mixture. (Alternatively, cut the cold butter into small pieces and add it to the flour mixture.) Use a pastry cutter to cut the butter into the flour mixture until it resembles coarse meal or sand.

4 Gradually pour in the buttermilk or milk, stirring continuously until the dough just comes together.

5 Turn the dough out onto a clean countertop and then form it into a ball. Press the dough flat until it is 1 inch (2.5cm) thick. Use a circle biscuit cutter or drinking glass to cut out the biscuits. Combine the leftover scraps and continue pressing and cutting until all the dough has been used.

6 Place the biscuits on an ungreased baking sheet and bake at 425°F (220°C) for 12 to 15 minutes or until the tops are nicely browned. Brush the tops with melted butter, if desired. Serve warm.

··· **NOTES** ···

* For extra-flaky results, keep the butter or shortening as cold as possible! (If needed, place it in the freezer for 10 to 15 minutes before using in the recipe.) Also, handle the dough as little as possible and work quickly to keep the dough cold. If needed, pop the formed biscuits into the fridge for 15 to 30 minutes to chill before baking.

SCAN TO WATCH

mom's quick buttermilk cornbread

½ cup salted butter, melted

⅔ cup granulated sugar

2 large eggs

½ tsp baking soda

1 cup buttermilk

1 cup cornmeal

1 cup all-purpose flour

½ tsp salt

This cornbread is fluffy, sweet, and so easy to put together. You can use this one recipe to make a pan of cornbread, cornbread muffins, or even skillet cornbread. All you need is a bowl, a whisk, and a handful of ingredients—all of which you most likely already have at home!

1 Preheat the oven to 375°F (191°C). Lightly grease a 9 x 9-inch (22 x 22cm) baking pan.

2 In a medium bowl, whisk together the melted butter and sugar until smooth, about 60 to 90 seconds. Whisk in the eggs until well blended, about 30 seconds more.

3 Add the baking soda and stir to combine, slowly pouring in the buttermilk as you stir. Add the cornmeal, flour, and salt. Continue stirring until well combined. Pour the batter into the prepared pan.

4 Bake for 20 minutes or until the top begins to brown.

·········· VARIATIONS ··········

Skillet Cornbread: Preheat an 8-inch (20cm) or 10-inch (25.5cm) cast-iron skillet in the oven. Once the batter is prepared, pour it into the hot skillet and return the skillet to the oven. Bake about 20 minutes for a 10-inch (25.5cm) skillet or up to 25 minutes for an 8-inch (20cm) skillet.

Cornbread Muffins: Line a muffin tin with cupcake liners or lightly grease the tin with nonstick cooking spray. Divide the prepared batter evenly into 12 muffin cups. Bake for 20 minutes.

SCAN TO WATCH

homemade soft pretzels

1¼ cups water

1 tbsp yeast

¼ cup light brown sugar

3–3½ cups all-purpose flour

¼ cup baking soda

1½ cups hot water

½ cup melted butter

Coarse salt

Just a few simple ingredients is all you need to make these homemade soft pretzels. This recipe has a warm, buttery, salty exterior and is delicious by itself or dunked in your favorite cheese dip!

1 Place 1¼ cups water in a small saucepan. Heat on low until it reaches a temperature of 105°F to 110°F (41°C to 43°C). (Alternatively, place the water in a small microwave-safe bowl and heat in 30-second increments, stirring in between, until the water is heated to the desired temperature.)

2 In a medium bowl, dissolve the yeast and brown sugar in the warm water. Add 3 cups flour and stir until well combined. Add additional flour, if needed, until a soft dough is formed. (There is no need to knead the dough.) Set the dough aside to rise in a warm location until it almost doubles in size, about 20 minutes.

3 Preheat the oven to 500°F (260°C). Divide the dough into golf ball–sized pieces. Roll each piece into a rope and then twist it into a pretzel shape (or whatever shape you'd like!).

4 In a small bowl, dissolve the baking soda in the hot water. Dip the pretzels in the solution and place them on a well-greased baking sheet.

5 Bake for about 6 minutes or until golden brown. Remove the pretzels from the oven and dip the faces in the melted butter and then sprinkle coarse salt over the tops. Serve warm.

SCAN TO WATCH

······································ **VARIATIONS** ································

Cinnamon-Sugar Pretzels: Omit sprinkling with the coarse salt. Combine 1 tablespoon ground cinnamon and ⅓ cup granulated sugar in a small bowl. Dip the pretzels in the melted butter and then dip them in the cinnamon-sugar mix.

quick breads

1 cup fruit purée (mashed bananas, pumpkin purée, or applesauce)

1 cup granulated sugar or brown sugar*

½ cup melted butter or vegetable oil

1 large egg

1 tsp vanilla extract

½ tsp salt

½ tsp baking soda

½ tsp baking powder

2 tsp ground spice (cinnamon or pumpkin pie spice)

1½ cups all-purpose flour

1 cup chopped nuts, mini chocolate chips, or chopped dried fruit or diced fresh fruit (optional)

This quick bread is delightfully moist and sweet and can be made into practically any flavor using this base recipe. I've included instructions in the notes for the three of the most popular flavors, but feel free to experiment with your own custom creations.

1 Preheat the oven to 325°F (163°C). Lightly grease a 4 x 8-inch (10 x 20cm) loaf pan.

2 In a large bowl, combine the fruit purée, sugar, melted butter or vegetable oil, egg, and vanilla extract. Whisk until well combined and creamy, about 60 to 90 seconds.

3 Stir in the salt, baking soda, baking powder, and ground spice. Stir until just combined. Add the flour and stir until everything is well incorporated. Fold in any additional nuts, chocolate chips, or dried or fresh fruit (if using).

4 Transfer the batter to the prepared loaf pan. Bake for 50 to 60 minutes or until a toothpick inserted into the center comes out clean.

NOTES

* Either brown sugar or granulated sugar can be used. Brown sugar contains molasses, which adds a warmer sugar flavor to the bread.

VARIATIONS

Banana Quick Bread: A classic quick bread favorite! Use freshly mashed, very ripe bananas, ground cinnamon, melted butter, and chopped walnuts (if you enjoy that bit of crunch).

Pumpkin Quick Bread: Use pumpkin purée, vegetable oil (vegetable oil produces the moistest pumpkin bread), and pumpkin pie spice. (Mini chocolate chips are also a fun add-in for pumpkin quick bread.)

Apple Quick Bread: We absolutely love this quick bread flavor! Use any applesauce you like, butter, and ground cinnamon. Swap out the granulated sugar for brown sugar. For this variation, I prefer to use a blend of ½ cup whole wheat flour with 1 cup all-purpose flour. You can also add some amazing texture with diced or dried apples.

SCAN TO WATCH

VG

READY IN 10 MINUTES • MAKES 8 SERVINGS

ultimate garlic bread

1 loaf French bread

½ cup salted butter, softened

2 tbsp olive oil

1 tbsp dried basil

1 tsp dried oregano

½ cup grated Parmesan cheese

4 garlic cloves, minced

½ tsp salt

¼ tsp black pepper

This is the garlic bread you've always craved! It has the perfect balance of garlicky, buttery goodness. It's bold and herbaceous and the kind of garlic bread that people will talk about for days. My dear friend Megan talked about it for years after trying it at my house!

1 Slice the bread loaf in half lengthwise and then place each half on a baking sheet.

2 In a small bowl, combine the butter, olive oil, basil, oregano, Parmesan, garlic, salt, and black pepper. Mix well to ensure the ingredients are well combined.

3 Spread the garlic butter in a generous, even layer over each half of the French bread.

4 Place the baking sheet underneath the broiler. Broil until the bread just begins to brown. (Watch it very closely, it will brown very quickly and should not take more than 5 minutes.) Devour warm!

SCAN TO WATCH

homemade bread

2¼ cup milk
  (whole, 2%, or 1%)

2 tbsp granulated sugar

2¼ tsp instant dry yeast

1 tbsp salt

3 tbsp salted butter,
  melted

5½–6 cups all-purpose
  flour, divided

This is the perfect homemade bread for slicing and sandwiches. It's moist and soft, with the perfect chewy crumb. (Scan the QR code for substitutions, including dairy-free options, whole wheat options, sugar replacements, and more. I've tested everything to make sure I have answers to all your questions and can help you bake the perfect loaf.)

1 Add the milk to a small saucepan. Heat over low heat until it reaches a temperature of 100°F to 110°F (38°C to 43°C).

2 In the bowl of a stand mixer fitted with a dough hook, combine the warm milk, sugar, yeast, salt, melted butter, and 5 cups of the flour. Knead on low speed for 1 minute and then slowly increase the speed while adding the remaining flour, ¼ cup at a time, until the dough forms a smooth elastic ball that is soft and tacky, but not sticky.

3 Transfer the dough ball to a large greased bowl. Cover with a tea towel or plastic wrap and set aside to rise for 90 minutes or until the dough doubles in size.

4 After 90 minutes, divide the dough into two equal pieces. Roll or press each piece into a 9 x 7-inch (23 x 18cm) rectangle. Roll each rectangle lengthwise into a tight roll and then pinch the ends shut.

5 Transfer each loaf to lightly greased 9 x 5-inch (23 x 13cm) bread loaf pans. Cover loosely with a tea towel or plastic wrap and set aside to rise for 1 hour more or until the loaves double in size.

6 Preheat the oven to 350°F (177°C). Bake for 35 to 40 minutes or until the tops are golden brown.

7 Remove the loaves from the oven and cool for 10 minutes before removing from the pans. Let cool completely before slicing.

SCAN TO WATCH

british scones

2 cups all-purpose flour

⅓ cup granulated sugar

1 tbsp baking powder

¼ tsp salt

½ cup very cold salted butter*

1 large egg (optional) **

1 cup plus 2 tbsp heavy cream

1 tsp vanilla extract

These perfectly flaky scones can be enjoyed plain or easily made into any flavor you'd like including blueberry, cranberry–orange, pumpkin, chocolate chip, cranberry, lemon, or cinnamon!

1 Preheat the oven to 425°F (218°C).

2 In a large bowl, stir together the flour, sugar, baking powder, and salt.

3 Using a cheese grater, grate the cold butter into the flour mix. (Alternatively, use a knife to cut the butter into small pieces.) Stir the butter into the flour mixture and then use a pastry cutter to cut the butter into the flour mixture until it resembles coarse meal or sand.

4 Add the egg (if using), 1 cup heavy cream, and vanilla extract. Stir just until the dough comes together.

5 Turn the dough out onto a clean countertop and shape it into a ball. Press the dough flat until it's a 2-inch (5cm) thick circle. Use a butter knife to cut the circle into 8 wedges.

6 Place the cut scones on an ungreased baking sheet and then brush the tops with the remaining 2 tablespoons heavy cream to create shiny tops

7 Bake for 12 to 15 minutes or until the tops are nicely browned. Serve warm or at room temperature.

SCAN TO WATCH

·········· NOTES ··········

* For extra-flaky results, keep the butter or shortening as cold as possible. (If needed, place it in the freezer for 10 to 15 minutes before using it in the recipe.) Also, try to handle the dough as little as possible and work quickly to keep the dough cold. If needed, pop the formed scones into the fridge for 15 to 30 minutes to chill before baking.

** Adding an egg to the batter changes the texture of the scones, creating a richer, more dense result. This recipe can still be made without the egg, so it's completely optional and can be omitted.

·········· VARIATIONS ··········

Blueberry Scones: Add 1 cup fresh blueberries.

Chocolate Chip Scones: Omit the vanilla extract and add 1 cup mini chocolate chips.

Cranberry–Orange Scones: Omit the vanilla extract and add ¾ cup dried cranberries and 2 tablespoons orange zest.

Pumpkin Scones: Omit the vanilla extract and replace half of the heavy cream with ½ cup pumpkin purée and 2 teaspoons pumpkin pie spice.

Cranberry Scones: Add 1 cup dried cranberries.

Lemon Scones: Omit the vanilla extract and replace ¼ cup of the heavy cream with ¼ cup lemon juice and 2 tablespoons lemon zest.

Cinnamon Scones: Omit the vanilla extract, replace the granulated sugar with brown sugar, and add 1 to 2 teaspoons ground cinnamon.

14 the delicious little extras

rachel's green sauce

2 cups fresh cilantro,
loosely packed

1–2 jalapeños, stems and
seeds removed
(seeding optional)

2 tbsp grated Parmesan
cheese

2 garlic cloves

2 tbsp red wine vinegar

2 tbsp lemon juice

½ cup olive oil

1 tsp salt

½ tsp black pepper

This versatile sauce can be served on just about anything! Use it as a bread dip or drizzle it over your favorite meat, seafood, or veggies. No matter how you use it, you are going to love it! I always have this condiment in the fridge and we are always finding new things to use it on. My sister described it as "the sauce she couldn't stop thinking about" once she tasted it.

1 Place all the ingredients in a blender or food processor.

2 Purée until smooth.

3 Transfer to an airtight container. Store in the fridge for up to 7 days.

·········· **NOTES** ··········

For a creamier sauce, replace the olive oil with ½ cup mayonnaise.

Jalapeños vary in spiciness, so you can add more or less based on your own heat preference.

SCAN TO WATCH

pickled red onions

1 large red onion, thinly sliced

1½ cups white vinegar

2 tbsp granulated sugar

1 tbsp salt

FLAVORING OPTIONS (PICK ONE OR MIX AND MATCH)

1 tsp black peppercorns

1 tsp allspice berries

2 sprigs fresh rosemary

2 sprigs fresh thyme

1 small hot red pepper

3 garlic cloves, peeled

1 tsp whole cumin seeds

These pickled red onions will add a punch of flavor to any dish! This recipe shows you how to make basic pickled red onions and also gives you several ways to flavor the pickling juice to create a variety of taste options.

1 Place the onions in a pint-sized Mason jar or other glass, plastic, or ceramic container with a sealable lid. Set aside,

2 In a small saucepan, stir together the vinegar, sugar, and salt. (If desired, add 1 or more of the flavorings options at this point or just leave the onions as is.) Bring the mixture just to a boil over high heat and then remove the pan from the heat.

3 Pour the hot mixture over the onion until the jar is full. Place the lid on the jar and let it cool to room temperature.

4 Transfer to the fridge and let the onions pickle for at least 12 hours before enjoying. These will stay good in the refrigerator for between 2 and 6 months.

································· NOTES ·································

You can use the same method to make pickled jalapeños by replacing the onion with 6 large jalapeños that have been sliced.

SCAN TO WATCH

GF · VG · VE

READY IN 10 MINUTES · MAKES 2 CUPS

easy chimichurri sauce

2 cups fresh flat-leaf
   parsley leaves
5 garlic cloves
1 tsp salt
½ tsp black pepper
½ tsp red pepper flakes
½ tsp dried oregano
½ cup extra virgin olive oil
3 tbsp red wine vinegar
3 tbsp lemon juice

This easy-to-make chimichurri sauce is perfect to use as a marinade or as an accompaniment to beef or other grilled meats. It's full of fresh herbs and tangy vinegar and brings a zesty flavor with a tiny hint of heat to a variety of foods.

1 In a food processor or blender, combine the parsley leaves, garlic cloves, salt, black pepper, red pepper flakes, oregano, olive oil, red wine vinegar, and lemon juice.

2 Pulse on high until puréed.

3 Transfer to an airtight container. Store in the fridge for up to 7 days.

SCAN TO WATCH

homemade gravy

2 tbsp fat (butter, coconut oil, vegetable oil, olive oil, margarine, or bacon fat)

¼ cup all-purpose flour or 2 tbsp cornstarch

2 cups broth (chicken, beef, turkey, or vegetable) or strained pan drippings

Make gravy of any kind with this simple recipe. I've got you covered, with instructions for making gravy from pan drippings or with canned broths or stocks.

1 In a medium saucepan, melt the butter over medium-high heat.

2 Whisk in the flour until well combined and no white specks remain. Cook 2 minutes.

3 Slowly pour in the broth and whisk well.

4 Simmer, whisking constantly, until thickened, about 2 minutes. Serve immediately or let cool and then transfer to an airtight container. Store in the fridge for up to 2 days.

.... NOTES ....

Any kind of broth, stock, or other liquid can be used in the same ratio to make gravy. For vegetarian gravy, use vegetable broth.

When using pan drippings from roasting a turkey, chicken, or beef roast, be sure to strain the drippings through a fine-mesh strainer to remove any gristle or fat. If you don't have enough drippings, you can supplement them with additional broths or stocks.

SCAN TO WATCH

homemade butter

1 cup heavy cream
   (38% fat)
Pinch of salt (optional)

Learn how to make homemade butter two different ways! It's easy, and the Mason jar version is a fun activity for kids. Take your next dinner party up a level by serving one of my bread recipes with your own homemade butter.

Mixer instructions:

1 Add the heavy cream to the bowl of a stand mixer fitted with a whisk attachment. (Alternatively, you can use a large mixing bowl and hand mixer.)

2 Begin beating the cream on low speed, gradually increasing the speed as the mixture thickens.

3 After several minutes, a whipped cream will form and the cream will begin to turn yellow and clumps of butterfat will form as the fat solids begin to separate from the liquids, leaving the sloshing liquid buttermilk in the bottom of the bowl. Strain the fat solids from the buttermilk using a fine mesh strainer or cheesecloth. (You can reserve the buttermilk and save it for later use in recipes.*)

4 Rinse the butter with cold water 3 times and then shape it into a ball.

5 Enjoy as is or add salt, honey, or herbs to create a flavored butter. Store in an airtight container at room temperature for 3 to 5 days or in the fridge for 7 to 10 days.

Mason jar instructions:

1 Add the heavy cream to a 16-ounce Mason jar, filling it halfway full. (Do not fill past the halfway mark.) Screw the lid on tightly so there are no leaks.

2 Shake the Mason jar vigorously for 5 to 7 minutes. (After a few minutes, the whipped cream will form.) Keep shaking until you hear a lump form inside the jar and then continue shaking for an additional 30 to 60 seconds or until you can clearly see that the fat solids have separated from the liquids.

3 Strain the fat solids from the buttermilk using a fine mesh strainer or cheesecloth. (You can reserve the buttermilk and save it for later use in recipes.*)

4 Rinse the butter with cold water 3 times and then shape it into a ball.

5 Enjoy as is or add salt, honey, or herbs to create a flavored butter. Store in an airtight container at room temperature for 3 to 5 days or in the fridge for 7 to 10 days.

SCAN TO WATCH

··· NOTES ···

* If you want to add salt or herbs to your butter and don't plan on using the rendered buttermilk for other recipes, you can just add the flavorings initially with the heavy cream.

nacho cheese sauce

2 tbsp salted butter

2 tbsp all-purpose flour

⅛ tsp cayenne

1 cup milk (whole, 2%, or 1%)

8oz (227g) grated cheddar cheese or diced processed American cheese

This amazing nacho cheese sauce is ridiculously easy to make and tastes so much better than the store-bought variety. Enjoy it as a dip for chips or veggies or layered over a plate of nachos.

1 Melt the butter in a saucepan over medium-high heat.

2 Whisk in the flour and cayenne. Cook for 1 to 2 minutes.

3 Whisk in the milk. Bring back to a simmer and then reduce the heat to low.

4 Add the cheese and stir continuously until the cheese is melted.

SCAN TO WATCH

buttermilk substitutes

OPTION 1

1 tbsp lemon juice

1 cup milk (whole, 2%, or 1%) or nondairy milk alternative

OPTION 2

1 tbsp white vinegar

1 cup milk (whole, 2%, or 1%) or nondairy milk alternative

OPTION 3

1¾ tsp cream of tartar

1 cup milk (whole, 2%, or 1%) or nondairy milk alternative

OPTION 4

¾ cup sour cream

¼ cup milk (whole, 2%, or 1%)

As you may have noticed, I love using buttermilk in my recipes. It adds a richness and flavor that you just can't quite get from regular milk. And the acidity of buttermilk can interact with baking powder and baking soda to give you a better rise in muffins, pancakes, waffles, and more. All of these substitutes will work equally well, so you can choose an option based on what you have on hand.

1 Stir or whisk the ingredients together in a small bowl.

2 Let stand for 5 minutes before using.

NOTES

Be sure to scale the amount of substitute you make to match the amount of buttermilk that is called for in the recipe.

If you don't want to use buttermilk in a recipe, plain yogurt can also be used as a direct replacement for buttermilk.

SCAN TO WATCH

overnight refrigerator pickles

1 large English cucumber

1½ cups white vinegar

2 tbsp granulated sugar

1 tbsp salt

1 tsp whole black
peppercorns

3 garlic cloves

3 sprigs fresh dill

These refrigerator pickles have just the right amount of salty, tangy goodness with the most perfect crunch. You are going to love making your own pickles at home!

1 Slice the cucumber or cut it into spears. Place the cucumbers in a resealable heat-resistant container or quart-sized Mason jar.

2 In a small saucepan over high heat, stir together the white vinegar, sugar, salt, black peppercorns, and garlic cloves. Bring just to a boil and then remove from the heat.

3 Pour enough of the hot vinegar mixture over the cucumbers to fill the container. Seal and let the pickles cool to room temperature.

4 Once cooled, add the fresh dill sprigs and reseal the jar. Refrigerate overnight before eating.

·········· **NOTES** ··········

I like my pickles strong! If you want to tone down the acidity in your pickles, you can replace up to half of the white vinegar with water.

SCAN TO WATCH

15 yes! soup for you!

easy street corn soup

4 tbsp butter

1 small white onion, chopped

2 jalapeños (1 minced and 1 sliced), divided

5 garlic cloves, minced

3 tbsp all-purpose flour

2 tsp ground cumin

1 tsp chili powder

4 cups chicken stock

6 cups (about 30oz [850g]) frozen corn kernels

1 tbsp granulated sugar

2 tsp salt

1½ cups heavy cream (you can also use half-and-half or whole milk)

1 cup chopped fresh cilantro

½ lb (227g) bacon, cooked and crumbled

½ cup crumbled cotija cheese

This corn soup has all the flavors you love from street corn, all bundled up into one comfort food soup that is to die for! It's loaded with corn and has heat from the jalapeños and flavor from the garlic, chili powder, and cumin. Don't skip the toppings because the cilantro, bacon, and cotija cheese add even more flavor!

1   Melt the butter in a large saucepan over medium heat. Add the onion and minced jalapeño. Sauté for about 5 minutes and then stir in the garlic. Cook for 1 minute more.

2   Stir in the flour, cumin, and chili powder. Cook 1 to 2 minutes and then add the chicken stock and stir until smooth. Increase the heat to high and bring to a boil. Add the corn, sugar, and salt. Stir. Once the mixture returns to a boil, reduce the heat to low and simmer for 10 minutes.

3   Stir in the heavy cream and cilantro and then remove from the heat. Serve topped with the crumbled bacon, cotija, and jalapeño slices.

SCAN TO WATCH

old-fashioned beef stew

2 lb (907g) beef stew meat, such as cubed chuck roast

4 tbsp cornstarch, divided

1 tsp salt, plus more to taste

¼ tsp black pepper, plus more to taste

2 tbsp olive oil

2 garlic cloves, minced

2 tbsp tomato paste

4 cups beef broth

¼ cup Worcestershire sauce

1½ lb (680g) red potatoes, cut into bite-sized chunks

10oz (283g) pearl onions

4 medium carrots, peeled and sliced

4 medium celery ribs, sliced

1 tsp granulated sugar

½ tsp dried basil

½ tsp dried oregano

½ tsp dried parsley

½ tsp paprika

¼ tsp allspice

¼ cup cold water

This stew is pure comfort in a bowl, with tender beef, hearty vegetables, and all the right herbs and spices. My stew can stand on its own!

1 Dust the meat with 2 tablespoons of the cornstarch and then season with the salt and black pepper.

2 In a large pot over medium-high heat, heat the olive oil. Add the meat to the pot and sear until all sides are browned, about 5 minutes.

3 Add the garlic and tomato paste. Cook for 1 to 2 minutes or until fragrant.

4 Pour in the beef broth and Worcestershire sauce to deglaze the pan. Add the red potatoes, pearl onions, carrots, and celery. Season with the sugar, basil, oregano, parsley, paprika, and allspice.

5 Bring to a boil over high heat and then reduce the heat to low. Simmer, covered, for 90 minutes, stirring occasionally.

6 After 90 minutes, mix together the remaining 2 tablespoons of cornstarch with the cold water in a small bowl. Stir until completely dissolved. Pour the mixture into the stew. Stir until the stew thickens.

7 Season with additional salt and black pepper to taste. Serve hot.

·········· NOTES ··········

Slow cooker instructions: Follow steps 1 through 3 to brown the meat and give an initial cook to the garlic and tomato paste. Transfer the meat and pot ingredients to a slow cooker and then add all remaining stew ingredients. Cook on low for 6 to 8 hours and then follow step 6 to create the cornstarch slurry. Add the slurry to the stew and cook another 30 minutes or until thickened.

SCAN TO WATCH

chicken noodle soup

1 tbsp olive oil

2 medium skinless, boneless chicken breasts

1 tsp salt, plus more to taste

½ tsp black pepper, plus more to taste

2 tbsp salted butter

1 cup sliced carrots

1 cup sliced celery

1 medium white onion, diced

1 tbsp freshly grated ginger or 1 tsp dried ginger

1 tbsp minced garlic

8 cups chicken broth

½ tsp dried thyme

½ tsp dried oregano

12oz (340g) egg noodles (dried or frozen)

3 tbsp chopped fresh parsley

This classic chicken noodle soup is so simple to make! It's ready in under 45 minutes and is loaded with tender veggies, juicy chicken, and fragrant herbs. I've also included a suggestion for a creamy version if that is what you prefer.

1 In a large 6-quart pot, heat the olive oil over medium-high heat. Season the chicken breasts with salt and black pepper. Sear for 3 to 4 minutes per side or until browned and then transfer to a plate. (Do not wipe the pot clean.)

2 Add the butter, carrots, celery, and onion to the pot. Sauté until the vegetables are just tender, about 5 to 7 minutes. Add the ginger and garlic and sauté for 2 minutes more.

3 Add the chicken breasts back to the pot. Pour in the chicken broth and season with the thyme and oregano. Bring to a boil over high heat and then reduce the heat to medium and let the soup simmer for 10 minutes.

4 Add the egg noodles and simmer until the noodles are cooked through. (Frozen noodles will take longer to cook than dried egg noodles.)

5 Transfer the chicken breasts from the pot to a cutting board. Use two forks to shred and then return the chicken to the soup. Taste and add additional salt and black pepper, if desired. Top with the chopped parsley.

NOTES

For a creamy version, add 2 cups heavy cream during the last few minutes of cooking.

If you want to increase the protein content, add 1 cup frozen peas to the soup and let them heat through while you shred the chicken breasts.

If you're short on time, you can replace the chicken breasts with 1½ to 2 cups of leftover precooked chicken breast that has been diced or shredded. Simply stir in the leftover chicken during the last 5 minutes of cooking to heat through.

SCAN TO WATCH

old-fashioned chicken and dumplings

1 tbsp olive oil

3 medium celery ribs, sliced

3 medium carrots, peeled and diced

1 medium white onion, diced

3 garlic cloves, minced

3 boneless, skinless chicken breasts

1 tsp salt

½ tsp black pepper

8 cups chicken broth

FOR THE DUMPLINGS

2 cups all-purpose flour

3 tsp baking powder

1 tsp salt

1 cup buttermilk

2 tbsp salted butter, melted

This chicken and dumplings recipe is just like mom used to make! It's full of old-fashioned homemade goodness. I've also included a rolled dumplings recipe in the notes section.

1 Heat a large Dutch oven pot over medium-high heat. Add the olive oil and heat for 1 minute. Add the celery, carrots, and onion. Sauté for 5 minutes or until the onion is soft and translucent. Stir in the garlic and cook 1 minute more.

2 Add the chicken breasts and then season with the salt and black pepper. Pour in the chicken broth. Bring to a boil and then boil 20 minutes or until the chicken is cooked through and easily shreds with a fork. (You can shred the chicken directly in the pot or remove it to a cutting board, shred it, and return it to the soup.)

3 Make the dumplings by whisking together the flour, baking powder, and salt in a large bowl. Slowly pour in the buttermilk and then stir until well combined. Drop the batter by the spoonful directly into the soup. Cover and simmer for 20 minutes. Serve hot.

······· NOTES ·······

For rolled dumplings: Decrease the amount of baking powder to ½ teaspoon and replace the melted butter with ⅓ cup very cold butter or shortening. Mix the flour, baking powder, and salt in a mixing bowl. Cut in the cold butter using a pastry cutter or food processor. Gradually pour in the buttermilk, stirring just until the dough comes together. Turn the dough out on a floured surface and work it just until everything is well combined. (The dough should not be sticky.) Roll the dough out about ¼-inch (.60cm) thick and then cut it into 1-inch (2.5cm) strips that are approximately 2 inches (5cm) in length. Boil the dumplings over medium heat in the soup base for 15 to 20 minutes before serving.

SCAN TO WATCH

creamy cauliflower vegetable soup

2 tbsp salted butter

1 tbsp extra virgin olive oil

1 large head cauliflower, cut into small florets

1 medium white onion, diced

3 medium celery stalks, sliced

3 medium carrots, diced

4 garlic cloves, minced

1 tsp dried thyme

1 tsp dried oregano

2 tbsp cornstarch

2 cups vegetable broth

2 cups milk (whole, 2%, or 1%)

Salt and black pepper to taste

This creamy soup is the most delicious comfort food for a cold, winter day. The combination of onion, celery, and carrots is called *mirepoix* and is used to sweeten and deepen the flavors of a dish. While the cauliflower is the star of this show, the other vegetables play an important supporting role to add nutrients and flavor.

1 Heat the butter and olive oil in a large pot over medium-high heat. Add the cauliflower, onion, celery, and carrots. Cook for 10 to 12 minutes, stirring occasionally, until the vegetables begin to soften. Add the garlic and sauté for 1 minute more.

2 Stir in the thyme, oregano, and cornstarch. Cook for 1 minute.

3 Pour in the vegetable broth and milk. Stir continuously until the mixture comes to a boil and then reduce the heat to low and simmer for 3 to 5 minutes or until the soup thickens. Season to taste with salt and black pepper. Serve hot.

SCAN TO WATCH

potato leek soup

½ cup salted butter

2 leeks, rinsed and sliced (white and pale green parts only)

2 tsp salt, divided

2 tbsp cornstarch

1 qt (946ml) chicken broth

4 cups diced Yukon gold potatoes

½ tsp black pepper

2 cups heavy cream or whipping cream

This potato leek soup is creamy, savory, and oh so satisfying. It is an easy-to-make classic that pairs beautifully with homemade bread. It's sure to become a family favorite! I'm giving you three ways to prepare this soup so you can enjoy it creamy, brothy, or puréed.

1 Melt the butter in a large pot over medium heat.

2 Add the leeks and season with 1 teaspoon of the salt. Sauté, stirring frequently, for about 10 minutes or until the leeks are soft.

3 Stir the cornstarch into the leek mixture until well combined. Slowly add the chicken broth and stir continuously until the cornstarch is dissolved.

4 Add the potatoes, remaining 1 teaspoon salt, and black pepper. Bring just to a boil and then reduce the heat to low. Stir in the whipping cream and simmer for 30 minutes or until the potatoes are tender. Serve hot.

·················· **NOTES** ··················

For a brothy, cream-free version, simply replace the heavy cream with 2 additional cups of chicken broth for a total of 6 cups of broth.

For a smoother texture, use an immersion blender to purée the soup in the pot before adding the cream.

SCAN TO WATCH

GF · VG · Q+E
READY IN 25 MINUTES · MAKES ABOUT 6 SERVINGS

tomato basil soup

1 tbsp olive oil

1 medium white or yellow onion, diced

4 garlic cloves, minced

1 cup chicken broth

29oz (822g) canned fire-roasted diced tomatoes

½ tsp salt, plus more to taste

½ tsp black pepper, plus more to taste

12 large fresh basil leaves,* cut chiffonade

½ cup heavy cream

This easy tomato basil soup is thick, creamy, and full of tomato flavor. This family-favorite soup is delicious on its own, but even better paired with a classic grilled cheese.

1 Heat the olive oil in a large saucepan over medium-high heat. Add the onions and sauté until soft and translucent, about 5 minutes. Stir in the garlic and cook 1 minute more.

2 Add the chicken broth, diced tomatoes, salt, and black pepper. Bring to a boil and then reduce the heat to medium and simmer for 15 minutes. Remove the pan from the heat and add the basil.

3 Using a handheld immersion blender, purée the soup until smooth. (Alternatively, you can purée the soup in a blender and then return it to the pot. However, if you do this, be sure to vent the steam so too much pressure does not build in the blender jar.)

4 Stir in the heavy cream. Season to taste with additional salt and black pepper, if desired. Serve hot.

·················· NOTES ··················

* If you don't have fresh basil, you can replace it with 1 teaspoon dried basil.

SCAN TO WATCH

creamy carrot soup

4 tbsp butter

2 shallots, sliced

1 medium white onion, diced

½ tsp salt, plus more to taste

8 garlic cloves, sliced

2 tsp Thai red curry paste

1 cup heavy cream

8 medium carrots, peeled and chopped

6 cups vegetable broth

This soup is so full of flavor, it may very well become your new favorite! Who knew that carrot soup could be this good?! Well, I did! I've won contests with this recipe. By the way, the Thai red curry paste is a game changer in this recipe. Don't skip it!

1 In a large saucepan, melt the butter over medium heat. Add the shallots and onion and sauté for about 5 minutes. Season with the salt.

2 Add the garlic and Thai red curry paste. Sauté for another 1 to 2 minutes to allow the flavors to release.

3 Add the carrots and vegetable broth. Bring to a boil over high heat and then reduce the heat to medium and simmer until the carrots are soft, about 20 minutes.

4 Purée the soup in the pot using an immersion blender or purée in batches in a food processor or blender. After the soup has been pureéd, return to low heat and add in the heavy cream. Season to taste with additional salt, if necessary. Serve hot.

SCAN TO WATCH

mom's chicken and rice soup

2 lb (907g) boneless skinless chicken breasts

1 tsp salt, plus more to taste

½ tsp black pepper, plus more to taste

2 tbsp olive oil, divided

1 medium white onion, diced

1 cup sliced carrots

½ cup sliced celery

1 cup white rice

1 tbsp freshly grated ginger

1 tbsp minced garlic

8 cups low-sodium chicken broth

1 tsp dried thyme

1 tsp dried oregano

1 cup heavy cream (optional)

¼ cup lemon juice

Mom's chicken and rice soup is healthy, hearty, flavorful, and a family favorite comfort food for those cold winter days. This recipe uses white rice, but I've included instructions for using brown rice or wild rice in the notes.

1 Season the chicken breasts with the salt and black pepper.

2 Heat 1 tablespoon of the olive oil in a large soup pot over medium-high heat. Sear the chicken breasts for 2 minutes per side or until lightly browned but not cooked through. Remove the chicken breasts from the pot to a plate.

3 Add the remaining 1 tablespoon of olive oil to the pot. Add the onion, carrots, and celery. Sauté for 4 to 5 minutes and then add the rice, ginger, and garlic. Sauté for 2 to 3 minutes and then return the chicken to the pot.

4 Pour in the chicken broth and season with the thyme and oregano. Simmer for 15 minutes or until the chicken is cooked through.

5 Use tongs to transfer the chicken breasts to a cutting board. Use two forks to shred the chicken and then return it to the pot. Pour in the heavy cream (if using). Cook for an additional 5 minutes or until the rice and vegetables are soft.

6 Remove from the heat and stir in the lemon juice. Season to taste with additional salt and black pepper, if desired. Serve hot.

· **NOTES** ·

If using brown rice, the rice will need to cook for approximately 50 to 60 minutes. If using wild rice, the rice will need to cook for 40 to 45 minutes.

If you want to use boneless, skinless chicken thighs instead of chicken breasts, you will need to simmer them for approximately 30 to 40 minutes. (Due to the longer cook time for thighs, they're actually preferred if you're also using brown or wild rice.)

If the rice absorbs too much liquid for your liking, you can add more chicken broth.

SCAN TO WATCH

GF · VG · FF

READY IN 30 MINUTES · MAKES ABOUT 6 SERVINGS

butternut squash soup

1 medium butternut squash

3 tbsp salted butter

1 medium white or yellow onion, diced

4 medium carrots, peeled and sliced

3 medium celery ribs, sliced

1 medium red or green apple, peeled, cored, and cubed

4 cups vegetable broth

1 tsp salt

½ tsp ground nutmeg

¼ tsp black pepper

1 cup heavy cream

This creamy butternut squash soup is a bowl of comfort food goodness. It's incredibly easy to make, full of healthy vegetables, and ready in just 30 minutes.

1 Place the squash in the microwave and heat on high for 3 minutes. Once it's cool enough to handle, use a vegetable peeler to remove the skin. Cut in half lengthwise and use a spoon to scrape out the seeds. Cut the squash into cubes. Set aside.

2 Melt the butter in a large pot over medium-high heat. Add the onion and sauté for 5 minutes or until the onion is soft and translucent.

3 Add the squash, carrots, celery, apple, and vegetable stock. Season with the salt, nutmeg, and black pepper. Bring to a boil and then reduce the heat to medium-low and simmer for 15 to 20 minutes or until the vegetables are tender.

4 Using an immersion blender, purée until smooth. (Alternatively, you can purée the soup in a blender. However, if you do this just be sure to vent the steam so too much pressure does not build in the blender jar.) Stir in the heavy cream. Serve hot.

SCAN TO WATCH

no-fuss chili

1½ lb (680g) lean ground beef

1 medium white onion, diced

2 garlic cloves, minced

3 tbsp chili powder

1 tsp ground cumin

1 tsp salt

1 tsp black pepper

14.5oz (411g) canned beef broth

30oz (850g) canned red kidney beans, rinsed and drained

14.5oz (411g) canned diced tomatoes

9oz (256g) canned green chilies

⅔ cup finely crushed tortilla chips

FOR SERVING

Shredded cheddar cheese

Chopped fresh cilantro

Sour cream

This easy chili recipe is full of flavor and satisfying with hearty beans and savory ground beef. It's perfect for those chilly fall days when a warm bowl of chili is just what the doctor ordered.

1 Preheat a large pot over medium-high heat.

2 Add the ground beef and cook until browned, about 5 minutes. Add the onion and sauté for 3 to 5 minutes until soft and translucent. Drain any excess grease and then return the pot to the heat.

3 Add the garlic, chili powder, cumin, salt, and black pepper. Sauté for 1 minute.

4 Stir in the beef broth, kidney beans, tomatoes, and green chilies. Bring to a boil and then reduce the heat to low. Simmer, covered, for 45 to 60 minutes, stirring every 10 minutes.

5 Turn off the heat, remove the lid, and stir in the tortilla chips. Let the chili rest uncovered for 10 minutes to thicken.

6 Transfer to bowls and serve hot topped with a sprinkle of shredded cheese, a sprinkle of chopped fresh cilantro, a dollop of sour cream, and additional tortilla chips, if desired.

SCAN TO WATCH

30-minute chicken tortilla soup

2 tbsp olive oil

1 medium white onion, diced

1 medium red bell pepper, diced

5 garlic cloves, minced

2 tsp chili powder

1 tsp ground cumin

1 tsp paprika

4 cups chicken broth

3 boneless, skinless chicken breasts

15oz (425g) canned tomato sauce

15oz (425g) canned fire-roasted diced tomatoes

15oz (425g) canned black beans, drained and rinsed

7oz (198g) canned diced green chiles

1½ cups corn kernels (frozen or canned)

½ cup chopped fresh cilantro

¼ cup lime juice

½ tsp salt

FOR SERVING

Tortilla strips or tortilla chips

Diced avocado

Shredded Monterey Jack cheese

Sour cream

This amazing chicken tortilla soup is absolutely delicious and also very easy to make. Tender chicken, black beans, and hearty Tex-Mex vegetables come together in this comfort food soup that's perfect for busy weekday evenings.

1 Heat the olive oil in a large pot over medium-high heat.

2 Add the onion and bell pepper. Sauté for 5 minutes and then add the garlic, chili powder, cumin, and paprika. Sauté for 1 minute more.

3 Pour in the chicken broth and add the chicken breasts. Bring to a boil and then reduce the heat to medium-low. Simmer until the chicken is cooked through, about 15 to 20 minutes.

4 Transfer the cooked chicken breasts from the pot to a cutting board. Use two forks to shred and then return the chicken to the pot.

5 Pour in the tomato sauce, diced tomatoes, black beans, green chiles, and corn. Return the soup to a simmer and let it simmer for 5 minutes.

6 Turn off the heat and stir in cilantro and lime juice. Season with the salt. Serve hot topped with tortilla strips, a sprinkle of diced avocado, a sprinkle of Monterey jack cheese, and a dollop of sour cream.

NOTES

Slow cooker instructions: Add all of the ingredients to the slow cooker except for the lime and cilantro. Cook on low for 6 to 8 hours or on high for 3 to 4 hours. Shred the chicken in the slow cooker and then add the lime juice and cilantro just before serving.

SCAN TO WATCH

16 let them eat cake!

the most amazing chocolate cake

3 cups all-purpose flour

3 cups granulated sugar

1½ cups unsweetened
cocoa powder

1 tbsp baking soda

1½ tsp baking powder

1½ tsp salt

4 large eggs

1½ cups buttermilk

1½ cups warm water*

½ cup vegetable oil

2 tsp vanilla extract

This cake is full of moist, chocolatey perfection! Frost with the chocolate version of the **Perfect Buttercream Frosting** (p. 305), **Whipped Chocolate Ganache** (p. 311), or any of your favorite frostings.

1 Preheat the oven to 350°F (177°C). Coat three 9-inch (23cm) round cake pans with butter and then dust with all-purpose flour or cocoa powder. Invert the pans and tap out the excess flour. (Alternatively, lightly grease the pans with nonstick cooking spray and line with parchment paper.)

2 In a stand mixer fitted with a whisk attachment (or in a large mixing bowl with a hand mixer), combine the flour, sugar, cocoa powder, baking soda, baking powder, and salt. Mix on low speed until combined.

3 Add the eggs, buttermilk, warm water, vegetable oil, and vanilla extract. Beat on medium until smooth, about 2 to 3 minutes.

4 Divide the batter evenly between the prepared pans. (I've found that adding just over 3 cups of the batter to each pan will divide it evenly.)

5 Bake for 30 to 35 minutes or until a toothpick inserted into the center of each cake comes out clean.

6 Transfer the cakes in the pans to wire racks to cool for 15 minutes and then turn the cakes out onto the wire racks to cool completely.

7 To assemble, frost between layers as you stack the cakes and then frost the top and outside of the cake.

SCAN TO WATCH

···················· • NOTES • ····················

* For a deeper, darker chocolate flavor, substitute an equal amount of brewed coffee for the warm water.

the most amazing white cake

This delicate white cake is light, airy, and absolutely gorgeous. It's the moist white wedding-style cake you've always dreamed of baking! You can mix and match this versatile cake with any of your favorite fillings and frostings.

1 Preheat the oven to 350°F (177°C). Grease two 9-inch (23cm) round cake pans with butter or nonstick cooking spray and then line the bottoms with parchment paper.

2 In a large bowl, use a hand mixer on high speed to cream the butter and sugar together until smooth and creamy, about 3 minutes. Beat in the almond extract and sour cream until just combined. Set aside.

3 Using a fork, combine the eggs and milk in a medium bowl or a 2-cup liquid measuring cup. Set aside.

4 In another medium bowl, stir together the cake flour, baking powder, and salt.

5 Add one third of the dry ingredients to the butter mixture. Mix with the hand mixer until just combined. Add half of the milk mixture and mix again to combine. Add another third of the dry ingredients and mix until combined, followed by the remainder of the milk mixture. Mix again. Add the remainder of the dry ingredients and mix until just combined, Using a rubber spatula, scrape the sides and bottom of the bowl to ensure all the ingredients are incorporated.

6 Divide the batter evenly between the prepared pans. Bake for 25 to 30 minutes or until a toothpick inserted into the middle of the cakes comes out clean. Let the cakes sit in the pans on a wire rack to cool completely before turning them out onto the rack.

7 To assemble, frost between the layers as you stack the cakes and then frost and decorate the top and sides.

1 cup salted butter, softened

1½ cups granulated sugar

2 tsp almond extract

½ cup sour cream, warmed to room temperature*

6 large egg whites, warmed to room temperature

1 cup milk (whole, 2%, or 1%) or buttermilk, warmed to room temperature

3½ cups cake flour

4 tsp baking powder

½ tsp salt

.... NOTES ....

* If you're not a fan of sour cream, you can omit the sour cream and simply use 1½ cups of milk or buttermilk.

If desired, this cake can also be made into three thinner layers.

SCAN TO WATCH

the most amazing vanilla cake

½ cup salted butter, softened

½ cup vegetable oil

1½ cups granulated sugar

1½ cups buttermilk, warmed to room temperature

3 large eggs, warmed to room temperature

1 tbsp vanilla extract

3½ cups cake flour

4 tsp of baking powder

½ tsp salt

This vanilla cake is so incredibly moist and flavorful; it's the perfect yellow cake to use for any special occasion and can be paired with any combination of fillings and frostings.

1 Preheat the oven to 350°F (177°C). Grease two 9-inch round cake pans with butter or nonstick cooking spray and then line the bottoms with parchment paper.

2 In a large bowl, use a hand mixer on high speed to cream the butter, vegetable oil, and sugar together until smooth and creamy, about 3 minutes. Add the buttermilk, eggs, and vanilla extract. Beat on low speed until combined.

3 Add the cake flour, baking powder, and salt. Mix until just combined. Use a rubber spatula to scrape the sides and bottom of the bowl to ensure all of the ingredients are incorporated.

4 Divide the batter between the prepared pans. Bake for 25 to 30 minutes or until a toothpick inserted into the center of the cakes comes out clean. Let the cakes sit in the pans on a wire rack to cool completely before turning them out onto the rack.

5 To assemble, frost between the layers as you stack the cakes and then frost and decorate the top and sides.

.... **NOTES** ....

While not entirely necessary, for a more even texture you can sift the flour, baking powder, and salt after measuring and before adding the dry ingredients to the batter.

SCAN TO WATCH

flourless chocolate cake

6oz (170g) semisweet chocolate chips

½ cup salted butter

¾ cup granulated sugar

½ cup unsweetened Dutch process cocoa powder

3 large eggs

1 tsp vanilla extract

FOR THE GANACHE

1 cup semisweet chocolate chips

½ cup heavy cream

Rich, dense, and fudgy, this cake is incredibly easy to make. It's a classic Italian chocolate cake recipe that just so happens to also be gluten-free.

1 Preheat the oven to 375°F (191°C). Lightly grease a 9-inch (23cm) round cake pan with butter or nonstick cooking spray and then line the bottom with parchment paper.

2 Place the chocolate chips and butter in a medium microwave-safe bowl. Microwave in 30 second intervals, stirring in between, until the ingredients are melted and smooth.

3 Add the sugar, cocoa powder, eggs, and vanilla extract. Use a hand mixer to beat the ingredients until just combined. (Do not over mix.) Use a rubber spatula to scrape the sides and bottom of the bowl to ensure all the ingredients are incorporated.

4 Pour the batter into the prepared cake pan. Bake 25 minutes. (The cake is ready when the center is still fudgy, but doesn't jiggle.)

5 Let the cake cool in the pan for 5 minutes and then run a knife around the edges to loosen. Turn the cake out onto a serving platter or cake stand. Let it cool completely.

6 While the cake is cooling, make the ganache by placing the chocolate chips in a medium bowl. In a small microwave-safe bowl, heat the heavy cream in the microwave until simmering, about 45 seconds. Pour the hot cream over the chocolate chips. Let stand 2 minutes and then stir until smooth.

7 Spread the warm ganache over the top of the cake. Let the ganache cool before slicing and serving.

SCAN TO WATCH

traditional pound cake

This pound cake is made the traditional way, with equal parts butter, sugar, eggs, and flour. Anything else is just a variation! But don't worry, I've still got you covered with several popular variations so you can enjoy a variety of delicious pound cake flavors.

1 Preheat the oven to 350°F (177°C). Lightly grease two 9 x 5-inch (23 x 13cm) loaf pans with butter and then dust with flour. Invert the pans and tap out the excess flour.

2 In a large mixing bowl, use a hand mixer to cream the butter until light and fluffy. Beat in the sugar until smooth.

3 Add the eggs, one at a time, and beat until smooth. Slowly add the flour, mixing the batter continuously as you add the flour. Pour the batter into the prepared loaf pans.

4 Bake for 1 hour. (Tent the cakes with aluminum foil if they start to brown too much.) Allow the cakes to cool in the pans for 15 minutes before turning them out onto a wire rack to cool completely.

2 cups salted butter, softened

2 cups granulated sugar

9 large eggs

3¼ cups all-purpose flour

········· NOTES ·········

This cake can also be baked in a Bundt pan. Add approximately 30 minutes more baking time if using a Bundt pan.

·············· VARIATIONS ··············

Vanilla Pound Cake: Add 2 teaspoons vanilla extract to the batter with the eggs. Make a vanilla glaze by whisking 1 cup powdered sugar with 2 tablespoons water and 1 teaspoon vanilla extract. Drizzle the glaze over the warm cake.

Almond Pound Cake: Add 2 teaspoons almond extract to the batter with the eggs. Make an almond glaze by whisking 1 cup powdered sugar with 2 tablespoons water and 1 teaspoon almond extract. Drizzle the glaze over the warm cake.

Sour Cream Pound Cake: Replace half of the butter with 1 cup (8 ounces [227g]) sour cream. (Sour cream will produce a more moist cake.)

Cream Cheese Pound Cake: Replace half of the butter with 8 ounces [227g]) cream cheese.

Rum Pound Cake: Add 2 teaspoons rum extract to the batter with the eggs. Make a rum glaze by heating ½ cup butter, 1 cup sugar, ¼ cup dark rum, and ¼ cup water in a saucepan over medium-high heat. Bring to a simmer, stirring continuously, until the sugar is dissolved. Use the handle end of a wooden spoon to poke holes in the baked cake. Drizzle the warm glaze over the warm cake.

Lemon Pound Cake: Add 2 tablespoons lemon juice or 1 teaspoon lemon extract to the batter with the eggs. Make a glaze by whisking together ⅓ cup lemon juice with ⅓ cup sugar until the sugar is dissolved. Drizzle the glaze over the warm cake.

Cornmeal Pound Cake: Replace half of the all-purpose flour with finely ground cornmeal.

SCAN TO WATCH

red velvet cake

3 cups all-purpose flour

3 cups granulated sugar

½ cup cornstarch

½ cup unsweetened cocoa powder*

1 tbsp baking soda

1½ tsp baking powder

1½ tsp salt

4 large eggs

1½ cups buttermilk

1¼ cups warm water

½ cup vegetable oil

1 tsp vanilla extract

1 tsp distilled white vinegar

2 tbsp red food coloring

This red velvet cake is moist, fluffy, has the perfect hint of tartness, and a mild cocoa flavor that gives the distinct flavor that is red velvet. Frost with the cream cheese variation of the **Perfect Buttercream Frosting** (p. 305) or the classic choice of **Ermine Frosting** (p. 312).

1 Preheat the oven to 350°F (177°C). Grease three 9-inch (23cm) round cake pans with butter and then dust with flour. Invert the pans and tap out the excess flour.

2 Using a stand mixer fitted with a whisk attachment (or using a large bowl with a hand mixer), mix the flour, sugar, cornstarch, cocoa powder, baking soda, baking powder, and salt at low speed until combined.

3 Add the eggs, buttermilk, warm water, vegetable oil, vanilla extract, white vinegar, and food coloring. Beat on medium speed until smooth, about 2 to 3 minutes.

4 Divide the batter equally across the prepared cake pans. Bake for 30 to 35 minutes or until a toothpick inserted into the middle of the cakes comes out clean.

5 Allow the cakes to cool in the pans for 15 minutes on a wire rack and then turn them out onto the racks to cool completely. Once cooled, frost the cakes as desired.

·········· NOTES ··········

* For a brighter red color, reduce the cocoa powder to ¼ cup.

SCAN TO WATCH

fresh berry chantilly cake

1 cup unsalted butter, warmed to room temperature

1½ cups granulated sugar

1¼ cups whole milk, warmed to 100°F (38°C)

3 large eggs, warmed to room temperature

¼ cup vegetable oil

2 tsp vanilla extract

3½ cups cake flour

4 tsp baking powder

½ tsp salt

FOR THE CHANTILLY CREAM

2 cups heavy cream

2 tsp vanilla extract

8oz (227g) cream cheese, softened

8oz (227g) mascarpone cheese, softened

2 cups powdered sugar

FOR THE BERRY FILLING

4 cups mixed fresh berries (any combination of strawberries, blackberries, raspberries, or blueberries), plus more to garnish (optional)

2 tsp lemon zest

2 tbsp lemon juice

⅔ cup seedless raspberry or strawberry jam

¼ cup water

Chantilly cake is a delicious vanilla sponge cake layered with fresh berries and topped with mouth-watering mascarpone Chantilly cream.

To make the cake:

1 Preheat the oven to 350°F (177°C). Grease two 9-inch (23cm) round cake pans with butter and then line the bottoms with parchment paper.

2 In a large bowl, use a hand mixer to cream the butter and sugar until creamy, about 2 minutes. Set aside.

3 Use a fork to combine the milk, eggs, vegetable oil, and vanilla extract in a medium bowl. In a second medium bowl, stir together the cake flour, baking powder, and salt.

4 Add one third of the dry ingredients to the butter mixture and then mix with the hand mixer until just combined. Add half of the milk mixture and mix again. Add another third of the dry ingredients and mix until combined, followed by the remainder of the milk mixture. Mix again and then add the remainder of the dry ingredients. Mix until all of the ingredients are just combined. Use a rubber spatula to scrape the sides and bottom of the bowl to ensure all of the ingredients are incorporated.

5 Divide the batter evenly across the prepared cake pans. Bake for 25 to 30 minutes or until a toothpick inserted into the middle of each cake comes out clean. Cool the cakes in the pans on a wire rack for 5 minutes and then turn them out onto the rack to cool completely. Set aside until you're ready to assemble the cake.

To make the Chantilly cream:

1 In a large bowl, combine the heavy cream with the vanilla extract. Beat with a hand mixer until stiff peaks form.

2 In a medium bowl, combine the cream cheese and mascarpone. Cream until light and fluffy, about 2 minutes, and then add the powdered sugar and beat until smooth.

3 Using a rubber spatula, fold the whipped cream and cream cheese mixtures together until just combined. Refrigerate until you're ready to assemble the cake.

SCAN TO WATCH

To make the berry filling:

1 Place the mixed berries in a medium bowl. Add the lemon zest and lemon juice. Toss to combine.

2 In a microwave-safe bowl, stir together the jam and water. Microwave until the jam is melted, about 30 seconds, and then stir again. Set aside until you're ready to assemble the cake.

To assemble the cake:

1 When you're ready to assemble the cake, slice each cake in half horizontally to create four even layers.

2 Spread one third of the jam filling onto the top of the bottom cake layer. Top with an even layer of Chantilly cream and then top the cream with ⅔ cup of the fresh berries.

3 Top the first layer with the next cake round and then continue layering the jam, Chantilly cream, and berries until all of the layers have been added.

4 Use the remaining Chantilly cream to frost the top and the outside of the cake. Garnish the top with additional fresh berries (if using).

strawberry cake
with strawberry chantilly cream

1lb (454g) fresh strawberries, hulled

¾ cup salted butter, softened

¼ cup vegetable oil

1½ cups granulated sugar

¼ cup sour cream

1½ tsp vanilla extract

1 tsp strawberry extract

3 large eggs, warmed to room temperature

1 cup buttermilk, warmed to room temperature

3½ cups cake flour

4 tsp baking powder

½ tsp salt

Pink food coloring (optional)

FOR THE CHANTILLY CREAM

2 cups heavy cream

1 tsp vanilla extract

1½oz (43g) instant strawberry gelatin

2 cups powdered sugar, divided

8oz (227g) cream cheese, softened

8oz (227g) mascarpone cheese, softened

Moist and full of strawberry flavor, this cake is topped with a decadent Chantilly cream. With fresh strawberries, strawberry extract, and strawberry gelatin in the Chantilly cream, this cake packs a serious strawberry punch. If you love strawberries, you will love this cake!

To make the cake:

1 Add the strawberries to a blender or food processor. Purée until smooth. Add the puréed strawberries to a small saucepan over medium heat. Simmer, stirring occasionally, until the mixture is thick and reduced by half, about 20 minutes. (You should end up with just about 1¼ cup of the reduced strawberry purée.) Set aside.

2 Preheat the oven to 350°F (177°C). Lightly grease two 9-inch (23cm) round cake pans with butter or nonstick cooking spray and then line the bottoms with parchment paper.

3 In a large bowl, combine the butter, vegetable oil, and sugar. Use a hand mixer on high speed to cream until smooth, about 3 minutes. Beat in 1 cup of the strawberry purée along with the sour cream, vanilla extract, and strawberry extract. (Reserve any remaining strawberry purée for the Chantilly cream.)

4 Use a fork to combine the eggs and buttermilk in a small bowl or 2 cup liquid measuring cup. Set aside.

5 In a medium bowl, stir together the cake flour, baking powder, and salt.

6 Add one third of the dry ingredients to the butter mixture and then mix with the hand mixer until just combined. Add half of the milk mixture and mix again. Add another third of the dry ingredients and mix until combined, followed by the remainder of the milk mixture. Mix again and then add the remainder of the dry ingredients. Mix until all of the ingredients are just combined. Use a rubber spatula to scrape the sides and bottom of the bowl to ensure all of the ingredients are incorporated.

7 Stir in the food coloring (if using) a few drops at a time until the desired color is achieved.

SCAN TO WATCH

8 Divide the batter evenly between the two prepared cake pans. Bake for 25 to 30 minutes or until a toothpick inserted into the middle of the cakes comes out clean. Cool the cakes in the pans on a wire rack for 5 minutes and then turn them out onto the rack to cool completely. Set aside until you're ready to assemble the cake.

To make the Chantilly cream:

1 Combine the heavy cream and vanilla extract in a large bowl. Use a hand mixer to whip the cream and extract while slowly adding the strawberry gelatin. Once the cream forms soft peaks, slowly add ½ cup of the powdered sugar. Continue beating until stiff peaks form and the ingredients are well combined.

2 In a separate medium bowl, beat together the cream cheese, mascarpone, and remaining ¼ cup of strawberry purée (from the cake recipe) until whipped and smooth, about 2 minutes. Add in the remaining 1½ cups powdered sugar. Mix until combined.

3 Use a rubber spatula to fold the whipped cream mixture in with the cream cheese mixture. Fold until just combined and no streaks remain.

To assemble the cake:

1 Place the first layer onto a cake stand, frost, and then add the second layer.

2 Frost the top and outside of the cake and decorate as desired.

gingerbread cake
with cream cheese frosting

¾ cup butter, melted

2 cups light brown sugar

2 cups molasses

1 cup warm water

1 cup buttermilk, warmed
 to room temperature

3 large eggs

2 tbsp ground ginger

1 tbsp ground cinnamon

¾ tsp ground cloves

1½ tsp salt

1 tsp baking soda

1½ tsp baking powder

4 cups all-purpose flour

FOR THE FROSTING

16oz (454g) cream cheese,
 softened

½ cup salted butter,
 softened

1 tbsp vanilla extract

6 cups powdered sugar

SCAN TO WATCH

Three layers of moist gingerbread are covered with a cream cheese frosting for an amazing dessert that will impress everyone. This is perfect for the holiday season, but can be enjoyed by gingerbread lovers anytime of the year.

1 Preheat the oven to 350°F (177°C). Lightly grease three 9-inch (23cm) round cake pans with butter and then line the bottoms with parchment paper.

2 In a large bowl, whisk together the melted butter, brown sugar, molasses, warm water, buttermilk, and eggs. Whisk in the ginger, cinnamon, cloves, salt, baking soda, and baking powder. Slowly add the flour while stirring continuously. Mix until just combined.

3 Divide the batter evenly between the prepared cake pans. Bake 30 to 35 minutes or until a toothpick inserted into the center of each cake comes out clean.

4 Let the cakes cool in the pans for 5 to 10 minutes before turning them out onto a wire rack to cool completely.

5 While the cakes are cooling, make the frosting by using a hand mixer to beat the cream cheese and butter on high speed until smooth in a large bowl. Add the vanilla extract and continue mixing until just combined. Slowly add the powdered sugar while mixing continuously on low speed until the desired consistency is achieved. (The frosting should be thick but spreadable.)

6 Stack the cakes, frosting in between layers, then frost the top and sides of the cake.

coconut cake

with coconut cream cheese frosting

½ cup vegetable oil

1½ cups granulated sugar

2 tsp coconut extract

6 large egg whites, warmed to room temperature

1½ cups coconut milk

¼ cup sour cream

3½ cups cake flour

4 tsp of baking powder

½ tsp salt

FOR THE FROSTING

16oz (454g) cream cheese, softened

1 cup salted butter, softened

1 tsp coconut extract

3 cups powdered sugar

3 cups coconut flakes

This cake is rich, full of bold coconut flavor, and topped with an amazing coconut cream cheese frosting. It will wow everyone in the room!

1 Preheat the oven to 350°F (177°C). Lightly grease three 9-inch (23cm) round cake pans with butter or nonstick cooking spray and then line the bottoms with parchment paper.

2 In a large bowl, use a hand mixer on high speed to cream the butter, vegetable oil, and sugar until smooth, about 3 minutes. Add the coconut extract and egg whites and beat on low speed for about 1 minute more. Add the coconut milk and sour cream. Mix until just combined.

3 Add the cake flour, baking powder, and salt. Mix on low speed until just combined.

4 Divide the batter across the three prepared cake pans. Bake for 25 to 30 minutes or until a toothpick inserted into the center of each cake comes out clean. Let the cakes cool in the pans for 5 minutes before turning them out onto a wire rack to cool completely.

5 While the cakes are cooling, make the frosting by using a hand mixer on high speed to beat the cream cheese and butter for 1 minute or until light and fluffy. Add the coconut extract and mix until combined, about 10 seconds.

6 Slowly add the powdered sugar, ½ cup at a time, until smooth, while mixing on low speed between additions.

7 Frost the top of one cake and then place the second cake on top of the first. Repeat with the third layer and then frost the entire cake. Coat the top and sides of the cake with the coconut flakes.

SCAN TO WATCH

angel food cake

3 cups powdered sugar, divided

¼ tsp salt

1 cup cake flour

12 egg whites

½ tsp vanilla extract

½ tsp almond extract

1½ tsp cream of tartar

This angel food cake is so light, airy, and deliciously sweet. It's the perfect angel food cake recipe! It's so easy to make this perfect sponge cake every time. You'll never go back to buying store-bought angel food cakes ever again!

1 Preheat the oven 350°F (177°C).

2 In a large bowl, sift together 1½ cups of the powdered sugar with the salt and cake flour. Set aside.

3 In another large bowl, use a hand mixer on high speed to beat together the egg whites, vanilla extract, almond extract, and cream of tartar. Whip with the hand mixer for 2 minutes and then slowly add the remaining 1½ cups of powdered sugar until stiff peaks form.

4 Sprinkle some of the flour mixture on top of the stiff egg peaks and gently fold the mixture in. Repeat until all of the flour mixture has been incorporated.

5 Use a rubber spatula to scrape the batter into an ungreased 9 to 10-inch (23 to 25cm) tube pan. (It's *very* important that the pan remain ungreased.)

6 Bake for 40 to 45 minutes or until the top is lightly browned and dry to the touch.

7 Remove the pan from the oven and immediately invert it on a cooling rack or place a glass bottle through the center of the pan and then invert it. Let the cake cool in the inverted pan for 1½ hours.

8 Gently tap the sides and bottom and of the pan to remove the cake from the pan.

SCAN TO WATCH

perfect buttercream frosting

1 cup salted butter, softened

1½ tsp vanilla extract

3 cups powdered sugar, divided

1 tbsp milk (whole, 2%, or 1%)

This buttercream frosting is an absolute classic for frosting cakes and cupcakes. This is the only buttercream frosting recipe you will ever need. It's perfection every single time!

1 In a large bowl, use a hand mixer or stand mixer to beat the softened butter until light and fluffy, about 2 to 3 minutes.

2 Add the vanilla extract and continue mixing until combined.

3 Add the powdered sugar, 1 cup a time, while mixing in between additions. After you've added 2 cups of the powdered sugar, add the milk and whip until smooth. Add the remaining 1 cup of powdered sugar and continue mixing until smooth.

4 Use immediately or store in an airtight container in the fridge for up to 7 days.

.... NOTES ....

Be sure the butter is softened completely by allowing it to sit at room temperature for 1 to 2 hours before using it to make the frosting. For best results, use a high-quality, high-fat butter.

.... VARIATIONS ....

Chocolate Buttercream Frosting: Add ½ cup unsweetened cocoa powder at the same time as the powdered sugar.

Cream Cheese Buttercream Frosting: Replace half of the butter with cream cheese.

SCAN TO WATCH

7-minute frosting

4 large egg whites
1¼ cups granulated sugar
1 tbsp water
¼ tsp salt
¼ tsp cream of tartar
1 tsp vanilla extract

This light and fluffy frosting has the perfect bright white color and, despite its name, takes about 10 minutes to make. It has a meringue or marshmallow-like texture that will practically melt in your mouth! You can use this frosting on any completely cooled cake or cupcake.

1 Make a double boiler by placing 2 inches (5cm) of water in the bottom of a medium saucepan and then placing a heat-safe metal or glass mixing bowl on top of the saucepan. (The edges of the bowl should rest securely on the edges of the saucepan so that the bottom of the bowl does not touch the water.)

2 Remove the bowl from the saucepan and bring the water to a boil over medium-high heat. Once boiling, reduce the heat to medium or medium-low and leave it at a simmer.

3 Add the egg whites, sugar, water, salt, and cream of tartar to the bowl.

4 Place the bowl over the simmering water. Use a hand mixer to beat the egg mixture for 7 minutes. (Alternatively, whisk the mixture vigorously by hand.)

5 After 7 minutes, carefully remove the mixing bowl from the saucepan and place it on the counter. Add the vanilla extract and beat it with the hand mixer for 1 to 2 minutes or until the frosting forms stiff peaks that hold their shape.

6 Use immediately or store in an airtight container in the fridge for up to 2 weeks.

SCAN TO WATCH

cooked chocolate fudge icing

½ cup salted butter

⅓ cup unsweetened
cocoa powder

⅓ cup buttermilk

3 cups powdered sugar

1 tsp vanilla extract

Gooey, chocolatey, and melty, this is hands-down the best chocolate fudge icing recipe for sheet cakes and brownies. It's so soft and fudgy, you may get the impression you're eating candy!

1 Melt the butter in a medium saucepan over low heat.

2 Whisk in the cocoa powder and then add the buttermilk. Increase the heat to medium-high and bring to a simmer while whisking constantly.

3 Once the mixture is simmering, remove the pan from the heat and whisk in the powdered sugar and vanilla extract. Whisk until smooth.

4 Pour the icing over the cake or brownies to cover. Use a rubber spatula to smooth and spread, if needed. (The cake or brownies can still be warm when you do this.)

··· NOTES ···

The yield of this recipe is perfect for icing a standard 18 x 13-inch (46 x 33cm) sheet cake or 9 x 9-inch (23 x 23cm) pan of brownies.

SCAN TO WATCH

sweetened condensed milk frosting
(two flavors)

FOR VANILLA SWEETENED CONDENSED MILK FROSTING

1 cup salted butter, warmed to room temperature

14oz (396g) can sweetened condensed milk* (chilled)

½ tsp vanilla extract

FOR CHOCOLATE SWEETENED CONDENSED MILK FROSTING

2oz (57g) unsweetened baking chocolate, roughly chopped

14oz (396g) can sweetened condensed milk

½ tsp vanilla extract

This recipe is a simple and easy way to make a creamy sweet frosting for all your favorite desserts. Whether you make the chocolate option or the vanilla option, it only takes three ingredients. If you like plain sweetened condensed milk, you'll love this frosting!

Vanilla Sweetened Condensed Milk Frosting

1 In a large bowl, use a hand mixer to whip the softened butter until light and fluffy, about 2 minutes.

2 Slowly whip in the sweetened condensed milk and then add the vanilla extract. Whip until thoroughly combined.

Chocolate Sweetened Condensed Milk Frosting

1 In a medium saucepan over medium heat, melt the chocolate into the sweetened condensed milk. Continue cooking, stirring constantly, until thickened, about 5 to 7 minutes.

2 Remove from the heat and stir in the vanilla extract. Allow to cool before using.

·········· NOTES ··········

* For the vanilla frosting, make sure you chill the can of condensed milk in the fridge for at least 2 hours before using, and preferably overnight. (It does not need to be chilled for the chocolate frosting.)

SCAN TO WATCH

chocolate ganache

DRIZZLE CHOCOLATE GANACHE (1:1 RATIO)

8oz (227g) semisweet chocolate

8fl oz (237ml) heavy cream

WHIPPED CHOCOLATE GANACHE* (1:1 RATIO)

8oz (227g) semisweet chocolate

8fl oz (237ml) heavy cream

FIRM CHOCOLATE GANACHE FROSTING (2:1 RATIO)

16oz (454g) semisweet chocolate

8fl oz (237ml) heavy cream

MILK CHOCOLATE GANACHE (2.5:1 RATIO)

20oz (567g) milk chocolate chips

8fl oz (237ml) heavy cream

WHITE CHOCOLATE GANACHE (3:1 RATIO)

24oz (680g) white chocolate chips

8fl oz (237ml) heavy cream

This ganache requires only two ingredients, so you will learn how to make a standard ganache for drizzling, a firm ganache, a whipped ganache, a milk chocolate ganache, and a white chocolate ganache. Each is a snap to make!

1 Place the chocolate in a glass or metal mixing bowl. (If using chocolate bars, roughly chop the bars into small chocolate chip–sized pieces.)

2 Heat the cream in a small saucepan over medium heat until it comes to a simmer. Once simmering, immediately remove from the heat and pour over the chocolate.

3 Let sit 2 to 3 minutes to allow the heat from the cream to melt the chocolate.

4 Use a rubber spatula to gently stir until the chocolate is completely melted and the ganache is smooth.

.... NOTES ....

* If you're making a whipped ganache, cover and chill the melted ganache in the fridge for 1 hour. After 1 hour, remove the ganache from the fridge and use a hand mixer to whip until light and fluffy, about 3 to 4 minutes.

Use the best quality chocolate you can get. I recommend Guittard, Ghiradelli, Lindt, or other widely available high-quality chocolate brands. Avoid using any chocolate with added stabilizers, as the ganache won't set up properly.

If the ganache is too thick, add heated cream, 1 tablespoon at a time, to thin it out.

If the ganache is too grainy, add the ganache to a heat-safe mixing bowl and place it over the hot water. (The edges of the bowl must rest on the edges of the pan and the bottom of the bowl should not touch the water.) Whisk the ganache until smooth.

If the ganache is too thin, create a double boiler and add additional chocolate in small amounts until the desired consistency is achieved.

SCAN TO WATCH

VG

READY IN 1 HOUR 15 MINUTES • MAKES ABOUT 4 CUPS

ermine frosting

2 cups granulated sugar

½ cup all-purpose flour

2 cups whole milk

2 cups unsalted butter, softened

1 tsp vanilla extract

Pinch of salt

Ermine is a type of buttercream frosting that is cooked on the stovetop. It's light, fluffy, and has just the right amount of sweetness. It's also decidedly less sweet than a standard buttercream frosting and pairs beautifully with practically any cake you can imagine! This is the traditional frosting used for **Red Velvet Cake** (p. 297).

1 In a medium saucepan over low heat, whisk together the sugar and flour. Cook for 2 minutes to let the flour toast briefly.

2 Increase the heat to medium. Slowly whisk in the milk and bring to a simmer. (A light layer of foam will form.) Once it reaches a simmer, continue cooking about 1 minute more or until the mixture develops a puddinglike consistency and then promptly remove from the heat.

3 Pour the mixture into a medium bowl and place plastic wrap directly on the surface of the mixture so no skin forms on the surface. Place in the fridge to cool for 1 hour.

4 In a large bowl, use a hand mixer to whip the butter until light and fluffy, about 2 to 3 minutes. Add the cooled milk mixture 1 to 2 tablespoons at a time, mixing well between each addition.

5 Once all the milk mixture has been added, beat in the vanilla and salt. Continue beating until the frosting is thick and creamy and everything is well combined, about 1 to 2 minutes more.

SCAN TO WATCH

perfect pastry cream

1 large egg

2 large egg yolks

¼ cup cornstarch

⅓ cup plus ¼ cup granulated sugar, divided

2 cups whole milk

2 tbsp butter

1 tsp vanilla extract

This simple pastry cream is easy to make at home and can be used in pastries, cakes, and other desserts. This classic filling, known as *crème pâtissière*, is the traditional filling for eclairs and cream puffs, as well as for Boston cream pie. You'll love this recipe!

1 In a medium bowl, whisk together the egg, egg yolks, cornstarch, and ⅓ cup sugar. Set aside.

2 In a large saucepan, stir together the milk and the remaining ¼ cup sugar. Bring to a simmer over medium heat.

3 Once the milk reaches a simmer, working quickly and carefully, pour half of the hot milk in a steady stream into the egg mixture, whisking constantly to avoid curdling or cooking the eggs. Immediately pour the egg mixture back into the saucepan and into the remaining milk mixture while whisking constantly. Increase the heat to medium and continue whisking until the mixture thickens.

4 Once the mixture thickens, remove from the heat and add the butter and vanilla extract. Stir until the butter is melted and then pour the mixture into a clean bowl.

5 Place plastic wrap directly on the surface of the pastry cream so no skin forms on the surface.

6 Cool in the refrigerator for at least 4 hours before using.

·············· **NOTES** ··············

To make a Boston cream pie, spread the pastry cream between two layers of **The Most Amazing Vanilla Cake** (p. 293) and then top the cake layers with the **Drizzle Chocolate Ganache** (p. 311).

SCAN TO WATCH

17 me want cookies!

bakery-style cookies
(six flavors)

1 cup unsalted butter, warmed to room temperature

¾ cup light brown sugar

½ cup granulated sugar

2 large eggs

1 tsp vanilla extract

1 cup cake flour

1¾ cup all-purpose flour

1 tsp baking powder

1 tsp baking soda

½ tsp salt

These cookies are so soft, thick, and full of delicious cookie goodness. This base recipe will enable you to create a wide variety of flavors with the variations. You can enjoy amazing cookies in the comfort of your home in less time than it would take to drive to a bakery!

1 Preheat the oven to 400°F (204°C). Line two baking sheets with parchment paper or silicone baking mats.

2 In the bowl of a stand mixer fitted with a paddle attachment, combine the butter, brown sugar, and granulated sugar. Mix on medium to high speed until smooth, about 1 minute.

3 Add the eggs and vanilla extract. Beat until just combined, about 30 seconds.

4 Add the cake flour, all-purpose flour, baking powder, baking soda, and salt. Mix until just combined.

5 Add any desired add-ins at this point (if using). Use a large spoon or rubber spatula to fold in the ingredients.

6 Divide the dough into 8 equal-sized pieces for large cookies or 24 equal-sized pieces for regular-sized cookies. Use your hands to roll the pieces into large balls and then place the balls on the prepared baking sheets.

7 Bake for 11 to 14 minutes for larger cookies or 8 minutes for regular-sized cookies. Bake until the tops are golden brown

8 Let the cookies cool on the baking sheets for 15 minutes and then transfer to a wire rack to cool completely before serving.

SCAN TO WATCH

Chocolate Chip–Walnut Cookies: Add 2 cups semisweet chocolate chips and 1 cup chopped walnuts.

Cowboy Cookies: Add 2 cups semisweet chocolate chips, 1 cup quick oats, ¾ cup chopped pecans, and ¾ cup unsweetened coconut flakes.

Oatmeal Raisin Cookies: Add 1½ cups quick oats and 2 cups raisins.

Dark Chocolate Chunk: Add ½ cup cocoa powder and 2 cups dark chocolate chunks or dark chocolate chips. (For a chocolate cookie dough base, reduce the flour to 1½ cups and add in ½ cup unsweetened cocoa powder.)

Dark Chocolate–Peanut Butter Chip: Add ½ cup cocoa powder and 2 cups peanut butter chips. (For a chocolate cookie dough base, reduce the flour to 1½ cups and add in ½ cup unsweetened cocoa powder.)

VG · FF

READY IN 1 HOUR 25 MINUTES · MAKES ABOUT 20 COOKIES

chocolate chip–shortbread cookies

1 cup salted butter, softened

⅔ cup powdered sugar

½ tsp vanilla extract

2 cups all-purpose flour

¾ cup mini chocolate chips

8oz (227g) melting chocolate wafers

These shortbread cookies feature all the goodness of melt-in-your-mouth shortbread combined with a touch of chocolate. Your family will absolutely love these cookies!

1 In a large bowl, use a hand mixer to beat together the butter and powdered sugar until light and fluffy. Add the vanilla extract and beat until combined.

2 Add the flour and mix just until the flour disappears. Fold in the mini chocolate chips.

3 Transfer the dough to a gallon-sized resealable plastic bag or place it between two layers of plastic wrap. Roll the dough until ¼ inch (.60cm) thick. Refrigerate on a flat surface until firm, about 1 to 2 hours.

4 Preheat the oven to 325°F (163°C). Line a large baking sheet with parchment paper.

5 Remove the dough from the plastic bag or plastic wrap and use a butter knife to cut it into equal-sized squares or rectangles. Transfer the cut pieces to the prepared baking sheet.

6 Bake for 18 to 20 minutes or until the edges are just lightly kissed with brown.

7 Microwave the dipping chocolate on high in a small microwave-safe bowl in 30 second intervals, stirring in between intervals, until the chocolate is melted and smooth. Dip the cookies in the melted chocolate, covering a third to half with the chocolate. Transfer the dipped cookies to parchment paper to cool and harden.

SCAN TO WATCH

perfectly soft sugar cookies

These sugar cookies are absolutely divine and come out perfectly soft every single time! This is the only sugar cookie recipe you'll ever need.

1 In the bowl of a stand mixer fitted with a whisk attachment, cream the butter, sugar, and cream cheese until light and fluffy.

2 Mix in the corn syrup, vanilla extract, almond extract, and egg until well combined. Use a rubber spatula to scrape the sides and bottom of the bowl to ensure all the ingredients are incorporated.

3 Switch the mixer attachment to a paddle or dough hook. Add the flour, baking powder, salt, and baking soda. Mix until well combined.

4 Wrap the dough with plastic wrap and refrigerate for 1 hour.

5 Preheat the oven to 375°F (191°C). Lightly grease a baking sheet with nonstick cooking spray or line with parchment paper.

6 Place the chilled dough on a lightly floured surface and roll out until ¼-inch thick. Use cookie cutters to cut shapes or a biscuit cutter to cut circles. Place the cookies on the prepared baking sheet.

7 Bake for 10 minutes and then remove from the oven to cool for 2 to 3 minutes on the baking sheet before carefully transferring the cookies to a wire rack to cool completely. Frost the cooled cookies, if desired, with **Perfect Buttercream Frosting** (p. 305).

1 cup salted butter, softened

1¼ cups granulated sugar

¼ cup cream cheese

2 tbsp corn syrup

1 tsp vanilla extract

¼ tsp almond extract

1 large egg

3 cups all-purpose flour

1 tsp baking powder

¾ tsp salt

¼ tsp baking soda

······································· **VARIATIONS** ·······································

Drop Cookies: Skip refrigerating the dough and pinch off 1 tablespoon of dough, roll it into a ball, and gently press it between your hands or fingers to flatten. Repeat with the remaining dough and then bake as instructed.

Chocolate Sugar Cookies: Omit the almond extract, increase the flour to 3½ cups, and add ⅔ cup melted semisweet chocolate chips and ⅓ cup unsweetened cocoa powder at the same time as you add the egg in step 2.

SCAN TO WATCH

rachel's perfect chocolate chip cookies

1 cup salted butter, softened

1 cup light brown sugar, tightly packed

½ cup granulated sugar

2 large eggs

2 tsp vanilla extract

1 tsp baking soda

½ tsp salt

2 ½ cups all-purpose flour

2 cups chocolate chips

This is the quintessential classic chocolate chip cookie recipe! These are perfectly soft and buttery and so easy to make. In fact, this is the cookie that started my journey into professional cooking all the way back at age twelve. The recipe has been perfected over the years and has become my signature recipe. Decades later it's finally in print for the world to enjoy!

1 Preheat the oven to 350°F (177C). Lightly coat two large baking sheets with nonstick cooking spray or line them with parchment paper.

2 In a large bowl, use a hand mixer to cream together butter, brown sugar, and granulated sugar. Add the eggs and vanilla extract. Beat until smooth.

3 Add the baking soda, salt, and flour. Mix until a nice dough is formed. Use a spoon to stir in the chocolate chips.

4 Take two tablespoons of the dough and use your hands to quickly shape it into a ball. Place it on the prepared baking sheet and repeat with the remaining dough. (You should have 12 cookies on each baking sheet.)

5 Bake for 10 to 12 minutes or until the cookies are just kissed with brown. (Be careful not to overbake!)

6 Remove the cookies from the oven and set aside to cool on the baking sheets for 3 to 5 minutes before transferring them to a wire rack to cool completely. Once cooled, store in an airtight container for 3 to 5 days.

.... **NOTES** ....

The dough can easily be frozen for future use. For best results, shape it into balls, freeze the balls on a baking sheet, and then transfer the balls to a resealable plastic freezer bag. Freeze for up to 3 months. When ready to bake, place the dough balls on a prepared baking sheet and let thaw slightly while the oven preheats. Bake 12 to 15 minutes.

SCAN TO WATCH

5-ingredient peanut butter cookies

1 cup creamy peanut
    butter
½ cup granulated sugar
½ cup light brown sugar
1 large egg
1 tsp vanilla extract

Get ready for the softest peanut butter cookies you've ever had! These come together with only five ingredients. Note that using conventional peanut butter will work best for this recipe, natural peanut butters may produce inconsistent results.

1 Preheat the oven to 350°F (177°C). Line a large baking sheet with a silicone baking mat or parchment paper.

2 In the bowl of a stand mixer or in a large bowl with a hand mixer, beat the peanut butter, granulated sugar, and brown sugar on high until smooth and creamy, about 2 to 3 minutes. Add the egg and vanilla extract. Mix until combined.

3 Scoop out a heaping tablespoon of the dough and roll it into a 1¼-inch (3.25 cm) ball. Place the ball on the prepared baking sheet. Repeat with the remaining dough, spacing the balls 2 to 3 inches (5 to 7.5cm) apart. Use a fork to press the cookies down and create cross-hatch patterns in the tops.

4 Bake for about 8 minutes and then remove the cookies from the oven and allow to cool completely before removing from the baking sheet. Store in an airtight container for 3 to 5 days.

SCAN TO WATCH

cinnamon roll cookies

1 cup salted butter, softened

1¼ cups granulated sugar

¼ cup cream cheese

2 tbsp corn syrup

1 tsp vanilla extract

¼ tsp almond extract

1 large egg

3 cups all-purpose flour

1 tsp baking powder

¾ tsp salt

¼ tsp baking soda

FOR THE FILLING

½ cup salted butter, softened

1 cup light brown sugar

2 tsp ground cinnamon

FOR THE GLAZE

2 tbsp cream cheese, softened

2 tbsp salted butter, softened

1 cup powdered sugar

½ tsp vanilla extract

1½ tbsp milk (whole, 2%, or 1%)

These cookies take all the goodness of cinnamon rolls and combine it with sugar cookies for one outrageously delicious cookie that people go absolutely crazy for!

1 In the bowl of a stand mixer fitted with a paddle attachment, cream the butter, sugar, and cream cheese until light and fluffy. Add the corn syrup, vanilla extract, almond extract, and egg. Mix until well combined. Use a rubber spatula to scrape the sides and bottom of the bowl to ensure all the ingredients are fully incorporated.

2 Add the flour, baking powder, salt, and baking soda. Mix until the ingredients are well combined.

3 Divide the dough into two equal pieces. Shape them into balls and then flatten them into disks. Wrap the disks in plastic wrap and chill in the fridge for 1 hour.

4 Preheat the oven to 375°F (191°C). Lightly grease a large baking sheet with nonstick cooking spray or line it with parchment paper.

5 Make the filling by combining the butter, brown sugar, and cinnamon in a small bowl. Use a hand mixer on high speed to beat the ingredients together, about 2 minutes.

6 On a lightly floured surface, roll each dough ball out into a 8 x 15-inch (20 x 38cm) rectangle. Spread the filling out in an even layer over each piece of dough. Working from the long ends, roll the dough sheets up tightly to form long logs. (For the best cookie shapes, wrap the dough logs in plastic wrap and chill for 1 additional hour.) Slice the logs into 1-inch (2.5cm) cookies. Place the cookies on the prepared baking sheet.

7 Bake for 10 minutes and then remove from the oven and cool for 2 to 3 minutes on the baking sheet before carefully transferring the cookies to a wire rack to cool completely.

8 While the cookies are cooling, make the glaze by using a hand mixer to whip the cream cheese and butter together until light and fluffy. Slowly beat in the powdered sugar, vanilla extract, and milk. Drizzle the glaze over the top of the cooled cookies. Once the glaze has set, transfer the cookies to an airtight container. Store at room temperature for 3 to 5 days.

SCAN TO WATCH

chocolate kiss cookies

12 tbsp unsalted butter, softened

1½ cups granulated sugar

½ cup light or dark brown sugar, tightly packed

4 large eggs

2 tsp vanilla extract

2½ cups all-purpose flour

1 cup unsweetened cocoa powder

1 tbsp baking powder

¾ tsp salt

2 cups powdered sugar (for coating)

3 dozen milk chocolate Hershey's Kisses, unwrapped

These fudgy, crackled, powdered sugar-coated chocolate cookies are topped off with milk chocolate Hershey's Kisses. These cookies are chocolate overload in the best possible way! If desired, you can omit the chocolate candy for a plain chocolate crinkle cookie.

1 Combine the butter, granulated sugar, and brown sugar in the bowl of a stand mixer. (Alternatively, you can use a large bowl and a hand mixer.) Beat the ingredients until well creamed and then add the eggs, one at a time, until they are completely incorporated. Mix in the vanilla extract.

2 In a separate large bowl, whisk together the flour, cocoa powder, baking powder, and salt.

3 Gradually add the dry ingredients to the wet ingredients, stirring until they're completely combined. Cover the bowl with plastic wrap and refrigerate at least 4 hours or overnight.

4 Preheat the oven to 350°F (177°C). Line three large baking sheets with parchment paper.

5 Scoop out 1½ tablespoon-sized pieces and then roll them into balls. Roll the balls in the powdered sugar to coat thoroughly. Place the balls on the prepared baking sheet.

6 Bake for 10 to 12 minutes or until the cookies are just set. (Do not overbake!) Remove the cookies from the oven and immediately and gently press a chocolate Kiss into the center of each cookie while they are still hot.

7 Allow the cookies to cool completely on the baking sheet. Store in an airtight container for 3 to 5 days.

SCAN TO WATCH

chocolate turtle cookies

1 cup salted butter, softened

½ cup granulated sugar

½ cup light brown sugar

2 large eggs

½ tsp vanilla extract

½ cup unsweetened cocoa powder

1 tsp baking soda

¼ tsp salt

2 cups all-purpose flour

1 cup milk chocolate chips

1 cup chopped pecans

14 baking caramels, unwrapped

1 tbsp heavy cream

These ultradecadent cookies are soft and delicious. Any chocolate lover will go crazy for them! They have rich chocolate flavor with morsels of melted chocolate, crunchy pecans, and a gooey caramel drizzle.

1 Line two large baking sheets with parchment paper. Set aside.

2 In the bowl of a stand mixer fitted with an paddle attachment or in a large bowl using a hand mixer, cream together the butter, granulated sugar, and brown sugar. Add the eggs and vanilla extract and beat until combined. Add the cocoa powder, baking soda, and salt. Beat until combined.

3 Use a spoon or rubber spatula to stir in the flour until combined and then stir in chocolate chips and pecans.

4 Scoop out a 2 tablespoon–sized chunk of the dough, roll it into a ball, and then place the ball on a prepared baking sheet. Repeat with the remaining dough until you have 24 cookies. Place in the freezer for 30 minutes.

5 While the dough is chilling, preheat the oven to 325°F (163°C).

6 Remove the cookies from the freezer and place in the oven. Bake for 12 minutes or until they are just barely set in the center.

7 While the cookies are baking, place the unwrapped caramels and heavy cream in a microwave-safe bowl. Microwave in 30 second intervals, stirring in between each interval, until the caramel is completely melted and smooth.

8 Remove the cookies from the oven and then drizzle the caramel sauce over the top of the cookies. Transfer to a wire rack to cool completely. Store in an airtight container in the fridge for 3 to 5 days.

SCAN TO WATCH

18 treat yo'self!

5-minute fudge

14oz (397g) can sweetened condensed milk

2 cups semisweet chocolate chips

1 tsp vanilla extract

This easy-to-make fudge takes just five minutes to make from start to finish and requires only a handful of ingredients. It's a simple recipe that yields perfectly smooth and creamy fudge every time.

1 Line an 8 x 8-inch (20 x 20cm) pan with parchment paper.

2 In a large microwave-safe bowl, combine the sweetened condensed milk, chocolate chips, and vanilla extract. Microwave in 30 second intervals, stirring in between, until the chocolate chips are completely melted and smooth.

3 Pour the mixture into the prepared pan. Use a rubber spatula to smooth.

4 Refrigerate until set, about 2 hours. Once set, remove the fudge from the pan and cut into small pieces for serving. Store in an airtight container in the fridge for 2 to 3 weeks.

·········· NOTES ··········

No microwave? No problem! Combine all ingredients in a medium saucepan over medium heat. Stir constantly until all ingredients are melted and the mixture is smooth. Pour the mixture into the prepared pan and refrigerate until set.

·········· VARIATIONS ··········

Nut Fudge: Stir in ½ cup roughly chopped nuts (pecans, walnuts, or almonds). If desired, replace all or part of the vanilla extract with the corresponding nut extract.

White Chocolate Fudge: Replace the semisweet chocolate chips with an equal amount of white chocolate chips.

Marbled Fudge: Make half of the recipe with white chocolate chips and the other half with semisweet chocolate chips. Spoon each into the prepared pan to dot the bottom and then use a butter knife or toothpick to swirl together.

Mint Chocolate Fudge: Replace the vanilla extract with an equal amount of mint extract.

Peanut Butter Fudge: Use ½ cup creamy peanut butter and 12 ounces (340g) white chocolate in place of the semisweet chocolate chips.

SCAN TO WATCH

READY IN 35 MINUTES • MAKES 9 SQUARES

best brownies ever

1½ cups milk chocolate chips, divided

10 tbsp salted butter, melted

1 cup granulated sugar

2 large eggs

2 tsp vanilla extract

¾ cup all-purpose flour

¼ cup unsweetened cocoa powder

½ tsp salt

These brownies have the perfect crackly top with bites of fudgy, chewy, chocolatey goodness. This one-bowl recipe is so easy that you'll never need to buy boxed brownie mix again! You can also use it as a base recipe for all sorts of different brownie variations.

1 Preheat the oven to 350°F (177°C). Line a metal 9 x 9-inch (23 x 23cm) baking pan with parchment paper.

2 Add ½ cup of the milk chocolate chips to a microwave-safe bowl. Microwave in 30-second increments, stirring in between, until the chocolate is melted and smooth.

3 Pour the melted butter into a large bowl. Whisk in the sugar until smooth, about 30 seconds. Add the eggs and vanilla extract. Whisk 1 minute more. Add the melted chocolate and whisk until combined and smooth.

4 Use a rubber spatula to stir in the flour, cocoa powder, and salt. Stir until just combined and then stir in the remaining 1 cup of milk chocolate chips.

5 Pour the mixture into the prepared pan and use a rubber spatula to smooth.

6 Bake for 30 minutes. Remove from the oven and let cool in pan for 30 minutes before slicing. Store in an airtight container for 3 to 5 days.

SCAN TO WATCH

cheesecake cupcakes

24 Oreo sandwich cookies

16oz (454g) cream cheese, softened

½ cup granulated sugar

½ tsp vanilla extract

2 large eggs

½ cup sour cream

1 pinch salt

½ cup **Hot Fudge Sauce** (p. 340)

Enjoy delicious cheesecake in cupcake form! This easy-to-make dessert utilizes an Oreo sandwich cookie base and is swirled with hot fudge.

1 Preheat the oven to 325°F (163°C). Line a large muffin tin with cupcake liners. Place a sandwich cookie in the bottom of each cup.

2 In a large bowl, use a hand mixer on high to beat the cream cheese and sugar together until smooth. Beat in the vanilla extract, eggs, sour cream, and salt. Continue beating until combined and smooth.

3 Spoon about 2 heaping tablespoons of the cheesecake batter into each muffin cup to fill the cup about three quarters full.

4 Warm the hot fudge sauce in the microwave for 20 seconds and then stir. Place a scant teaspoon of the warm sauce on top of each cupcake. Use a toothpick or butter knife to gently swirl the fudge into the cheesecake mix.

5 Bake for 40 to 45 minutes or until the filling is set and no longer jiggles in the center. Cool completely in the muffin tin before removing. Store in an airtight container in the fridge for 3 to 5 days.

·········· NOTES ··········

Other flavors of sandwich cookies can be used in place of the Oreos for this recipe to create different flavor options.

You can replace the **Hot Fudge Sauce** with caramel sauce or any flavor of jam. (Lemon cookies with strawberry jam is a personal favorite, but feel free to be creative and experiment!)

SCAN TO WATCH

old-fashioned cobbler

3 lb (3.6kg) fresh fruit, cleaned, cored, and sliced (if using berries, do not slice)

Zest and juice of 1 lemon

2 tsp cornstarch

½ tsp vanilla extract

⅓ cup granulated sugar

2 cups all-purpose flour

¾ cup powdered sugar

1 tbsp baking powder

1 tsp salt

½ cup very cold salted butter, diced

1 cup half-and-half

Get ready for the best cobbler of your life! This made-from-scratch cobbler is super easy to make and completely delicious. And with only 10 minutes of prep, you're sure to be making this frequently. You can use a variety of fruits with this recipe including peaches, berries, apples, or even combinations of fruits.

1 Preheat the oven to 350°F (177°C). Spray a 9 x 13-inch (23 x 33cm) baking pan with nonstick cooking spray.

2 In a medium bowl, toss the fruit with the lemon zest, lemon juice, cornstarch, vanilla extract, and granulated sugar. Spread the fruit across the bottom of the prepared baking pan.

3 In a large bowl, stir together the flour, powdered sugar, baking powder, and salt. Use a pastry cutter to cut in the butter until it resembles a course meal. (Alternatively, you can pulse the ingredients in a food processor.)

4 Pour in the half-and-half. Stir to form a thick batter.

5 Scoop the batter in large clumps on top of the fruit to form a nice cobbler crust.

6 Bake for 1 hour and then transfer to a wire rack to cool completely. Once cooled, stored covered in the refrigerator for up to 5 days.

.... NOTES ....

If you're using frozen fruit instead of fresh fruit, the end result may a bit more liquidy since frozen fruit produces extra moisture once it's thawed. To compensate for this, double the amount of cornstarch In the recipe.

To reheat, spoon a serving onto a plate or into a bowl and microwave on high in 30-second intervals until warmed through. (This recipe is also delicious eaten cold.)

.... VARIATIONS ....

Spiced Cobbler: To create a spiced cobbler like cinnamon-apple cobbler, add 1 teaspoon of ground cinnamon in with the fruit when you add the cornstarch. ¼ teaspoon of nutmeg is also a yummy addition.

SCAN TO WATCH

homemade churros

There's nothing quite like freshly fried homemade churros! These are flaky and warm and practically melt in your mouth. And they are incredibly easy to make at home!

1 Line a large plate with paper towels. Combine the sugar and cinnamon in a resealable plastic bag. Set aside.

2 Add the oil to a large pot. Heat to between 350°F and 375°F (177°C and 190°C).

3 While the oil is heating, make the dough by heating the water, butter, vanilla extract, and salt in a large saucepan over medium-high heat. Once the butter is completely melted and the mixture begins to simmer, remove from the heat and stir in the flour with a wooden spoon.

4 Add the eggs, one at a time, stirring and mashing the dough together until each egg is fully incorporated. Transfer the mixture to a large pastry bag fitted with a large star-shaped tip.

5 Working in batches of 3 to 5 at a time, pipe the dough directly into the hot oil, using scissors to trim the churros to the desired length.

6 Cook until the dough puffs and turns golden brown, turning the churros halfway through so all sides cook evenly, about 2 to 4 minutes. Use tongs to carefully transfer the churros from the oil to the paper towel–lined plate. Drain the churros for 1 to 2 minutes or until they're just cool enough to handle.

7 Once the churros are cool enough to handle, put them in the bag with the cinnamon sugar mixture, two at a time, and gently shake until the churros are coated in the mixture. Serve warm.

1 cup granulated sugar

1 tsp ground cinnamon

4 cups vegetable or canola oil, for frying

1 cup water

½ cup salted butter

1 tsp vanilla extract

¼ tsp salt

1 cup all-purpose flour

3 large eggs

SCAN TO WATCH

grandma's homemade caramels

1 cup unsalted butter

14oz (397g) can sweetened condensed milk

1 cup corn syrup

2 cups light brown sugar

2 tsp vanilla extract

¼ tsp salt

If you can stir, you can make homemade caramels! These caramels are soft, chewy, and so easy to make. You can wrap them to give away or you can keep them all to yourself!

1 Liberally butter a 9 x 13-inch (22 x 33cm) baking pan. Set aside

2 Melt the butter in a large saucepan over medium heat. Once melted, add the sweetened condensed milk, corn syrup, and brown sugar.

3 Use a rubber spatula to stir the mixture continuously until it begins to simmer, scraping the sides and bottom regularly. Continue at a constant simmer, stirring continuously, until the caramel reaches the soft-ball stage temperature range of 235°F to 245°F (113°C to 118°C) on a candy thermometer.* (At higher elevations, use the lower end of the range; at lower elevations, use the upper end of the range.)

4 When the caramels reach the desired temperature for the soft-ball stage, immediately remove the pan from the heat and stir in the vanilla extract and salt. Pour the caramel into the prepared baking pan.

5 Allow to cool completely in the pan before cutting into 1-inch (2.5cm) squares. Wrap the individual pieces in wax paper for individual servings, if desired.

·········· NOTES ··········

* If you don't have a candy thermometer, you can determine if the caramel is ready the old-fashioned way by filling a drinking glass or bowl with cold water and adding just a drop of the caramel from the pan to the water. For the soft-ball stage, the caramel should form a small round ball in the cold water and should flatten when it is removed from the water.

SCAN TO WATCH

luscious lemon bars

FOR THE CRUST

1 cup salted butter, sliced

½ cup granulated sugar

2 cups all-purpose flour

FOR THE LEMON CURD

1½ cups granulated sugar

¼ cup all-purpose flour

4 large eggs

1 cup lemon juice (about 4–5 lemons)

2 tbsp powdered sugar, for dusting (optional)

It only takes a handful of ingredients to make these perfectly luscious lemon bars. This recipe is the perfect balance between tart and sweet.

1 Preheat the oven to 350°F (177°C). Line a 9 x 9-inch (23 x 23cm) baking pan with parchment paper.

2 In a medium bowl, make the crust by using a pastry cutter to combine the butter, sugar, and flour. (Alternatively, you can pulse the ingredients in a food processor.) Press the dough into the bottom of the prepared baking pan. Place the crust in the oven and bake for 15 minutes.

3 About 5 minutes before the crust is done baking, begin making the lemon curd by mixing together the granulated sugar and flour and then whisking in the eggs and lemon juice.

4 Remove the crust from the oven. Gently pour the lemon curd mixture over the baked crust and then return the pan to the oven. Bake until the lemon layer is set, about 40 to 50 minutes.

5 Remove from the oven and allow to cool completely before dusting the top with the powdered sugar (if using). Cut into 9 squares. Store in an airtight container for 3 to 5 days.

SCAN TO WATCH

READY IN 15 MINUTES · MAKES ABOUT 2 CUPS

hot fudge sauce

½ cup salted butter

⅓ cup unsweetened cocoa powder

⅔ cup milk chocolate chips

2 cups granulated sugar

12fl oz (354ml) can evaporated milk

1 tsp vanilla extract

The hot fudge sauce is so easy to make and it beats the store-bought options—no contest! It's thick, gooey, fudgy, and delicious. It's perfect served over ice cream or any other treat that calls for a dose of chocolate!

1 Combine the butter, cocoa powder, chocolate chips, sugar, and evaporated milk in a medium saucepan over medium-low heat. Stir until combined and then increase the heat to medium-high. Bring the mixture to a boil and then immediately reduce the heat to low and simmer for 7 minutes, stirring continuously.

2 After 7 minutes, remove from the heat and add the vanilla extract.

3 Pour the mixture into a blender. Blend for 2 minutes or until smooth, making sure to vent the blender so pressure does not build from the steam.

4 Serve warm or allow to cool before transferring to an airtight container. Store in the fridge for up to 1 month.

······· NOTES ·······

To reheat, spoon the desired portion into a microwave-safe bowl and microwave in 10 second intervals until warm.

SCAN TO WATCH

easy crème brûlée

This easy, classic crème brûlée will hit the sweet spot with a rich, thick vanilla custard and caramelized sugar topping. This is so exquisite—your guests won't believe you made this at home!

1 Preheat the oven to 300°F (149°C). Place six 6-ounce (171g) ramekins in the bottom of a 9 x 13-inch (22 x 33cm) baking pan or roasting pan.

2 In a large bowl, use a hand mixer on medium speed to beat together the egg yolks and granulated sugar until smooth and velvety, about 3 to 5 minutes.

3 Pour in the heavy cream and vanilla extract or scraped vanilla seed. (If using a vanilla bean pod, split the pod open lengthwise and scrape the seeds directly into the egg mixture.) Beat on low until combined, about 1 to 2 minutes.

4 Strain the custard through a fine mesh strainer to remove any egg bits. Pour the custard into the prepared ramekins, filling each ¼ inch (.60cm) from the top. Pour enough hot tap water into the pan to surround the ramekins with ½ inch (1.25cm) of water. (Be careful not to get any water in the custards.)

5 Carefully transfer the pan to the oven. Bake for 45 to 50 minutes or until the custards are set.

6 Very carefully transfer the pan from the oven to a wire cooling rack. Let the custards cool slowly in the pan with the water until completely cooled, about 1 hour. Remove the cooled ramekins from the pan, cover with plastic wrap, and refrigerate for at least 4 hours.

7 Just before serving, sprinkle a scant tablespoon of the superfine sugar over each ramekin. Use a kitchen torch to melt the sugar until caramelized or place the ramekins 2 to 3 inches (5 to 7.5cm) under a broiler. Broil 1 to 2 minutes or until the sugar is caramelized with a deep brown color. (Watch carefully to ensure you do not burn the sugar.)

8 large egg yolks

½ cup granulated sugar

2 cups heavy cream

2 tsp vanilla extract or
1 vanilla bean pod

⅓ cup superfine sugar*

SCAN TO WATCH

··· **NOTES** ···

* If you don't have superfine sugar, you can use regular sugar or even brown sugar instead. Superfine sugar simply melts more quickly and evenly due to its small crystal size.

The ideal ramekin size for crème brûlée is 6 ounces (171g). These dishes have a diameter of approximately 5 inches (13cm) and are about 1 inch (2.5cm) deep. Other ramekin sizes can also be used, but the cooking time will be determined by the depth of the liquid.

foolproof pie crust

2 ½ cups all-purpose flour

2 tbsp granulated sugar

1 tsp salt

¾ cup very cold unsalted butter

½ cup very cold vegetable shortening

¼ cup ice-cold water

¼ cup vodka*, chilled

This buttery, flaky pie crust is totally foolproof thanks to the addition of vodka, which doesn't impart any flavor, but it prevents the formation of gluten, allowing you to roll and re-roll the crust as many times as you need to without losing that perfectly flaky texture. This recipe yields two crusts, so you can either make one pie with a top and bottom crust or two pies with no top crusts.

1 In a large bowl, stir together the flour, sugar, and salt.

2 Cut the butter and shortening into small cubes. Add the cubes to the flour mixture in small batches (so the cubes don't stick together) while using a pastry cutter to cut the butter and shortening into the flour mixture until it forms the texture of a coarse meal or sand.

3 Combine the cold water and chilled vodka in a liquid measuring cup. Slowly pour the mixture into the flour mixture about a tablespoon at a time, stirring between additions, until all the liquid has been added and the ingredients are just combined. (Do not overwork.)

4 Use your hands to press the dough into a ball. Divide the dough into two equal pieces. Lay two 12-inch (30.5cm) pieces of plastic wrap on a flat surface. Place the dough balls in the center of one piece of the plastic wrap. Cover the dough with the second piece and then flatten each ball into a 2-inch-thick (5cm-thick) disc. Wrap the discs tightly with plastic wrap and refrigerate for at least 1 hour before rolling out.

5 Unwrap the chilled dough and transfer to a lightly floured surface. Use a rolling pin to roll the discs out into 12-inch (30.5cm) circles, rolling from the center each time to keep the thickness even.

6 Gently transfer one crust to an ungreased pie plate, allowing the crust to hang over the edges of the plate. (Crimp the edges of the crust if you're not using a top crust.) Use a fork to prick holes in the bottom of the crust. Fill the bottom crust with the desired fillings and then top with the second crust (if using). Trim away any excess dough and pinch the edges of the two crusts together. Bake as instructed.

·· NOTES ··

* The alcohol in the vodka will burn away during baking, but if you still don't want to use alcohol, you can omit the vodka and just use an additional ¼ cup of ice-cold water.

For a prebaked pie crust, place parchment paper on top of the crust to create a bowl. Fill with pie weights or dried uncooked beans to prevent the crust from sliding or bubbling.) Bake in a 400°F (204°C) oven for 12 to 15 minutes or until the crust is lightly browned.

The dough can be frozen for up to 3 months. Thaw overnight in the fridge before using.

SCAN TO WATCH

homemade lemonade

This old-fashioned, freshly squeezed lemonade will knock your socks off! It's super easy to make. I've even included instructions for making sugar-free lemonade and honey-based lemonade, as well as instructions for flavored lemonades. It's easy to mix and match various fruits and flavor combinations to quench your thirst with this old-fashioned treat!

1 Cut the lemons in half and juice each through a strainer and into a large measuring cup. Keep juicing until you have 2 cups of lemon juice.

2 Add the water to a medium saucepan over medium-high heat. Stir in the sugar. Continue cooking, stirring continuously, until the sugar is dissolved and the liquid is clear, about 2 to 3 minutes.

3 Combine the sugar solution with lemon juice to create a lemonade concentrate.

4 When ready to serve, add cold water to the lemonade concentrate to taste. (For a stronger lemonade, add less water; for a less sweet and more sour lemonade, adjust the ratio of simple syrup to lemon juice by adding more lemon juice or less simple syrup in step 2.)

5 lb (2.25kg) fresh lemons
2 cups water
2 cups granulated sugar

························· NOTES ·························

The concentrate can be frozen for later use. Just pour it into a gallon-sized resealable bag and lay it flat in the freezer. When ready to serve, thaw and add water to taste.

························ VARIATIONS ························

Honey-Based Lemonade: Replace the sugar with 2 cups honey.

Sugar-Free Lemonade: Replace the sugar with ¼ cup stevia powder.

Fruit-Flavored Lemonade: For strawberry lemonade, add a 1 pound (454g) of hulled strawberries or 1 pound (454g) fresh raspberries to your prepared lemonade and then blend it in a blender.

SCAN TO WATCH

slow cooker apple cider

8 large Gala apples,
   quartered

1 medium navel orange,
   thickly sliced (optional)

4 cinnamon sticks

1 tbsp whole cloves

1 tsp whole allspice berries

10 cups water

½ cup brown sugar

Cuddle up and stay warm with a mug of warm spiced apple cider! This cider is made from scratch and can be frozen to enjoy all winter long.

1 Combine the quartered apples, orange slices, cinnamon sticks, cloves, allspice and water in a slow cooker. Cook on high for 3 hours.

2 After 3 hours, use a potato masher to mash the apples. Add the brown sugar and cook an additional 1 to 3 hours on low.

3 Strain the solids from the cider and discard the solids. Enjoy warm or transfer the cider to an airtight container. Store in the fridge for up to 1 week or freeze for up to 3 months.

·· **NOTES** ··

I love a sweeter cider, so I actually like to use a mix of Gala and Red Delicious apples when I make this recipe. If you prefer a more tart cider, Pink Lady or Braeburn varieties would work well. Experiment with a variety of apples to see what suits your taste preferences.

You can add alcohol to apple cider for a spiked adult beverage. Popular choices for spiked apple cider are rum, bourbon, and whiskey. (Please drink responsibly.)

SCAN TO WATCH

decadent italian-style hot chocolate

This Italian-style hot chocolate is rich, thick, and full of real chocolate. It's not for the faint of heart! It's the kind of hot chocolate you make when you want to truly indulge. You can use dark chocolate, semisweet chocolate, or milk chocolate—whichever is your favorite!

1 Melt the butter in a medium saucepan over low heat.

2 Whisk in the cornstarch, 1 teaspoon at a time, until the desired thickness is achieved and the cornstarch is well combined and melty. (For a thinner hot chocolate, use 1 teaspoon; for a thicker hot chocolate that will coat your mouth, use 2 to 3 teaspoons.)

3 Add the milk and sugar. Increase the heat gradually to medium-high and cook until the mixture begins to simmer, stirring constantly. (Adjust the amount of sugar based on how sweet you prefer your hot chocolate.)

4 When the mixture begins to thicken, turn the heat down to low and add the chocolate chips. Stir continuously until the chocolate chips are melted completely.

5 Serve hot! (Keep the leftovers because it is also amazing, if not better, served cold!) Store any leftovers in an airtight container in the fridge for 3 to 5 days.

2 tbsp salted butter

1 to 3 tsp cornstarch

2 cups milk (whole, 2%, or 1%)

2 to 4 tbsp granulated sugar

1 cup chopped chocolate or chocolate chips

.... NOTES ....

The amount of sugar and type of chocolate you use depends on how sweet you want your hot chocolate. For a darker hot chocolate, use dark or semisweet chocolate chips and 2 tablespoons of sugar. For the most sweet hot chocolate, use milk chocolate chips and 4 tablespoons of sugar.

SCAN TO WATCH

old-fashioned eggnog

2 ½ cups milk (whole, 2%, or 1%)

4 cinnamon sticks

⅛ tsp ground cloves

2 ½ tsp vanilla extract, divided

7 egg yolks

¾ cup granulated sugar

2 cups heavy cream*

⅛ tsp ground nutmeg

Decadent and thick, this old-fashioned eggnog is so easy to make. You can whip up a batch of this holiday favorite drink in no time. And it's way better than the store-bought stuff!

1 Combine the milk, cinnamon sticks, cloves, and vanilla extract in a large saucepan over low heat. Simmer for 5 minutes.

2 In a medium bowl, combine the egg yolks and sugar. Whisk for 1 minute.

3 Increase the heat under the milk to medium-high. Remove the cinnamon sticks.

4 Slowly whisk in about one quarter of the hot milk mixture into the egg-and-sugar mixture and then pour all of the egg and sugar mixture back into the saucepan. Whisk to combine, adjust the heat to medium, and continue whisking for 3 minutes or until the eggnog thickens a bit.

5 Pour the hot eggnog into a large bowl or beverage container and let it cool for 1 hour. If desired, add the cinnamon sticks back to the eggnog.

6 After 1 hour, stir in the heavy cream and nutmeg. Transfer to the fridge to chill for at least 4 hours before serving. Store in an airtight container in the fridge for up to 7 days.

···················· **NOTES** ····················

* For a lighter version, substitute an equal amount of half-and-half for the heavy cream.

For an uncooked version, whisk the egg yolks, sugar, cloves, and nutmeg in a large mixing bowl. Replace the cinnamon sticks with ½ teaspoon ground cinnamon that is whisked in with the egg yolks. Slowly pour in the milk, heavy cream, and vanilla extract. Whisk until thoroughly combined.

If desired, you can add alcohol to taste before serving. Dark rum, cognac, and bourbon are all traditional options.

SCAN TO WATCH

INDEX